W9-BNR-112

Accounting and Finance for Your Small Business

Accounting and Finance for Your Small Business

E. JAMES BURTON
STEVEN M. BRAGG

WILEY
John Wiley & Sons, Inc.
New York • Chichester • Weinheim • Brisbane • Singapore • Toronto

This book is printed on acid-free paper. ∞

Copyright © 2001 by John Wiley & Sons. All rights reserved.

Published simultaneously in Canada.

No part of this publication may be reproduced, stored in a retrieval system or transmitted in any form or by any means, electronic, mechanical, photocopying, recording, scanning or otherwise, except as permitted under Sections 107 or 108 of the 1976 United States Copyright Act, without either the prior written permission of the Publisher, or authorization through payment of the appropriate per-copy fee to the Copyright Clearance Center, 222 Rosewood Drive, Danvers, MA 01923, (978) 750-8400, fax (978) 750-4744. Requests to the Publisher for permission should be addressed to the Permissions Department, John Wiley & Sons, Inc., 605 Third Avenue, New York, NY 10158-0012, (212) 850-6011, fax (212) 850-6008, E-mail: PERMREQ @ WILEY.COM.

This publication is designed to provide accurate and authoritative information in regard to the subject matter covered. It is sold with the understanding that the publisher is not engaged in rendering legal, accounting, or other professional services. If legal advice or other expert assistance is required, the services of a competent professional person should be sought.

Library of Congress Cataloging-in-Publication Data:

Burton, E. James
    Accounting and finance for your small business / Eric James Burton, Steven M. Bragg.—2nd ed.
      p.   cm.
    Rev. ed. of: The total business manual. c1991.
    ISBN 0-471-32360-8 (pbk. : alk. paper)
    1. Industrial management—Handbooks, manuals, etc. 2. Business enterprises—Finance—Handbooks, manuals, etc. 3. Small business—Management. 4. New business enterprises—Management. I. Bragg, Steven M. II. Burton, E. James. Total business manual. III. Title.

HD31.B852 2000
658—dc21   00-020096

Printed in the United States of America.

10 9 8 7 6 5 4 3

About the Authors

E. James Burton, Ph.D., CPA, CFE, is dean of the College of Business and a full professor of accounting at Middle Tennessee State University. He has founded, owned, managed, and sold a number of businesses in a variety of areas from service to manufacturing. He received a Bachelor of Arts degree from MacMurray College in economics/business, a Master of Business Administration degree from Murray State University in management, and a Ph.D. in accountancy from the University of Illinois at Urbana-Champaign. In addition to over 50 journal articles, he has written *Total Business Planning: A Step-by-Step Guide with Forms* that has continued through three editions and translation into Norwegian. He resides in Murfreesboro, Tennessee.

Steven M. Bragg, CPA, CMA, CIA, CDP, CSP, CPM, CPIM, has been the chief financial officer or controller of four companies, as well as a consulting manager at Ernst & Young. He received a master's degree in finance from Bentley College and an MBA from Babson College. He has also written *Just-in-Time Accounting, Advanced Accounting Systems, Financial Analysis, Outsourcing, Accounting Best Practices,* and *Managing Explosive Corporate Growth,* and has coauthored *Controllership* and *The Controller's Function.* Mr. Bragg resides in Englewood, Colorado.

Contents

Preface

This book has been written for business owners and managers who want to refine the financial and accounting operations of their companies. It provides detailed information about how to run these operations, track cash flows, conduct analyses, analyze key financial information, determine insurance requirements, and compile tax liabilities—in short, all of the key accounting and financial information required to operate a small business.

Chapter 1 describes the cost-volume-profit relationship, which is a crucial method for determining the sales volumes required to achieve a profit, given various levels of fixed costs. This is one of the best ways for a small business owner to determine how much money can be made (or lost) at various revenue levels.

Chapter 2 reveals how to set up a budgeting procedure and use standard budgeting formats to ensure that revenues are properly projected and matched to related costs. This is a very important issue for those cyclical industries in which expenses may be incurred well in advance of sales receipts and is also a highly necessary method for controlling such key expense areas as staff hiring and inventory levels.

Chapter 3 covers the budgeting techniques used for capital acquisitions, such as discounted cash flows and payback analysis. We also note how to modify capital budgeting reviews to account for high-risk expenditures and how to stratify a set of possible acquisitions in terms of which is the most desirable.

Chapter 4 turns to the analysis of cash flows. In it, we cover the creation of cash forecasts, the management of cash, and exceptions to expected cash flows, which can have a serious impact on actual cash flows. This is a critical area for the small business, which typically operates with minimal cash reserves.

Chapter 5 describes the various sources of financing that are available. This includes internal cash sources, such as zero working capital, and external ones, such as debt or equity financing, as well as a number of variations that are useful in specific circumstances. Since loans tend to be the chief form of financing, we also note how to obtain bank loans, as well as describe many of the key terms to be found in loan agreements.

Chapter 6 notes a large number of financial and operating ratios that are of great use in determining trends in corporate performance. We describe how to calculate each of the most common ratios and how to interpret them.

Chapter 7 includes coverage of a number of key areas that few small business owners want to address but that can impact their business in a negative manner. These issues include the management of tax liabilities, the management of a number of risks throughout the organization, and the careful use of insurance to mitigate those risks.

Chapter 8 covers the four main areas of reporting that are of concern to the small business owner. These are reports to the Federal government, State government, creditors, and for internal management. We spend the bulk of our time on internal management reports, because these can be used with great effectiveness if properly structured to reveal the most crucial information about ongoing operations and financial results.

The most effective way to use this book is as a reference source. We suggest that you first read the book through once, implementing the concepts section by section; it is not casual reading but rather a manual, intended for a reading-doing-reading-doing approach. Then, when you have trouble or concerns in a particular area, consult the specific chapter addressing that problem to find solutions.

Though not everything covered in a business school MBA curriculum is covered here, the most relevant topics are; therefore, the book serves as an update for those who have business school training and an introduction to many business concepts for those who have not.

Best wishes for improving, implementing, and benefiting from your decisions—and for making lots of money.

E. James Burton, Ph.D.
Steven M. Bragg
December 2000

Accounting and Finance for Your Small Business

Preparing to Operate the Business

The first section of the book covers those tasks that should be accomplished prior to the start of a business, or as ongoing analysis after it has been founded. It accomplishes this objective in three chapters.

The first chapter deals with the cost-volume-profit relationship, which the business owner must thoroughly understand before starting a business, since the relationship of these three items will drive the ability of the organization to create a profit. The information in this chapter should also be reviewed regularly thereafter, as a business progresses through its various stages of growth, to ensure that it is still capable of spinning off profits.

The second chapter covers the budgeting function. The issues addressed here, such as the format of a budget, its components, and how it should be compared to actual results, are critical to the overall management of a business, and should be firmly in place before the organization is created. It must also be regularly monitored and controlled to ensure that actual results do not stray from the plan.

The third chapter covers investments in large-dollar items, which are known as capital items. It covers the steps one should follow in order to investigate the need for a capital item, compare it to other capital requests, and determine what should be purchased. This is a key factor not only in the beginning of a business, but also in the renewal of key assets over time, as they gradually wear out and require replacement.

Chapter 1

Cost-Volume-Profit Relationships

The most common utilization of the cost-volume-profit relationship (C-V-P) has been to determine a break-even point. Business schools generally teach that the C-V-P relationship is a straight-line function. That is, you break even at the point of intersection of the total cost line and total revenue line. In certain situations, that is an accurate reflection of reality. In other circumstances, the truth is a bit more complex.

Figure 1.1 shows a typical straight-line version C-V-P relationship—the traditional break-even analysis. But break-even analysis can be a far more functional tool than a simple straight-line determination of a quantity where breakeven occurs. The familiar equation for this graph is the sales quantity at which sales revenue equals the sum of fixed costs plus variable costs:

BE sales revenue = Fixed costs + Variable costs

Another way to look at the two individual lines is to say that total cost (*TC*) is equal to the fixed cost (*FC*) plus the variable cost per unit (*VC*) times the quantity (*Q*):

$$TC = FC + (VC \times Q)$$

FIGURE 1.1

Traditional Break-Even Analysis

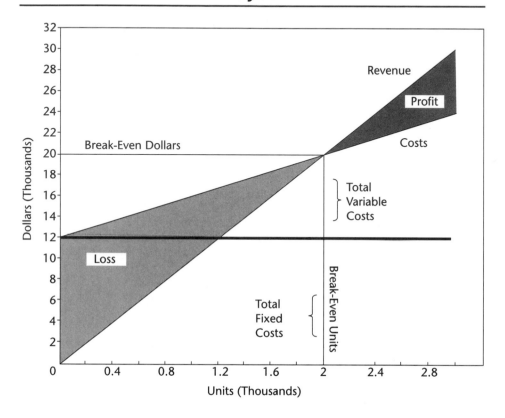

The equation for the total revenue (*TR*) line is simply the price (*P*) times the quantity sold:

$$TR = P \times Q$$

The break-even point occurs where total revenue (*TR*) exactly equals total cost (*TC*):

$$TR = TC$$

After the break-even point, total revenue exceeds total cost, and profits accrue.

Another way to present the information about a company's break-even point is through a table, such as the one shown in Figure 1.2. Though this format is based on the same information used for a break-even chart, it also itemizes the exact levels of margins and fixed costs that a company is currently experiencing, which is more precise information for the management team to use in planning ways to improve the break-even point. In the example, we list an increasing series of revenue levels that comprise the minimum and maximum sales levels that a company can reasonably expect to achieve in the near future. Then we multiply these sales levels by the current gross margin percentage, which gives us the gross margin dollars at each sales level, as shown in the third column. We then subtract from this gross margin all the company's fixed costs, which are shown in column four, which results in a profit or loss, as noted in the final column. The break-even point is at an approximate sales level of $60,000 and is noted in bold in the example.

The table format carries with it the added advantage of being usable in an electronic spreadsheet format for "what if" analysis. Any manager could use the model to alter margin percentages or fixed costs to determine their impact on profit levels. For example, if the sales manager were to assume that higher sales levels can be attained only by lowering the price of the product, this information could be

FIGURE 1.2

Break-Even Table

Revenue	Margin (%)	Margin ($)	Fixed Costs	Profit
$10,000	32%	$3,200	$18,000	–$14,800
20,000	32%	6,400	18,000	–11,600
30,000	32%	9,600	18,000	–8,400
40,000	32%	12,800	18,000	–5,200
50,000	32%	16,000	18,000	–2,000
60,000	32%	19,200	18,000	**1,200**
70,000	32%	22,400	18,000	4,400
80,000	32%	25,600	18,000	7,600
90,000	32%	28,000	18,000	10,800

added to the "Margin (%)" column in the table, which would automatically create a modified profit for that specific sales level.

The graph, the table, and the equation are, however, much more versatile tools than just break-even predictors. They can help you answer questions such as:

- What price is necessary if given quantities are predicted?
- What sales level is necessary to produce a given profit?
- What effect will changes in variable costs have on profits?
- What increase in sales volume is necessary to cover an increase in costs?
- What effect does a change in fixed costs have on profit and break-even?

Although the answers to these questions are extremely useful, there are severe limiting assumptions associated with the straight-line model:

- The selling price remains constant regardless of the quantity sold.
- All costs are classifiable as strictly fixed or variable.
- The fixed costs remain constant for all levels of production up to capacity.
- Total variable costs vary directly with the volume produced.
- The cost of inputs, policies, and technologies remain constant.
- Production is always equal to sales (i.e., no inventory is carried).

In most cases, you cannot meet the conditions of these assumptions; therefore, this graph and equation may be of limited help. However, each condition and each assumption can be compared to the actual situation and a judgment made as to how well the graph represents it. The usefulness of any forecasting tool is measured by how reliable and accurate it is as a predictor. If the tool is an accurate predictor, you should evaluate the cost of compiling the necessary data against the benefits derived from making better decisions. If the tool is not accurate, it is not worthwhile no matter how small the cost.

As with any tool, the more it is pushed, the more complex its application becomes and the more costly the compilation of needed data. Fortunately, to a point, as the complexity increases, the reliability and accuracy also increase. By making the use of the tool just a little more complex, the following helpful questions may be answered:

- What selling price yields the greatest profits?
- What effect would a change in the selling price have on revenues or on profits?
- Should the firm attempt to raise its sales volume?
- At what volume should the firm consider raising capacity?

In order to answer these questions, the model must be changed from the classic straight-line model to the curved-line model, which will be addressed later in the chapter.

It is clear that the simple break-even analysis can be useful in determining the point in units or in dollars where breakeven occurs. In addition, the model has certain strategic planning and analysis value for solving capital budgeting problems and as an aid in making other management decisions.

Some Basic Uses for Cost-Volume-Profit Relationships

C-V-P can be used as an inexpensive screening device. Other financial models, such as discounted cash flow, require the use of more expensive, harder-to-get data. Before incurring the cost of gathering this data, a simple C-V-P analysis may initially tell whether it is worthwhile to do more intensive and costly analysis.

C-V-P can be used as a simple test for product specifications and designs. Each design has cost implications and costs often affect price and market feasibility. C-V-P analysis based on projected costs and expected selling prices permits comparison of possible designs before specifications are frozen and product or process lines are implemented. For example, C-V-P analysis can be used for a new product with an uncertain projected sales volume; the decision can be made whether to build parts on a temporary hand-tooled basis or to invest in expensive automated production tooling.

The hand-tooled method typically has higher variable costs but lower fixed costs. This will often result in a lower break-even quantity for a project, lower risks, and lower potential profits. Generally, the more automated and technology-intensive a process is, the higher the sales necessary for breakeven. The obvious cause is that the initial fixed cost is significantly higher than in hand-tooling but the variable cost per product unit is correspondingly less. C-V-P analysis permits the examination of these trade-offs; alternatives may be compared and evaluated against one another.

One can also use C-V-P analysis as a substitute for estimating an unknown factor in making project decisions. In any decision concerning a project, there are many variables that one must consider and estimate in reaching a decision (demand, cost, price, and other factors). Usually, costs can be approximated for a process or product, and only two variables remain: selling price and demand.

Because selling price and demand are related, demand is difficult to estimate. If demand can be estimated, profit is a simple calculation. The break-even point occurs at zero profit; therefore, it is simple to calculate the minimum demand above which a project becomes a reasonable undertaking. Of course, simply having calculated the demand estimate does not assure you the market share required. But breakeven does give you a way to look at uncertainty and to fix a reasonable target quantity.

Applying C-V-P to Other Areas

While one use of C-V-P is to determine the sales necessary to generate a given profit level, you can also use the model to determine other useful information, such as the maximum out-of-pocket costs that should be put into the product.

For an understanding of how these different functions work, certain factors need to be defined.

Contribution on a per-unit basis (*CM*) is defined as the selling price per unit (*P*) minus the variable cost per unit (*VC*):

$$CM = P - VC$$

Break-even volume is equal to the total fixed cost (*FC*) divided by the contribution on a per-unit basis. Thus, break-even volume (*BV*) equals fixed cost divided by contribution margin:

$$BV = \frac{FC}{CM}$$

Contribution margin as a percent of revenue (CM%) is equal to the selling price per unit (*P*) minus the variable cost per unit (*VC*) divided by the selling price (*P*):

$$CM\% = \frac{(P - VC)}{P}$$

Breakeven in terms of dollars (B$) is equal to the total fixed cost (*FC*) divided by the contribution margin percentage (*CM%*):

$$B\$ = \frac{FC}{CM\%}$$

For example, if the selling price of an item is $10.00, with a variable cost of $7.50, the contribution on a per-unit basis is equal to:

$$CM = \$10 - \$7.50 = \$2.50$$

If the fixed costs necessary to manufacture such an item are $250,000, the break-even volume would simply be:

$$BV = \frac{\$250,000}{\$2.50} = 100,000 \text{ units}$$

The *CM%* would be

$$(CM\%) = \frac{(\$10 - \$7.50)}{\$10} = 25\%$$

The *B$* would be:

$$B\$ = \frac{\$250,000}{.25} = \$1,000,000$$

Using the formulae that have been generated, we will now look at the maximum out-of-pocket cost problem.

Problem

Suppose you can forecast sales with a reasonable degree of assurance and estimate you can sell 150,000 items per year. What out-of-pocket expenses can you incur and still break even? First, we change the break-even formula to find and use those factors we know. Take the formula:

$$BV = \frac{FC}{CM}$$

Multiply both sides by *CM* to get:

$$BV \times CM = FC$$

Then solve for *CM:*

$$CM = \frac{EC}{BV}$$

Now we simply find the contribution margin for the product:

$$CM = \frac{\$250,000}{150,000 \text{ units}} = \$1.67$$

By subtracting the *CM* of $1.67 from the selling price of $10.00, we get $8.33, the variable cost the firm can incur on each unit and still break even at 150,000 units and a $10.00 selling price.

Determining Potential Selling Price for a Product

Again, assume the variable cost for producing the product is $7.50 per unit, and there are $250,000 in fixed costs. Add to that data the "known" sales volume of 150,000 units and a desire to make a profit of $100,000 per year. What is the minimum selling price? The *CM* is equal to the fixed costs, divided by the break-even volume (*CM* = *FC/BV*). In our example, *CM* would be equal to $250,000 of fixed costs plus $100,000 of profit (treated as a fixed cost) divided by 150,000 units. Therefore: *CM* = $350,000/150,000, or *CM* is equal to $2.333. The minimum price should equal the variable cost plus the fixed cost: $7.50 + $2.333 = $9.833. (Remember: Up to the *BV* point, all of the *CM* goes to meet *FC*. Therefore, the $2.333 per unit on the first 150,000 units is *FC* per unit.) Therefore, $9.84 is the selling price, which can be compared to the existing market price to determine whether the product has a good chance of selling or if specifications must be altered to get the price down. This approach works well as an initial basis for bidding on projects.

Advertising Decisions

Advertising decisions may also be evaluated using C-V-P. Advertising is generally a contractually fixed cost. Any additional fixed costs raise the firm's break-even point, and thus require additional revenues or lower variable costs to compensate for the increase in expenditures. As already shown, the money for fixed-cost coverage comes from the contribution margin.

In our example, the contribution margin is 25 percent. Four additional dollars of revenue are required to cover each additional dollar of fixed cost. So, if you make a $25,000 expenditure for additional advertising, you would need to recover four times $25,000, or $100,000, in additional sales just to cover the cost of the additional advertising. You are not trying to guess how much sales will be generated from the additional advertising; you are evaluating the necessary increase in sales to justify an incremental expenditure for advertising.

Analysis of Credit Request

The model may also be used to determine whether to grant a request for credit. All that is required is an understanding of how to evaluate a credit application.

For example, a potential distributor for a product approaches you and requests to be considered for credit purchases. This distributor expects to purchase 400 units per month and requests terms of net 30 days, and conservatively estimates his account will turn over eight times per year. How do you evaluate whether to extend credit to this potential distributor?

Whenever a new account is taken on, the potential loss to you is the variable cost of the balance carried. The fixed costs are considered "sunk," and taking on an additional credit customer does not significantly affect the sunk costs. However, you incur the additional cost of carrying and administering the account. If we assume the carrying costs amount to 10 percent of the average balance, and the administrative costs are fixed at $1,000 per year for each new account, the average expected balance is found by taking total sales and dividing by turnover. The average expected balance in our case would be equal to 400 units times $10 per unit times 12 months, divided by 8 (expected turnover per year).

$$\text{Average expected balance} = \frac{\$48,000}{8} = \$6,000$$

The fixed cost associated with taking on this account is 10 percent of the average balance, plus the administrative costs:

$$FC = (\$6,000 \times 10\%) + \$1,000 = \$1,600$$

To these fixed costs must be added the variable cost of the average balance. Therefore, in this case, 75 percent of the $6,000 would be the associated variable cost. The variable cost would be equal to:

$$VC = \$6,000 \times 75\% = \$4,500$$

The 75 percent is derived when the $7.50 per unit variable cost is divided by the selling price of $10.00. As noted earlier, you incur $2.50 per unit fixed cost up to the break-even point, regardless of whether credit is granted or, for that matter, any of the product is sold. Therefore, the potential total cost, including possible loss of the outstanding balance, is:

$$\$4,500 + \$1,600 = \$6,100$$

Going back to an earlier analysis where we determined the contribution margin percentage of this product to be 25 percent, we concluded that it required four additional dollars of revenue to cover one dollar of additional total cost. The marginal break-even analysis for taking on this new customer would be four times the expected total cost. Therefore, the *B$* for the account is equal to four times $6,100, or $24,400.

Thus, the firm needs $24,400 in sales to the distributor to ensure that the account will at least break even if properly paid. Since the expected yearly sales are calculated as 400 units times $10.00 per unit times 12 months, or $48,000, the firm should reach break-even in approximately six months. It is at this point that managerial judgment should consider whether a six months' breakeven is a reasonable period for a distributor and the probability that this distributor will pay properly.

Although this is not a statistically sophisticated approach to granting credit, it does show a measure of the expected exposure to loss that an account will incur. Break-even analysis may be used to evaluate competing credit applications. A simple test could be which application has the shortest break-even time. To ensure a good decision, comparative decisions between competing potential distributors can be made using past experience.

Other Applications

C-V-P analysis can also be used to compare variable cost changes and fixed-cost changes for various products. It is applicable to determinations and analysis of such variable costs as material, labor, and overhead. By looking at the contribution margin percentage, you can readily determine the marginal sales required to break even on the costs of additional labor increments, material cost increases, or even the addition of a new supervisor or other managerial position.

Profit Margins

In our original example, we determined that the contribution margin percentage for our product was 25 percent (*CM%* = 25%). This assumed you were operating at zero profit (the necessary assumption for breakeven). Now, if you wish to determine at what quantity level a 10 percent profit margin could be expected, the model can be modified to accommodate that question.

Because the model assumes zero profit at CM = 25 percent, to calculate the break-even quantity for a 10 percent profit, we simply assume that the 25 percent contribution margin percentage is reduced by the profit percentage; in other words, we wish to find the quantity that produces a contribution margin percentage of 15 percent. The formula: $BE = FC/CM\%$ is used. Because the fixed cost in the original model was $250,000, we divide it by 15 percent to get the break-even dollars of $1,666,670. Because the selling price was $10.00 per unit, the break-even quantity would be 166,667 units.

Of course, you must be careful to determine whether that break-even quantity is within plant capacity and whether it can be sold within your market share. If you do not control enough of a market share to sell 166,667 units, it would do little good to produce them and expect a profit.

Proof		
At 166,667 units		
Total revenue @ $10/unit		$1,666,670
Total costs:		
Fixed costs:	$ 250,000	
Variable costs @ 7.50/unit:	1,250,003	1,500,003
Net profit before tax		$ 166,667

$$\text{Net profit \%} = \frac{\$166,667}{\$1,666,670} = 10\%$$

Alternative Application of the C-V-P Analysis

In periods when competition for market position and sales becomes fierce and when cash flow is restricted, C-V-P analysis can be employed to evaluate cash or near-cash items to test or screen whether to discontinue, divest, or drop a product or location that might be detrimental from a cash flow standpoint. Cash flow C-V-P analysis can be done quickly and easily when trying to make shut-down decisions.

Assume that Jones Ice Cream Company has four retail locations. Location 2 is in an area that is being redeveloped and where new roads are being put in. Traffic has been significantly cut, and entry and exit from the location is very difficult. All construction should be completed in nine months.

The Curved-Line C-V-P Analysis

	Cash Costs per Month Open	Cash Costs per Month Closed	Relevant Cash Costs
Rent	$1,200	$1,200	-0-
Insurance	300	200	$ 100
Minimum Personnel	1,600	200	1,400
Utilities	800	100	700
	$3,900	$1,700	$2,200

Assuming the gross margin on ice cream sales is 50 percent, the location must create $2,200/.50 = $4,400 sales per month for Jones Ice Cream Company to be as well off keeping Location 2 open as it would be to close it for the construction period. (Costs that do not differ between alternatives are not relevant to the decision.)

Curved-Line C-V-P Analysis

Assumptions

The curved-line C-V-P analysis does not have some of the restrictive assumptions applicable to the straight-line case. The relevant limiting assumptions for the curved-line model are:

- Policies, technology, and prices are constant.
- Product mix is constant.
- Production is equal to sales (no inventory level changes).

In this case, it is no longer necessary to have a constant selling price, costs that are strictly fixed or variable, a constant fixed cost for all volumes, a direct relationship between variable cost and volume, or constant prices for raw materials and other inputs. If the assumptions for the curved-line C-V-P analysis do not fit the model you are trying to evaluate, it is better to try another evaluation method than to force the facts into the analysis.

One of the more interesting nonlinear pricing problems is the cost of quantity discounts. The question seldom asked is: "How do we determine how to set quantity discounts?" One answer to this question may be: "We determine quantity discount policies by estimating the economic order quantity (EOQ) for the buyers of our product." This can be done by determining buyers' periodic demands from our records, and estimating their holding costs. Another method is using the EOQ techniques and the pricing guides to develop price breaks for use in maximizing profits.

What Does It Look Like?

The curved-line C-V-P analysis is also commonly called the economist's description of the total cost/total revenue relationship. It looks more complex than the linear version, and to some degree it is. However, with the advent of the graphing programs on microcomputer spreadsheets, the construction of the curved-line model is no more difficult than the linear model, provided you have the data.

Figure 1.3 shows how a computer-generated curved-line break-even graph might look. Note that it has two break-even points: one at a relatively low volume and one at a higher volume, which is likely to be close to capacity. One of the difficulties of constructing this graph from actual data is that most people try to stay in the most profitable range and therefore have little actual data at the lower or higher ends of the scale.

In order to generate this curve, some hypothetical data may have to be added to actual data that are available. If so, there are some cautions you should observe. First, unless the market demand is extremely strong for your product or service, you probably have to decrease your selling price to increase your unit sales. Failing to factor these price reductions into your data will result in inflated

FIGURE **1.3**

Break-Even Graph

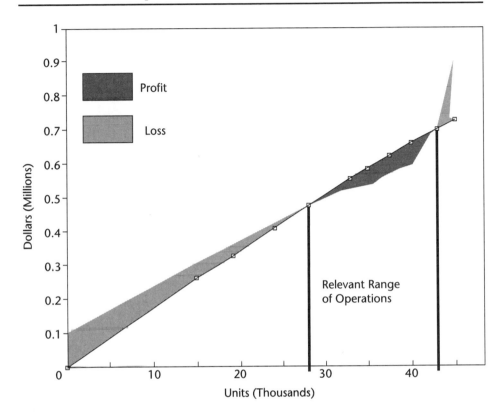

revenue estimates at high volumes. Second, as you approach capacity production, costs have a tendency to increase, sometimes dramatically (overtime, expediting, premiums for materials). Failing to factor in these cost increases will result in deflated cost estimates at high volumes. This combination of high-revenue estimates and low-cost estimates might indicate decisions that could prove unhealthy. Beware of these tendencies. It is important that you get good data.

Data Generation

The quality of the data you use has a direct relationship to the quality of the information generated by that data. The following method can be employed with little modification to many sales and revenue data collection problems.

Step 1. Identify the person or persons most likely to be the best predictors of sales for your products.

A good candidate may be your regional sales manager. As an example, the regional sales manager may have had a good career with the company starting as field repairman and working his way up through sales to his current position. If so, he probably knows the products well and may have kept good records on sales of products for the last few years.

Step 2. Identify the range of selling prices around which you intend to gather information. (You may have to go back and change these prices later if there is a market share problem).

Example: Smith Company has decided to market its "Fairy-Tale" cassettes in the $12.50 to $17.50 price range based on a market survey of competitive products.

Step 3. Pick several equally spaced prices within the price range relevant to the product.

Example: Smith decides to get sales quantity estimates for $1 increments between and including $12.50 to $17.50. They assume there are different markets into which they can sell at different price points. Obviously, they plan to sell as many units as possible at the highest price points before dropping the price. Therefore, each price drop will create marginal unit sales that Smith would not get at the higher price points.

Step 4. Have the selected person(s) predict the total quantity the firm could expect to sell at each selected price point.

Example: the estimator(s) gave the following:

Price/Unit	Total Units	Marginal Units
$17.50	15,000	15,000
16.50	28,000	13,000
15.50	35,000	7,000
14.50	40,000	5,000
13.50	43,000	3,000
12.50	45,000	2,000

Step 5. Multiply the price/unit by the marginal units to obtain marginal revenue (additional revenue generated from sales obtained by dropping the price).

Obtain the total revenue by a stepwise addition of the marginal revenue column (the total revenue at $15.50 is the marginal revenue at $17.50 + the marginal revenue at $16.50 + the marginal revenue at $15.50):

Price/ Unit	Total Units	Marginal Units	Marginal Revenue	Total Revenue
$17.50	15,000	15,000	$262,500	$262,500
16.50	28,000	13,000	214,500	477,000
15.50	35,000	7,000	108,500	585,500
14.50	40,000	5,000	72,500	658,000
13.50	43,000	3,000	40,500	698,500
12.50	45,000	2,000	25,000	723,500

The resulting Total Revenue line is shown in Figure 1.4. If you were to assume that all 45,000 units could be sold at $17.50 per unit, the revenue estimate would be $787,500. Figure 1.5 shows the resulting inflated revenue estimate from this error.

Sometimes a price-based method will prove to be ineffective. The predictors might say that it is easier to predict the price given the quantities desired.

Example: The products of the Evans Company are educational and foreign language lesson tapes. An alternative method for determining the curve is to proceed with the following method.

After identifying the persons within the organization:

Step 1. Identify the relevant range of sales and stick closely to that in gathering information. (Here the market share question is not a problem.) Assume the per-unit costs are lowest when production is in a range of 25,000 to 30,000 units per year.

Step 2. Pick several equally spaced points in the quantity range that are relevant for the product. In our example, Evans

FIGURE 1.4

Incremental Pricing

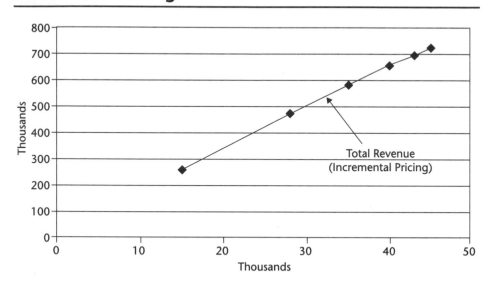

FIGURE 1.5

Constant Pricing

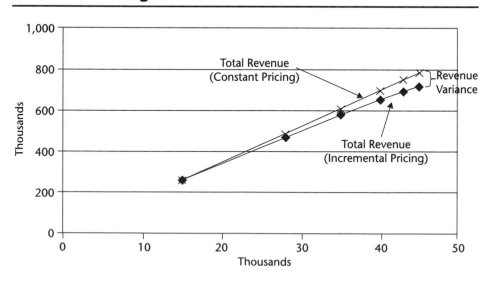

decides to use 1,000 unit increments in the range of 25,000 to 30,000.

Step 3. Ask the selected predictors what price would be necessary to sell the quantity selected.

The predictor comes up with the following prices:

Units	Price/Unit
25,000	$60.00
26,000	58.00
27,000	55.00
28,000	51.00
29,000	46.00
30,000	40.00

Step 4. Multiply the selling prices by the corresponding quantity to produce the expected revenue for each selected quantity. In this instance, we assume that the market is very competitive and there is virtually perfect information flow. Therefore, Evans can set only one price with which it will have to stick. They cannot "cream the market" as in a previous example.

The expected revenues for the educational tapes would be:

Units	Total Revenue
25,000	$1,500,000
26,000	1,508,000
27,000	1,485,000
28,000	1,428,000
29,000	1,344,000
30,000	1,200,000

Step 5. Plot the points representing the revenues and quantities on a graph as before.

In this case, we are using the quantity as the independent variable and determining price as the dependent variable. In the first example we were using price as the independent variable and making quantity the dependent variable. In either case, we expect (and hope) to get a curve (see Figure 1.6) Setting the quantity and estimating the price may be a better planning tool, because we can often generate better cost figures if we work within efficient production levels.

It is obvious that this market is very sensitive to price. Evans is better off, from a total revenue point of view, at lower volume/higher price. In fact, if costs are more than $8 per unit, they may be better off at 25,000 units.

Generating the Cost Line

As with the revenue line, there are several methods to generate the cost line.

1. The simplest method is to obtain an estimate of total costs for an expected volume. This is the first information needed. Draw a line

FIGURE 1.6

Total Revenue

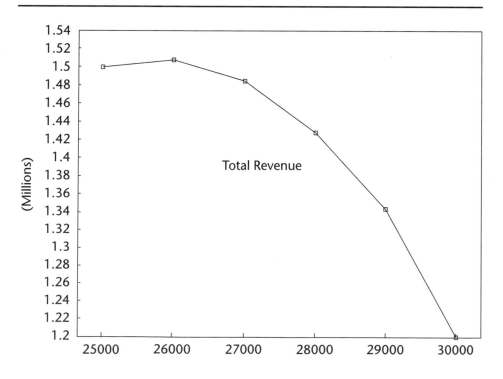

from that total cost point (point A) to the point on the vertical axis associated with the fixed costs, assuming zero production (point B). This is often called *standby costs* because it indicates expenditures that would continue in the short term even if operations were to be shut down (see Figure 1.7).

In this manner, we arrive at a linear approximation based on two pieces of data. But why use only two data points when more are available?

2. Obtain total cost figures and quantity figures for several previous periods and plot these points on a graph, as has been done in Figure 1.8. This approach should be used with some caution:

FIGURE **1.7**

Cost Graph

FIGURE **1.8**

TLAR

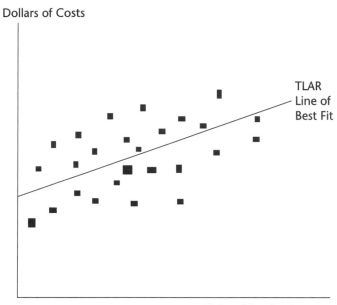

Dollars of Costs

TLAR
Line of
Best Fit

Units of Production

- Short periods of time should be used to minimize the effects of inflation.
- In looking at those periods you should assure yourself that significant learning effects have already taken place and that the process has stabilized.

Once you have obtained several cost figures and associated quantity figures and have plotted the points, draw a line that seems to fit the data best. There are two easy methods for doing this:

1. *The eyeball approximation, or TLAR (that looks about right) method.* In this method, you try to fit a line that to you seems to best approximate the relationships.
2. *Linear regression.* Most electronic spreadsheet programs can easily calculate the linear regression from a set of input data. In the appendix to this chapter, we include step-by-step instructions for

doing so in Microsoft Excel, as well as a copy of the graphical result.

What Does It All Mean?

Plotting the total cost and total revenue curves on the same graph generates useful information for planning. Before getting into the strategic planning implications of the C-V-P relationships, it should be noted that there are three points of interest on the curve shown in Figure 1.9. There is the break-even point at the lower end of the curve, BE1, where, for the first time, a quantity production will put

FIGURE **1.9**

Profits

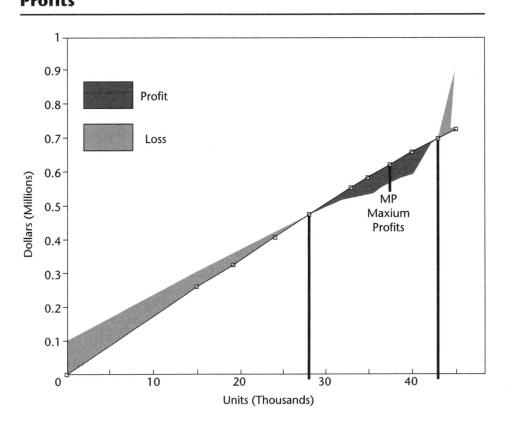

the firm in a position where total revenues equal total costs. From this point, as the quantity produced increases, total revenues exceed total costs, and there is a profit. Ultimately, a second break-even point, BE2, is reached. Again, total costs equal the total revenues and above this level of production the business incurs a total loss again.

A third point of interest is where the vertical distance between the total revenue and the total cost curves is at a maximum. It is at this point that maximum profits are achieved. The old concept that more sales are better holds true only until the quantity sold reaches the quantity at which profits are maximized.

After the point MP is reached, the firm has diminishing returns for each additional unit of production (see Figure 1.9). When the firm reaches break-even point (BE2), it is no longer realizing any profits. It would be very interesting to know exactly where maximum profits exist. In the estimating process, we can, if our curves are accurate, get a fairly good approximation of the point at which maximum profits occur.

There is good news and bad news relative to this point, MP. The good news is that the economic definition of the point MP is quite precise. It is that quantity of units sold where the additional cost to produce the last unit (marginal cost) is exactly equal to the additional revenue derived from selling that unit (marginal revenue). The bad news is that those numbers are normally difficult to attain in actual practice. Building the graph helps you to narrow your focus on this range, however.

Using C-V-P Relationships for Strategic Planning

Going through the analytical process of generating the cost and revenue curves necessary for a C-V-P analysis is, in itself, a useful exercise. You will have been able to identify where on the cost curve you are probably operating. With this information, you can estimate whether you are above or below the maximum profit point. There may be situations in which you are willing, in the short term, to forgo maximum profits now in order to ensure a better position in the future. This is where the use of the C-V-P model is helpful for strategic planning.

For example, you may believe that a competitor will fill the void if, rather than increasing production and selling at a lower marginal price, you choose to try to stay at the profit-maximizing quantity. Therefore, to forestall that competition, you may decide to produce and sell a higher quantity at a total profit lower than you could manage. However, you would probably do this only if you expected either to increase overall capacity or otherwise to alter the cost curve in such a way as to return toward optimal profitability in the longer term.

You might do this when you know that in the next year you will be opening a new plant with additional capacity. Once the plant opens, and you are meeting that additional demand from another facility, the cost curve will change beneficially and, with luck, return you toward the point of maximum profits. So you might take a lesser short-term profit to maintain market share from which you would later profit.

Another strategic issue involving production capacity is the anticipation of changes in the corporate break-even point as the result of adding extra capacity. When new facilities or equipment are added, the amount of fixed costs increases in a single, large surge called a "step cost"—the fixed cost structure increases, or steps, to a higher level. This concept is shown graphically in Figure 1.10, in which the level of production utilization for the existing facility peaks at 80 percent, after which the level of fixed costs increases, due to the acquisition of new facilities and machinery. Because of this jump in costs, the profit level is at its highest just prior to the addition of new facilities, which may give a company some strategic reason for stopping short of adding them. Once the new facilities are added, the break-even point increases, so the management team must be certain that it can sustain a higher level of sales volume to support the new costs.

In order to evaluate where on the curve you should be operating, you simply use the discounted cash flow method or the internal rate of return method found in the capital budgeting chapter to ascertain the current costs of operating above the maximum profit point in terms of future cash flows.

FIGURE 1.10

Break-Even Chart Including Impact of Step Costing

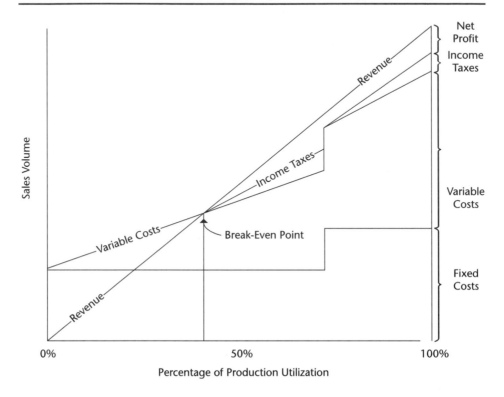

Source: Steven M. Bragg, *Controller's Guide to Financial Analysis* (New York: John Wiley & Sons, 2000). Reprinted with permission.

Sensitivity Analysis

People often banter around the expression "sensitivity analysis" as if it contains some mystique. In truth, sensitivity analysis is nothing more than an evaluation of how much change occurs in costs or revenue relative to changes in other variables. Sensitivity analysis is often used as a test of the underlying assumptions. For example, if we assume that the variable cost does, in fact, vary directly with the quantity produced, we could test the reasonableness of this assumption by looking at those variable costs associated with different production levels. One method of doing this is to look at historical variable costs actually incurred at different levels of production.

(Remember, if the points are selected at too divergent periods, there may be a factor of inflation to take into consideration.) If the relationship is approximately linear, then the assumption is accurate. However, if the costs tend to fluctuate greatly on a per-unit basis, we can say that the cost relationship does not support the assumption.

Other Problems

The graphical curves we have constructed for both cost and revenue represent a relatively stable product or process configuration. The model assumes that production is equal to sales and policies, that the new product mix, technologies, and other factors are constant.

Realizing the weaknesses of some of these assumptions allows you to determine their relative impact on the model. For instance, one problem is the allocation of overhead to various products in the mix. You may use a burden or overhead rate to allocate these charges based on direct labor man-hours, in much the same way as labor rates are used directly to allocate labor costs. Changes in allocation affect the break-even point(s) significantly.

Sales need not be exactly equal to production. However, if production and sales are relatively constant, or there is a gradual building or reduction of inventory, the problem is not of such a nature to affect critically the reliability of the model. But there are other problems which must be considered:

Taxes. If the firm is only considering breakeven, there may be no taxes. At breakeven, total revenue equals total cost, and profits are equal to zero. Therefore, it is of only academic interest to operate in a break-even situation. The usual way to treat taxes in the C-V-P analysis is simply to ignore them. Taxes can be subtracted from the net profit picture later.

Fixed vs. variable cost. It is difficult to be really honest with ourselves concerning what or who is really a fixed expense. This is especially true when considering closing down a product or process line. What overhead do you *really* eliminate? Almost all costs that are considered fixed may in fact be variable. Assignment of costs to either the fixed or the variable category should at least be attempted. You should be careful to analyze and make distinctions between fixed and variable costs. This distinction is necessary in order to get an accurate picture of a total cost curve.

Summary

C-V-P relationships (break-even analysis) have generally been used to determine the level of production above which the firm will operate profitably. The simple linear model has several limiting assumptions that tend to narrow the applicability of the model. However, as a model, it does have sound applications that should not be overlooked in favor of more flashy or sophisticated (and hence more costly) techniques.

The straight-line model has applications as a screen for making financial decisions. Its advantages are speed and low cost. The numbers are readily obtainable and the model is not difficult to manipulate. As a simple mathematical model, it has powerful applications in other areas where business decisions have to be made. It is a decision screen simple to use for advertising, credit policies, and comparability of alternative plans.

In the more complex configurations, the curved-line case has fewer limiting constraints and even more applications. With its power comes more difficulty in generating the cost and revenue lines. The curved lines are generated from cost and volume relationships estimated for varying prices and varying sales quantities. Properly done, however, these curves can give you a better understanding of where you are and of how pricing and selling decisions may affect your profitability.

One important application of the analysis is the determination of where on the cost curve you are operating or planning to operate. The curves can generate information relative to whether increasing or decreasing production will improve profitability.

Appendix: Regression Analysis

It can be quite difficult to plot an accurate line of average values through a scattergram of data. Fortunately, most electronic spread-

FIGURE 1.11

Data for Use in Regression Analysis

Month	Units Produced	Total Costs
January	500	$1,200
February	200	700
March	300	1,100
April	600	1,500
May	100	600
June	400	1,100
July	500	1,500
August	200	500
September	400	1,000
October	450	1,200
November	300	800
December	550	1,700

sheets can handle this chore quite easily. In this appendix, we will enter a set of raw data into a Microsoft Excel worksheet, and convert it into a regression analysis that plots an average trend line through the data. We begin with a listing of the total costs required to produce a number of units in each month of the year, which are listed in Figure 1.11.

We then copy this information into Microsoft Excel, as noted in Figure 1.12. This is a "screen print" of what the data looks like after having been entered in Excel.

Once we have entered the data in Excel, we highlight it, then click on the **Insert** command in the menu and select the **Chart** option. We then pick the **XY Scatter** option from the menu that then appears on the screen and select the scattergram option that does not attempt to plot a line through the data. The preliminary result is the graph shown in Figure 1.13.

Then press the **Next** button on the next two successive screens, and then the **Finish** button to complete our preliminary graph. However, there is still no regression line on the chart, just a scattering of dots that represent every data point that we initially entered. To obtain the regression line, we click on any data point in the resulting graph, and then press the right mouse button to locate a series of chart

FIGURE 1.12

Data Entry in Excel

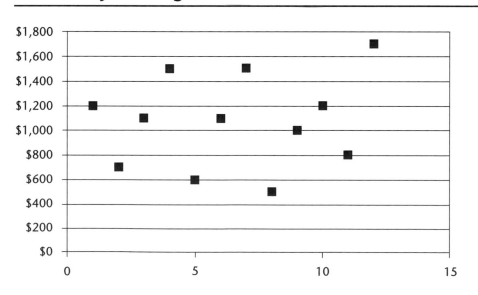

	A	B	C
1	January	500	$1,200
2	February	200	700
3	March	300	1,100
4	April	600	1,500
5	May	100	600
6	June	400	1,100
7	July	500	1,500
8	August	200	500
9	September	400	1,000
10	October	450	1,200
11	November	300	800
12	December	550	1,700

FIGURE 1.13

Preliminary Scattergram of Plotted Data

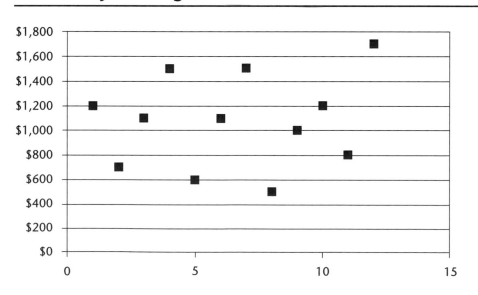

FIGURE **1.14**

Regression Line Based on Scattergram

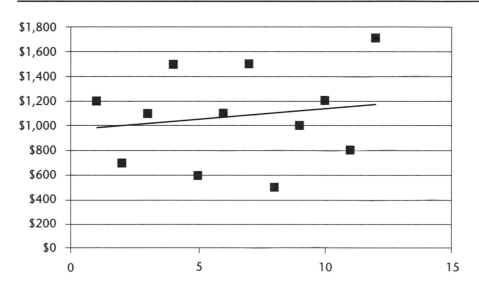

modification options. Pick the **Add Trendline** option, select the **Linear** chart type, and press **OK**. This results in the trend line shown in Figure 1.14.

Though we now have a regression line, we do not know the formula that Excel created from the original data in order to generate the line. To obtain it, click on the regression line, and then press the right mouse button. Select the **Format Trendline** option from the menu that appears on the screen, and then select the **Options** menu. Click in the **Display Equation on Chart** box, and press **OK**. These steps result in the final regression chart, which is shown in Figure 1.15. This one includes the Excel formula for the regression line, which is located in the lower right corner of the graph.

The entire process of entering data into a spreadsheet and using a few spreadsheet commands to arrive at a regression line, with the underlying formula, is a matter of a few minutes' work. This can be

FIGURE **1.15**

Regression Line with Formula

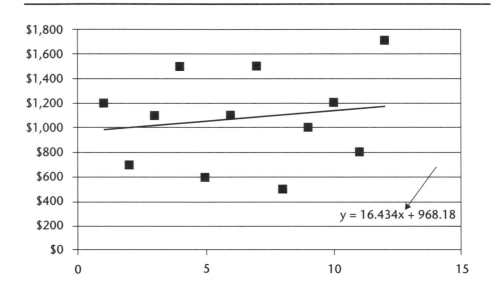

$$y = 16.434x + 968.18$$

of great assistance in the calculation of trend lines for many types of data.

The question is: How much variation can we accept before the assumption is rejected? In essence, that is the nature of sensitivity analysis: It tries to determine how sensitive an assumption is to variation.

Chapter 2

Budgeting for Operations

Operating budgets, sometimes called operating plans, are used by many manufacturing firms, retail stores, service companies, and governmental agencies for planning, operating, and control functions. To improve your probability of success, you should engage in not only long-range but also operational budgeting/planning. The fulfillment of the planning process requires marketing planning, product planning, capital planning, and financial planning. We want to emphasize that your plans should drive the budget and not the reverse. However, the process is not complete until it is quantified—that is, until budgets, as an outcome of the plan, have been prepared.

Definition or Purpose of an Operating Budget

An operating budget is a quantification of a company's business plan. It is a projected, and hopefully realistic, number picture of your income and cost objectives for a period.

Usually, operating budgets are constructed for a year, by months. Some people construct five-year operating budgets with varying reporting periods. Such budgets are often constructed monthly for the first two years, quarterly for the next two years, and annually or semi-annually for the remaining year. However, a one-year budget that is extended quarterly so that it again projects a full year is probably adequate for most uses.

As with any plan, the ensuing actual performance can be compared with the operating budget to defect "off-target" performances and to direct attention to troubled areas. In this way, the operating budget serves both as a planning tool and a control device. All functions of the business should be included when structuring the operating budget. By including all of the operating costs, more performance measures and controls are possible. The costs incurred to increase the level of preparation detail will relate favorably to realization of cost savings through better control.

Since measurements of performance many be devised according to an operating budget, there is a natural tendency for people to "adjust" the budget process. The potential consequences should be considered: Sales managers may make overly optimistic assessments of the market, thus reducing the reliability of the cash allocations and expenses anticipated for that level of production and sales. Some manufacturing managers may "pad" a budget to build in a safety margin or premium. In a tight market or competitive sales conditions, this pad could make a product look less attractive than competing products. The concern should be to get the budget as realistic and accurate as possible because a reasonable budget based on a reasonable plan encourages reasonable performance.

Signs of Budget Ineffectiveness

Some signs that the budget or budget process is less than optimally effective are:

- *Management or supervisory inattention to the budget.* Since a budget is, or can be used as, a measurement tool, accountability and review are necessary for control. Without review, there can be little corrective action and thus there is a loss of control. If management is not using the budget as a control tool, determine whether the problem is with the budget or with the management.
- *A lack of complete participation by all levels of management within the firm.* Budgets dictated from upper management without input from the accountable people may have negative effects on the psy-

chology of the employees and lower management. An attitude of "It's their budget, let's see them make it!" may develop.

- *Uncorrected large variances between planned performance and budget objectives.* Large budget variances may indicate one of several weaknesses:
  - Poor estimates
  - Poor feedback and lack of timely, corrective action
  - Ineffective management policies concerning budget mainte-nance
- *Lack of participation in the operation of the business by those who actively prepare the budgets.* Without a working knowledge of the dynam-ics of the operations of the business, it is difficult to maintain a working knowledge of current operational status. The amount or frequency of contact with operating departments is usually directly related to the stability of processes. The greater the varia-bility in the operations of the business the more frequently those who prepare the budget should observe and experience the oper-ating environment.
- *Supervisors or first-line managers do not know how their budgets were determined nor what is contained within their budget.* In such cases, department managers do not know how performance is being evaluated, how well they are performing to expectations, where they may be doing well, and where they are experiencing unplanned difficulties.

Budgets of all types are good planning tools and can also serve a very valuable control function. In order to be used for control, other systems have to be built to supplement the budget process.

- Creating the budget itself does not cause programs to be installed to implement the budget. A feedback loop is necessary to direct attention to areas where difficulties may be encoun-tered in meeting the business plan. Periodic budget reports should generate feedback on performance against budget. These reports should trigger action. If the budget and related perfor-mance against budget reports do not flag attention to problem areas, you are missing the opportunity for needed improve-ments.

- The feedback loop requires continuous measurement of performance to budget estimates. For feedback to work properly, it should be regular, expected, and consistently reported. Comparisons are most effective when they are done regularly, consistently, and timely. Trend analysis of budget performance is a good early warning device. Of course, benefits of the budget reporting process must outweigh the costs. However, the ongoing evaluation process is one of the places where you should realize substantial savings.

Improvements to the Budgeting System

Some of the budgeting problems outlined in the last section can be eliminated or mitigated by implementing a sound budgeting procedure that is closely followed by the management team throughout the year. In this section, we discuss a simple budgeting procedure that is useful for ensuring that the annual budget is constructed using a sufficient amount of time, and in the correct order. Later, we also note the monthly schedule to be followed to ensure that the management team reviews the comparison of budget to actual results. However, these are strictly procedural matters—the management team must still be committed to following the dictates of the budget, which is largely up to the senior management team to enforce.

The following budget procedure is a guideline for the sequential steps a company should follow to ensure that all components of the budget are completed in the correct order, and reviewed by those people who will be responsible for budget results. The dates noted in the procedure are based on the assumption that a company is on a calendar year-end; for those companies with a different year-end, just shift the dates to match it. The procedure is as follows:

1. *Expense update.* As of mid-November, issue to each department a listing of its expenses that are annualized based on actual expenses through October of the current year. The listing should include the personnel in each department and their current pay levels. Request a return date of 10 days in the future for this information, which should include estimated changes in expenses.

2. *Revenue update.* As of mid-November, issue to the sales manager a listing of revenue by month by business unit, through October of the current year. Request a return date of 10 days in the future for this information, which should include estimated changes in revenues.

3. *Capital expenditure update.* As of mid-November, issue a form to all department heads, requesting information about the cost and timing of capital expenditures for the upcoming year. Request a return date of 10 days in the future for this information.

4. *Automation update.* As of mid-November, issue a form to the manager of automation, requesting estimates of the timing and size of reductions in headcount in the upcoming year that are due to automation efforts. Request a return date of 10 days in the future for this information. Be sure to compare scheduled headcount reductions to the timing of capital expenditures, since they should track closely.

5. *Update the budget model.* This task should be completed by the end of November. See below.

   - Update the numbers already listed in the budget with information as it is received from the various managers. This may involve changing "hard coded" dollar amounts, or changing flex budget percentages. Be sure to keep a checklist of who has returned information, so that you can follow up with those personnel who have not returned requested information.
   - Verify that the indirect overhead allocation percentages shown on the budgeted factory overhead page are still accurate.
   - Verify that the Federal Insurance Contributions Act (FICA), State Unemployment Tax (SUTA), Federal Unemployment Tax (FUTA), medical, and workers' compensation amounts listed at the top of the staffing budget are still accurate.
   - Add job titles and pay levels to the staffing budget as needed, along with new average pay rates based on projected pay levels made by department managers.
   - Run a depreciation report for the upcoming year, add the expected depreciation for new capital expenditures, and add this amount to the budget.
   - Revise the loan detail budget based on projected borrowings through the end of the year.

6. *Review the budget.* Print out the budget and circle any budgeted expenses or revenues that are significantly different from the annualized amounts for the current year (do this by comparing the last two columns on each page). Go over the questionable items with the managers who are responsible for those items.

7. *Revise the budget.* Revise the budget, print it again, and review it with the president. Incorporate any additional changes. If the cash balance is excessive, you may have to manually move money from the cash line to the debt line to represent the pay down of debt.

8. *Issue the budget.* Bind the budget and issue it to the management team.

9. *Update accounting database.* Enter budget numbers into the accounting software for the upcoming year. All tasks should be completed by mid-December.[1]

Once the budget has been completed, there must be a feedback loop that sends budget variance information back to the department managers. The best feedback loop is to complete a budget to actual variance report that is sorted by the name of the responsible manager (see Figure 2.8 on page 56) as soon as the financial statements have been completed each month. The controller should take this report to all of the managers and review it with them, bringing back detailed information about each variance, as requested. Finally, there should be a meeting as soon thereafter as possible between the responsible managers and senior management to review variance problems and what each of the managers will do to resolve them. The senior managers should write down these commitments and return them to the managers in memo form; this document forms the basis for the next month's meeting, which will begin with a review of how well the managers have done to attain the targets to which they are committed. A key factor in making this system work is the rapid release of accurate financial statements, so that the department managers will have more time to respond to adverse variance information.

---

[1]Reprinted with permission from *The Design and Maintenance of Accounting Manuals, 1999 Supplement,* John Wiley & Sons, 1999, pp. 64–66.

Responsibility Accounting

Responsibility accounting means structuring systems and reports to highlight the accountability of specific people. The process involves assigning accountability to departments or functions in which the responsibility for performance lies.

Specific responsibility is a necessary concept of management control. Accounting has grown to encompass at least three purposes: financial reporting, product or service cost reporting, and performance evaluation reporting. The third function of accounting, the performance measurement function, is closely related to the operational function of the business. Since many businesses now evaluate and manage employees by objectives, the need for more sophisticated performance measurement tools has increased.

In a management by objectives (MBO) system, one critical element is to ensure that the individual has the authority necessary to carry out the responsibility he or she is asked to execute. Without the necessary authority, a person cannot, and should not, be expected to meet the responsibilities imposed. Since this is not intended to be an argument for an MBO system, we will assume that the manager has an appropriate balance of authority and responsibility.

Within this level of responsibility, a person can be evaluated only when the performance reporting system is tied to the expected level of performance. A person's actual performance is keyed to this budget expression of expected performance.

Responsibility accounting should not be restricted to any one level but should measure expected performance throughout the hierarchy of the business. Key indicators can be built into the system to evaluate performance and to trigger reactions to unanticipated results. In this way, management at each level is called upon to intervene only when it is necessary to correct problems or substandard performance. This management by exception system frees up significant time for managers to plan and coordinate other essential business functions.

Contrasted with financial accounting, responsibility accounting does not simply group like costs, but instead segments the business into distinct responsibility centers. A measurement process is established to compare results obtained against objectives established for the segment prior to the end of a plan/budget period. These objectives are part of the operating budget and comprise the targets of operation for every segment of the business.

To be effective, responsibility accounting must be tailored to each individual business. The accounting system must be adjusted to conform with the responsibility centers established. The revenue and expense categories must be designed to fit the functions or operations that management believes are important to monitor and evaluate. For example, the use of electricity by a particular machine may be significant, and excessive use may be an early warning sign of a process problem. Management would want to meter electricity consumption and have the expense reported as a line item to be measured against standard consumption rates by machine or by department.

In a service business, it may be important to accumulate and evaluate costs for "expedited" mailings as a distinct item not included in the "postage expense" numbers. Such costs might indicate inefficient operations in the mail room.

Another function of the responsibility accounting system is to compile the individual centers' performance reports into successively aggregated collective reports to identify broader categories of responsibility. Behind these groupings is still a great deal of detailed information available for analysis.

Developing Responsibility Centers

A responsibility center has no standard size. It can be as small as a single operation or machine or as large as the entire business. The business is, after all, the responsibility center of the chief executive of the business. Typically, the business is broken down into a large number of centers or segments that, when plotted in successive layers or groupings, appear as a pyramid. This pyramiding represents the hierarchy of authority and responsibility of the business. Various types of responsibility centers may be established for various purposes. The nature of the centers or segments can also vary.

If a person is charged with only the responsibility for the costs incurred in a process or operation, a *cost center* has been established. Cost centers can be line operations (such as painting) or staff functions (such as recruiting). The emphasis of a cost center is on producing goods or providing specific services in conjunction with other physical measures of performance. Usually, there is no direct revenue production measurement by that center because the center does not produce final product.

Another segment is a unit held responsible for the profit contribution it makes. This responsibility center is aptly named a *profit center.* Profit centers are often larger units than cost centers because a profit center requires the production of a complete product or service to make a contribution to the profit. (However, a salesman could be considered a profit center.) The establishment of a profit center should be based on established managerial criteria of revenues and costs.

Other divisions can be established such as *revenue centers* and *investment centers.* Revenue centers, for instance, are segments of the larger profit centers charged with the responsibility of producing revenue. Sales departments are a typical example. An investment center is a profit center that also has the responsibility of raising and making the necessary investment required to produce the profit. This added investment step would require the use of some rate-of-return test as an objective measure of the center's performance.

The appropriate establishment of cost centers, profit centers, and the like is a critical element of the responsibility reporting system, and as such must be performed carefully and accurately.

Establishing Costs

Another important aspect of responsibility accounting is the accumulation of costs. Accountants have labeled the standard types of costs typically encountered: fixed, variable, and semivariable. Within these classifications, some costs may be incurred at the discretion of specific levels of management whereas others are nondiscretionary at given levels of management. Sometimes, costs relate to more than one center and must be allocated between them. The most effective system will probably result when responsible management has been an active participant in the determination of the allocation of costs and the maintenance of the reporting system.

One complication of accumulating costs is the problem of transfer pricing. In manufacturing businesses, a cost center's performance is a function of the added costs and the intracompany movements of raw materials, work-in-progress, finished goods, and services performed. A market price may not be available or may be too uncertain, because of fluctuations, to use as an objective measure of performance. Some compromise is often necessary to establish transfer prices among departments.

Fixed Costs. A fixed cost is one that does not vary directly with volume. Some costs are really fixed, such as interest on debt. Other typically identified fixed costs, such as depreciation expense, may vary under some circumstances. Generally, over a broad range of operations, total fixed costs are represented as step functions because they are incurred in increments as production or the number of services increases.

This characteristic of fixed costs should not present any great difficulty. Since production or sales is predicted for a budget period, the level of fixed costs can be established from graphs such as that in Figure 2.1. Unfortunately, fixed costs, because of their apparent static behavior, are not always reviewed regularly and critically to determine reasonableness. Like all other costs, the larger the amount of individual fixed costs, the more frequently they should be reviewed. Insurance premiums are a good example. Insurance premiums may

Figure 2.1

Fixed Costs

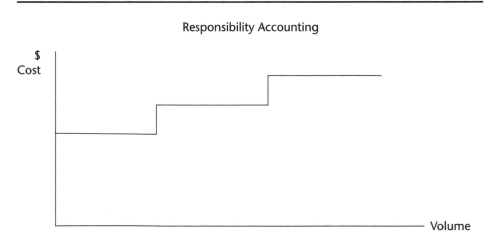

Responsibility Accounting

vary little, if at all, from year to year and be paid without reconsideration, particularly in good times. A schedule of review should be set up based on a two-factor analysis.

Figure 2.2 represents the relationship between the magnitude of a particular fixed cost and the frequency with which it should be reviewed. When making such an assessment for yourself, you should be aware of such factors as the cost of reconsideration in setting the time periods for "seldom" through "often." The process of reevaluating your insurance coverage may be a significant task, requiring a major allocation of time and resources. However, the returns could be equally significant if you realize substantial savings resulting from a renegotiation of the insurance policy and rates.

Another concern with fixed costs is the method of allocation of those costs among your different products or services. Fixed costs are often assigned in an arbitrary manner, creating an unrealistic profit or loss statement for each product. Otherwise, nonprofitable products

FIGURE 2.2

Relationship of Cost to Review Frequency

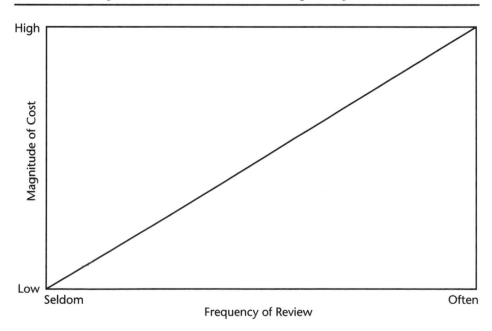

are sometimes carried by an "average fixed cost" allocation, which may not accurately depict costs associated with the product. Accurate decisions are unlikely without correct information concerning a product's costs. You should undertake to allocate fixed costs properly through the preparation of an operating budget. Your accountant should have a reasonable understanding of the magnitude of the costs and which products or services are affecting the amount. Also, you should determine how varying activity levels influence the costs you incur for different products and services.

When analyzing fixed costs, you should determine what causes that cost to be incurred and what causes it to change in amount. This analysis will go a long way toward identifying to which product(s) or service(s) the cost should be assigned and in what manner that allocation should be made.

For some fixed costs, this will be a very difficult process. Some administrative costs may simply not be identifiable with any one product or service. Successive allocations through your costing hierarchy may be needed to arrive finally at a "product-attributable" status.

One may treat such costs as variable and determine a rate at which to assign these costs against labor hours. In determining this burden or overhead rate, such fixed costs are divided by an estimate or projection of the anticipated direct labor hours and are allocated proportionately. However, this method may unfairly assign costs to labor-intensive products, ignoring that more fixed costs should perhaps be allocated to products with large capital or fixed investments. Furthermore, this assignment could underrecover fixed costs by misestimating projected direct labor hours. Or, equally likely, an overrecovery of fixed costs could occur.

A realistic approach should be taken in the allocation of these costs. If a direct hour allocation is realistic, then use it. If fixed costs can be identified to particular product(s) or service(s), it is appropriate to do so.

Variable Costs. In order to be properly classified as variable, a cost should meet two distinct criteria: no cost should be incurred until an activity begins, and a direct relationship should exist between the amount of the cost and the level of activity. An example of a purely variable cost is a sales commission. As sales increase or decrease, the amount of commission varies in direct relationship to the level of sales.

The relationship between the cost and the level of production may be a straight-line relationship, or the cost rate may increase as the level of output increases. When plotted, this increasing cost relationship will appear as a curvilinear (or curved shape) graph.

Although this relationship is common to variable costs, Figure 2.3 is not the usual way it is shown. The more usual case is the straight-line relationship. Often, setup costs are spread over production, in which case there is a curvilinear relationship; but that is not the same case. In the setup cost allocation, a fixed cost is spread over varying units of output, decreasing as the length of the production run increases. The earlier example is an increasing cost per unit as the number of units produced increases.

Typically, costs such as direct labor, scrap costs, packaging, and shipping are treated as variable costs. However, direct labor and other costs may not be purely variable. For example, the assumption that

FIGURE 2.3

Actual Relationship between Variable Cost and Level of Production

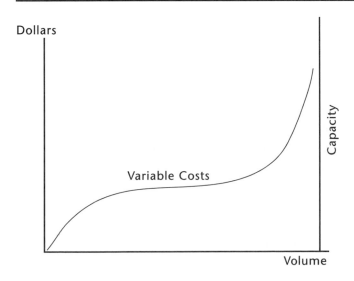

direct labor varies directly with the number of units produced relies on the divisibility assumption. But labor is not infinitely divisible. If an employee can produce 1,600 units in a standard eight-hour work-day but only 1,200 units are required, unless that employee can be used in another operation, he or she has been used at a 75 percent utilization level. Either this idle-time labor can be effectively used in other places or 25 percent of these (unutilized) efforts are assigned to fewer units produced. In most cases, direct labor and direct materials are treated as variable costs for budget purposes even if they are not perfectly divisible.

If you have established labor standards for your operations, these can be used for budgeting purposes. By accumulating data and establishing labor standards, you can begin to target costs. The difficulty is establishing objective labor-hour targets for the planning period. Reliance solely on historical data may bias projections, ignore the effects of the learning curve on efficiency, and avoid consideration of past inefficiencies.

For planning purposes, remember that the graph of these fixed and variable costs appears reversed *when they are assigned on a per-unit basis*. When variable costs are assigned on a per-unit basis, they are constant and fixed per unit. When fixed costs are assigned on a per-unit basis, they vary as production levels change.

Mixed Costs.   Mixed costs are those that behave as if they have fixed and variable components. Many items of cost fall into this category. Some people treat mixed costs as fixed costs. If you do so, you must assume an average or projected level of output and allocate the cost over that level. This may over- or underrecover that component of fixed cost. Some might say that it is not important because the over- or underrecovery will be insignificant.

A consistent bias toward underrecovery of the fixed component of one mixed cost may be equally true about an underrecovery of the fixed component of every mixed cost, allocated on the basis of that misestimated output level. If this biased data is used to make capital investment decisions, marketing and pricing decisions, and expansion or contraction decisions, one may experience serious problems.

It is sometimes difficult to determine what portion of a mixed cost is fixed and what portion is variable. Fortunately, this allocation can usually be established from historical data. As an example, data for the consumption of electricity in one department were tabulated for the previous six months (Figure 2.4).

Plotting this consumption (Figure 2.5), with the Y axis being kilowatt hours (kWh) consumed and the X axis being the units produced, the Y intercept is 5,000 kWh. This indicates that for zero production, the department still consumes 5,000 kWh of electricity each month, the fixed component of cost.

The variable component can then be determined by using the formula:

$$Y = MX + B$$

Because B, the Y intercept, is 5,000:

$$Y = MX + 5{,}000$$

Substituting any set of values from the table into the equation:

$$7{,}500 = M(400) + 5{,}000$$

and solving for (M), $M = 6.25$. Therefore, each unit of production has a variable component of 6.25 kWh in electrical consumption. By applying the electric rate to each component of electrical usage, the fixed- and variable-cost components of the mixed cost are determined. Sometimes, the equation is not so straightforward and linear regression may have to be used to project the line. This can be done using the linear regression "least squares" model discussed in Chapter 1.

Historical Data. One major concern of using historical data as a basis for future prediction is that the firm may be perpetuating past inefficiencies. However, historical data may be the best or even the only data available. When using historical data, one should be sure that:

FIGURE 2.4

Consumption of Power Table

	kWh Used	Units Produced
Jan	7,500	400
Feb	8,000	480
Mar	8,250	520
Apr	8,750	600
May	9,500	720
June	8,750	600

FIGURE 2.5

Consumption of Power Graph

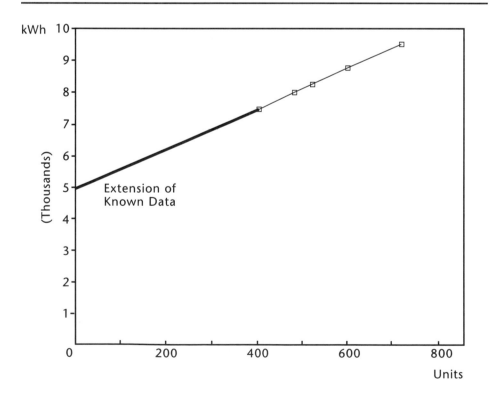

- Historical data accurately state the past. An examination must be made of the conditions under which data were collected, and what is and is not contained in the data.
- Historical data are relevant to what the firm is trying to predict. To the extent current conditions are not the same as past conditions, historical data become more difficult to use in projecting the future.
- The use of the data encourages performance that improves on the past performance.
- The effects of inflation are properly considered.

Further *practical points* in the use of historical data include:

- Avoid using historical data more than 12 months old in periods of high inflation or deflation.
- Be consistently objective. Do not bias the data by summarily rejecting data that seem to be out of line. There may be a reason for unusual numbers.
- Be creative; try not to be bound by traditional thinking. Some of the relationships between costs and activities may not seem direct and quantifiable. This could be the result of delayed billings or nontraditional billings.
- Consider and try using moving averages for data that tend to be nonlinear or scattered.
- Use extrapolation to project data for future estimated production or service levels.
- Never use tools past the point that common sense tells you is meaningful.

Projecting Revenues

Often, firms want a forecast of earnings for the entire enterprise to compare with the operating budgets. This forecast of revenues should be reconciled with the operating budget.

The basis of all revenue projections is a sales forecast. Many companies start the operating budget process by first generating this sales forecast. The sales forecast is exploded with lead and lag times added so that departmental schedules are created. This departmental scheduling of activities is then used to create the operating budget. For example, Fruit Crate Manufacturing Co., Inc., has a maximum production capacity of 1,000 crates per week and expects the following sales forecast.

	July	Aug
Type A crate	2,000	3,000

To produce a type A crate, the firm's process breaks down into three steps: sawing, curing or drying, and assembly. The sawing and curing is done in batches of 1,000 crates and the rate of production is:

Sawing   1,000 crates/1 week
Drying   1,000 crates/3 weeks
Assembly   1,000 crates/1 week

Since all sales are shipped on the first of each month, the exploded production schedule shown in Figure 2.6 is used for budgeting.

Armed with this operating schedule, the company can plan its equipment, labor, and materials scheduling, and a budget of expenses can be generated. Without carrying the example too much farther, it is easy to see how much of each operation must be done and when. For example, in May, two weeks of sawing and one week of drying must be budgeted; in June, three weeks of sawing, eight weeks of drying, and two weeks of assembly; and so forth.

As manufacturing and related costs are pushed back in time, the receipt of payments (cash flows) is pushed forward in time. If Fruit Crate Manufacturing Co., Inc., offers a 2/10, N/30 payment schedule (Two percent discount if paid within 10 days of invoice, the net amount due within 30 days), it will ship on July 1, having incurred expenses in May and June, but not expect payment until July 10 or August 1. The timing of cash flows, the revenue portion, and the expense portion of the plan, must be coordinated to ensure that adequate funds are on hand (cash flow budget) to meet expected operations. For this example, there is a negative cash flow for at least two and a half months.

FIGURE **2.6**

Exploded Production Schedule

Production Schedules
1,000-Crate Batches

MAY			JUNE			JULY			AUGUST			
S				A								
	D	D	D									
	S				A							
		D	D	D								
		S				A						
			D	D	D							
			S				A					
				D	D	D						
				S				A				
					D	D	D					
					S				A			
						D	D	D				

Budget Tracking and Maintenance

So far, this chapter has emphasized establishing responsibility and developing a budget and accounting system that conforms to an allocation of responsibility. The cardinal principle behind this system is that those who are to be measured by the system understand how it works and agree that the objectives are attainable *through their efforts.*

The first requirement should be an integration of your objectives, goals, and tactics to the managerial level involved. One method for integration is to have each manager participate in establishing and maintaining the objectives and goals. The test of reasonableness should apply. That is, there should be a reasonable likelihood of obtaining the objective in order to motivate compliance.

An element that often impedes effective budgeting and attainability is the inability to identify controllable and uncontrollable costs or expenses. Controllable costs should be identified and targeted. If elements of uncontrollable costs are included in a responsibility-based budget, they may have a negative motivation factor. Practically, all revenue and expense factors are controllable by some manager at some point. However, such expenses as property taxes may influence profits, yet be beyond the control of an operations manager. Such items as administrative overhead allocation are uncontrollable within departments of the firm. As a general rule, these items should be assigned and accounted for separately, so as not to indicate responsibility of the manager (e.g., heating, lighting, janitorial).

The final element in the budget tracking plan is variance analysis and reporting. Variance reporting can take many forms, but the most common is to compare monthly actuals to monthly projections with year-to-date comparisons as well. Often, the report will contain space for an explanation of the variance from budget. The report can be generated in many forms, including by product, by operation or group, by labor, and by materials. A typical report could look like the one shown in Figure 2.7.

The report shown in Figure 2.7 compares budgeted to actual costs by account category, such as repair supplies or insurance. Though this format is good for determining trends in certain cost categories, it does not assist in targeting which managers are responsible for specific costs. An example of a report that includes this information is shown in Figure 2.8. In this example, we have used the same expense line items but also added a column that lists the name of the manager who is responsible for each expense. Further, we have sorted the report by the names of those managers. This sorting has two purposes: One is to divide the report into separate pages for each manager, so that each one can easily group together the expenses for which he or she is responsible; the other reason is that sorting the report by manager

FIGURE 2.7

Budgeted versus Annual Costs

	Month			Year-to-Date			Explanations
	Budget	Actual	% Var	Budget	Actual	% Var	
A. Controllable							
Direct Labor							
Operating Supplies							
Repair Labor							
Repair Supplies							
Heat, Light, Power							
Subtotal							
B. Raw Materials							
Subtotal							
C. Overhead							
Supervisory Salaries							
Corporate Overhead							
Taxes							
Insurance							
Depreciation Expense							
Subtotal							
Total							

FIGURE 2.8

Comparison of Budget to Actual, Sorted by Responsibility

Expense Description Variance	Responsible Manager	Month				Year-to-Date		
		Budget	Actual	% Variance		Budget	Actual	%
Direct Labor	D. Hendricks	25,400	23,000	–9%		177,800	161,000	–9%
Repair Labor	D. Hendricks	8,000	7,250	–9%		56,000	50,750	–9%
Supervisory Salaries	D. Hendricks	7,250	7,000	–3%		50,750	49,000	–3%
Totals		40,650	37,250	–8%		284,550	260,750	–8%
Operating Supplies	R. Olbermann	1,450	1,500	3%		10,150	10,500	3%
Repair Supplies	R. Olbermann	3,300	3,500	6%		23,100	24,500	6%
Depreciation Expense	R. Olbermann	500	520	4%		3,500	3,640	4%
Totals		5,250	5,520	5%		36,750	38,640	5%
Heat, Light, Power	T. Abrams	3,200	1,700	–47%		22,400	11,900	–47%
Raw Materials	T. Abrams	89,450	79,500	–11%		626,150	556,500	–11%
Corporate Overhead	T. Abrams	55,000	56,000	2%		385,000	392,000	2%
Taxes	T. Abrams	11,500	10,250	–11%		80,500	71,750	–11%
Insurance	T. Abrams	27,050	26,000	–4%		189,350	182,000	–4%
Totals		186,200	173,450	–7%		1,303,400	1,214,150	–7%

allows one to summarize variances for each person, so that senior managers can determine which managers are doing the best job of keeping their costs within designated goals, which can be of assistance when determining the size of manager bonuses.

In Figure 2.8, the report reveals that the only manager who is consistently failing to achieve actual costs that are less than the budget is R. Olbermann, whose cumulative variance performance is 5 percent worse than the budget.

When the management team reviews revenue and expense variances, it does not have time to review what may be hundreds of individual accounts. Instead, it only has sufficient time to analyze a small proportion of the largest variances. Accordingly, the accounting staff can issue a summarized version of Figure 2.8 that lists only line items for which variances exceed a certain monthly or year-to-date dollar amount or percentage. The remaining accounts can still be issued as an addendum to the variance report. This slight format change will focus management's attention on the few largest variances that are most in need of correction.

This form of reporting consistently shows management the variations from budget, with an explanation of causes and circumstances. It thus meets the second and third objectives of a budget, to keep score and direct attention.

Parts of an Operating Budget

Budgets are what you make of them. There are no hard-and-fast rules for what budgets must look like. To assist you in better operating the business, budgets should be devised specifically. Some typical elements of operating budgets are discussed below.

Sales Forecast

Providing for all potential service(s) or sales may determine the amount of product to have on hand or the personnel needed for the provision of services. Thus, the foundation of operational planning is an estimate of how much you expect to sell and when. A sales forecast provides data for these two questions. Because it is the basis of a forecast of earnings, many people first develop a sales budget. These budgets are scrutinized to ensure that the volume is attainable under economic conditions expected in the budget year. Marketing experts or personnel may be called in to compare their budgets with forecasts prepared by sales personnel, since the latter are sometimes unrealistic in the evaluation of economic and market conditions.

The sales forecast is then exploded to include major product lines so as to consider production planning requirements and manufacturing capacity. The forecast may be refined to:

- Separate forecasts of physical units and price per unit (in lieu of total sales dollars).
- Recognize seasonal variation.
- Utilize daily or weekly averages.

Cost of Goods Sold Budget

For a specified level of production, a budget can be prepared if two pieces of data are assembled: a complete bill of materials and an objective set of labor-hour standards. If subassemblies or parts are received from a vendor, a market price must be established. This will probably include a component for in-house receipt, storage, and handling. For example, Fruit Crate Manufacturing Co., Inc., for a projected *manufacturing* cost estimate, has established the costs, labor components, transfer prices, and overhead shown in Figure 2.9 for the assembly of a type A crate for a projected three-month period.

Variable Manufacturing Budgets

As seen in Figure 2.9, the manufacturing cost element provides a useful cost evaluation tool to manufacturing managers, but it should also relate the manufacturing activity to the profit forecast. The variable manufacturing budget relates the various costs in a department or cost center to ranges of possible production. These budgets use a probabilistic or statistical method for establishing costs. This can be compared with the fixed operating expense budget shown in Figure 2.9.

FIGURE 2.9

Manufacturing Cost Estimate

**Parts of an Operating Budget
Fruit Crate Mfg. Co., Inc.
Manufacturing Cost Estimate, Type A Crate, May–July**

Labor	May	June	July
Trimming slats/finishing	.04 hrs.	.04 hrs.	.03[a]
Slats to nailing frame	.025	.025	.025
Cutting and nailing	.033	.030[b]	.025[b]
Attached stiffeners	.020	.018[b]	.017[b]
Attach label and move to storage	.040	.040	.040
Total direct labor hours	.158	.153	.137
Labor rate	$4.25/hr	$4.25/hr	$4.50/hr[c]
Total Labor Cost	$.672	$.650	$.617
Materials			
Slats 3 board feet @ $200/1000	$0.600	$0.600	$0.600
Wire/nails	0.060	0.065[d]	0.065
Labels	0.025	0.025	0.025
Total Materials Cost	$0.685	$0.690	$0.690
Overhead			
Plant & equipment	$0.15	0.15	0.15
Supervisory salaries	0.03	0.03	0.03
Taxes and insurance	0.010	0.010	0.015[e]
Utilities and maintenance	0.015	0.015	0.015
Total Overhead	$0.205	0.205	0.210
Total Manufacturing Cost	$1.562	$1.545	$1.517

[a]High-speed sander becomes operational.
[b]Effects of learning.
[c]New labor contract goes into effect.
[d]Projected cost increase of steel impacting fabricated steel parts.
[e]New taxes due to become effective as a result of change in state's budget year.

Payroll Budget

Some organizations—especially those in the service sector—have very few expenses besides payroll. Even for traditional manufacturing companies, there are probably a sufficiently large number of employees outside of the direct labor category to warrant some extra budgeting detail. For these situations, we have a payroll budget, such as the one shown in Figure 2.10. In Figure 2.10, all positions are categorized by department, and then the average pay level per position, the number of employees per position, and the overtime percentage to be expected (if the position is an hourly one) are noted. These columns are then multiplied to arrive at the gross pay level by position, which is noted in the Gross Pay column. In the next six columns, the various tax or benefit costs noted at the top of the columns are multiplied by the gross pay levels for each position to arrive at the total taxes and benefits the company must pay for each position. Then, in the three columns to the far right of the spreadsheet, the costs for all positions within each department are summarized into three categories—labor, taxes, and burden—which can then be entered into the various departmental budgets.

The payroll budgeting approach outlined here is superior to one that identifies individual employees, because they may change positions during the year, whereas the position titles are much more easily identifiable. Also, this format lends a small degree of confidentiality to the payroll figures, since an unauthorized reader cannot discern from it the precise pay level of an employee, unless there is just one employee within a job classification.

Need for Budget Updating

Flexible or variable budgets should be kept current so that targets are realistic and accurately reflect deviations from expected costs. Budgets, however, may lose their effectiveness as a measuring and control device if they are adjusted for every small change in operating costs. There is no rule of thumb for triggering a budget adjustment. However, budgets should be adjusted for changes in product mix,

Figure 2.10

Sample Payroll Budget

Description	Pay	Overtime	No. of Employees	Gross Pay	FICA 7.60%	SUTA 1.00%	FUTA 0.78%	Medical per Person $1,500	W/C Mfg. 3.00%	W/C Admin. 1.50%	Dept. Totals	Total Labor	Total Taxes	Total Burden
Assembly														
Inspectors	21,500	15%	3.0	74,175	4,902	645	503	4,500	1,935	—				
Manager	75,500	—	1.0	75,500	5,738	755	589	1,500	2,265	—				
Supervisor	45,000	—	1.0	45,000	3,420	450	351	1,500	1,350	—				
Planner/Scheduler	40,000	—	1.5	60,000	4,560	600	468	2,250	1,800	—				
Warehouse Staff	20,000	15%	4.0	92,000	6,080	800	624	6,000	2,400	—	Assembly	346,675	30,485	25,500
Engineering														
Engineer	58,000	—	3.0	174,000	13,224	1,740	1,357	4,500	5,220	—	Engineering	174,000	16,321	9,720
Maintenance														
Maintenance Lead	45,000	15%	1.0	51,750	3,420	450	351	1,500	1,350	—				
Maintenance	31,000	15%	2.0	71,300	4,712	620	484	3,000	1,860	—	Maintenance	123,050	10,037	7,710
Production														
VP/General Mgr.	105,000	—	1.0	105,000	7,980	1,050	819	1,500	3,150	—				
Plant Manager	72,000	—	1.0	72,000	5,472	720	562	1,500	2,160	—				
Shift Coordinator	45,000	—	3.0	135,000	10,260	1,350	1,053	4,500	4,050	—	Production	312,000	29,266	16,860
Quality														
Quality Engineer	55,000	—	1.0	55,000	4,180	550	429	1,500	1,650	—				
Quality Staff	28,000	—	5.0	140,000	10,640	1,400	1,092	7,500	4,200	—	Quality	195,000	18,291	14,850
Selling, Gen., Admin.														
Accounting Staff	24,000	—	3.0	72,000	5,472	720	562	4,500	—	1,080				
Admin. Assistant	26,500	15%	1.0	30,475	2,014	265	207	1,500	—	398				
Controller	75,000	—	1.0	75,000	5,700	750	585	1,500	—	1,125				
Customer Service	27,500	—	3.0	82,500	6,270	825	644	4,500	—	1,238				
Human Resources	32,000	—	1.0	32,000	2,432	320	250	1,500	—	480				
MIS Coordinator	50,000	—	1.0	50,000	3,800	500	390	1,500	—	750				
President	150,000	—	1.0	150,000	11,400	1,500	1,170	1,500	—	2,250				
Sales Manager	85,000	—	1.0	85,000	6,460	850	663	1,500	—	1,275	SG&A	576,975	53,747	26,595

major changes in cost levels, and schedule variations that significantly alter cost relationships.

On a departmental level, budget performance reflects actual departmental cost behavior, and budget gains or savings directly result in improvements in profits. The budget becomes an individual department's profit and loss expectation based on responsibility accounting. In emphasizing profit, the key is to ensure that quality output, good service, and employee morale are maintained.

One area in which potential problems may not be recognized is deferred maintenance. When increased output or profit is being emphasized, periodic maintenance is often deferred to "keep the wheels turning." This may be short-sighted, resulting instead in deferred costs when breakdowns occur.

Summary

The operating budget is a tool that can be integrated into overall operations. It can give an indication about the delays between cash outlays for manufacturing and sales receipts. This delay can be quantified in the budget and thereby permit one to plan for carrying or acquiring additional cash for predictable periods.

As with any good planning tool, the operating plan and related budget points up the opportunity for capital expenditures or the need for tightening capital investments. Because sales predictions are the driving force behind budget numbers, you will plan sales forces, marketing objectives, advertising budgets, sales quotas, credit policies, and many other factors as parts of operational budgeting/planning.

Finally, manpower planning and allocation can be computed straightforwardly from the production schedule and direct labor rates. The formula is simply a direct allocation of hours per operation per product, times the number of units of product scheduled for production, summed over all operations. For example, in the Fruit Crate case:

- The total labor hours per crate was .158 hours in May.
- In May, the firm scheduled 2,300 crates (equivalent) for production, which represents 363.4 direct labor hours.

- There were 176 hours (gross) per worker available in the month. The firm planned for 81 percent utilization in hours as a result of breaks, sickness, leave, and fatigue.
- The firm calculates 142.6 hours per man per month effective work time.
- By dividing 363.4 by 142.6, the firm arrives at 2.5 direct laborers necessary to produce the crates.

Using such an analysis, the firm can also break out, by operation, the number of employees needed for each task.

As a control device, an operating plan or budget can provide needed information and direct attention where variances have occurred.

Chapter 3

Investing in Long-Term Assets and Capital Budgeting

Most capital investment decisions should be made in two parts: first, the investment decision; then, the financing decision. You should first decide what facilities, equipment, or other capital assets you will acquire, when to acquire them, and what to do with them. Then you should decide where and how to get the money. This chapter will consider only the investment decision; the financing issues are left to Chapter 5.

The term *capital budgeting* may be defined as planning for an expenditure or outlay of cash resources and a return from the anticipated flow of future cash benefits. The necessary elements to be considered for this decision are:

- Expected costs and their timing.
- The flow of anticipated benefits.
- The time over which those funds will flow.
- The risk involved in the realization of those benefits.

Each of these elements has distinct characteristics associated with a company's management philosophy. Tools have been developed that use the numbers generated by management to help answer questions and to make reasoned decisions among competing business opportunities for the use of scarce investment dollars. In this chapter, we will look at the capital budgeting process as part of a cycle, not as an isolated exercise. We begin with an idea for a new product and proceed through to the discontinuance of that product and into the next generation. Although we are using a specific example, you will note that the concepts have a general application.

Parenthetically, it is interesting to note that capital budgeting can also be defined in almost the same precise words as the definition of *economics:* the study of the allocation of scarce resources to competing ends over time to maximize utility.

Definitions

Before attempting an explanation of the capital budgeting process, we need to be familiar with several terms. The common financial terms used in this chapter are:

Present value. The present value of an item is the value *today* of an amount you expect to receive or to pay at some future date. For example, if you expect to receive $100 one year from today, and you can get 12 percent for your money, that stream of income has a *present* value of $89.29 because $89.29 invested today at 12 percent return *will be* $100.00 one year from today.

Annuity (regular or ordinary). The receipt or payment of a series of equal payments made at the end of each of a number of fixed periods. The receipt of $100 on December 31 of each year for 10 years is an ordinary annuity. (An "annuity due" means payments are received at the beginning of each period rather than at the end.)

Payback period. The payback period indicates how long it takes for you to get your money back. In other words, it is the time necessary for net cash inflows to amortize an original investment. Interest or the time value of money is often not considered in simple payback calculations. However, a more appropriate form of payback calculation, called the discounted payback period, does consider the time value. In discounted payback, the present value of the inflows is considered in determining how long it takes to get the investment back.

Net present value (NPV). The present value of inflows of cash minus the present value of the outflows of cash. This is normally "after-tax cash flows."

Present value index. The net present value divided by original investment (this index is useful only for positive net present values).

Internal rate of return (IRR). The discount (interest) rate, which when used in calculating NPV results in NPV being zero. This is sometimes called the true rate of return.

There are other accounting and financial tools and models one can use to analyze possible investments in a product or project. These models consider mostly the same information in different ways and can be found in investment or finance textbooks. The six mentioned above will be sufficient for our purposes.

Overview and Use of Capital Budgeting

Budgets, a frequently used tool, have been around for a long time. Operating budgets seem to be the most common. Although seldom used to their potential, operating budgets are ordinarily among the first budgets attempted. The numbers for these budgets are not difficult to obtain, and most managers will give at least some credence to their usefulness. Operating budgets are discussed in detail in Chapter 2.

Cash budgets are not greatly different from operating budgets in their preparation and use. In cash budgeting, attention is focused on the receipt and expenditure of cash. However, cash budgets are often limited to use by fewer people within a business and often are not formalized until required by shortages of cash or the high cost of maintaining cash reserves. In periods of better financial conditions, the inefficiency of having too much cash is often overlooked. As a result, cash budgets sometimes fall into disuse during periods of prosperity.

Capital budgeting, however, does not fare well with many businessmen. This is due in part to the difficulties of preparing a capital budget. Estimates of cash flows must be pushed farther into the future and unfamiliar terms such as *weighted average cost of capital* and *internal rate of return* creep into the terminology. The calculations associated with these terms are often unfamiliar; many businessmen have learned to operate with no formal capital budget. However, used properly, a capital budgeting process can help to reduce the risk of making the wrong decision.

Capital budgeting is useful as a decision tool. Accountants, and some of your staff and some managers, have probably been trained to make the calculations necessary for determinations of present values, internal rates of return, and payback periods. These calculations are fairly simple and can be done using the forms provided in the appendix to this chapter. Some inexpensive calculators can do most of the calculations with ease. The critical work is the gathering of the information necessary to make the capital budgeting process more understandable and useful to the business.

Life Cycles

Products and projects, like people, have life cycles, as shown in Figure 3.1. They all go through similar stages: conception, birth, growth, maturity, decline, and ultimately death. Each stage requires a certain

FIGURE **3.1**

Project Life Cycle

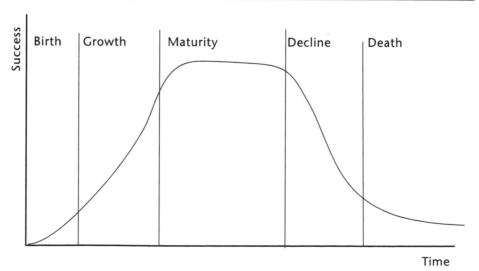

degree of attention. The applicability of capital budgeting concepts to new projects or new products extends beyond application to new ventures. It can be used to consider the replacement of existing product lines and even to cost reductions in existing lines in the current or future periods.

Capital Budgeting Sequence

There are four basic sets of actions that occur in a capital budgeting plan: proposal solicitation or generation, evaluation, implementation, and follow-up. We shall examine each in some detail.

Proposal Solicitation or Generation

1. The first step in proposal generation is evaluation of your present status. Many factors should be considered when making an evaluation of status. It is particularly important to pay attention to your position with respect to the availability of management talent, technological talent, financial and market positions, sources of labor, and the availability of markets for your product.

   Example: Assume you manufacture heavy cast iron cylinders for which "the market" is located primarily in southeastern sunbelt states. Therefore, one particularly important factor is the cost of transportation of the product to the ultimate user. At least two alternatives are available: Locate the plant in the area where the product is consumed or acquire manufacturing facilities on low-cost transportation networks such as rail or water.

   Another option may be to redesign the product. For example, assume you find that you can manufacture the cylinders out of aluminum with the installation of a tooled steel sleeve instead of the cast iron cylinder. The product now requires different raw materials, different processing and handling, and different packaging and shipping. The new product may change your marketing plans, and a proposal for capital expenditures may result.

2. The questions that you should answer are standard business planning questions: "What do we do best?" and "Where are we

going?" These require an evaluation of your business plan. The objectives formulated as a result of these questions may point out potential projects requiring capital expenditures.

Decisions relative to capital expenditures may be made at various levels within the organization depending on their size and significance. Rules for decision making should be consistently applied at whatever level of management you have established.

3. Cost reduction programs may be a rich source of capital budgeting projects. Cost reduction programs generally carry with them less risk than any other form of project. In most cases, cost reduction programs have obvious cost justifications. Potential payback periods and returns on investments can be readily calculated because the programs are intended to improve the cost efficiency of existing projects. Such programs, if adopted, help make employees feel that they are a part of the decision-making process, because a large part of these proposals are usually generated from line employees.

4. Ideas from employees and customers are also often low-risk sources for increased profitability. Marketing or sales personnel meet with customers on a regular basis. They should be able to determine current market needs and may assess demands not being met. Often, these opportunities can be exploited with little additional cost to you. By taking advantage of unmet market needs head-on, competition can be avoided and you may successfully expand your market presence. To encourage new ideas and market opportunities you may use either or both of the following avenues: (a) Encourage entrepreneurship by allowing self-interest to work for you. Monetary incentive programs for sales staff and other employees are extremely effective in generating growth-producing ideas. (b) Surveys of customer needs can be made on a regular basis to inform you of potential growth possibilities.

5. Competitors are often a good source of potential growth-producing ideas. Sometimes, it is beneficial to let competitors pioneer certain new products. Letting them take the risks often eliminates these products from your consideration as a result of their lack of profitability or outright product failure. Of course, this gives the competitor a head start on successful ventures.

6. Product matrix analysis will sometimes disclose holes in the market. A full discussion of product matrix analysis is given in the chapter on marketing.

7. Often, new ideas are available through purchase from independent research and development (R&D) firms or may be generated by your own R&D efforts.

8. Trade shows, conventions, seminars, and publications are good sources of potential ideas. In this case, you are not paying for the development of ideas but instead are picking other people's brains.

9. You may decide on vertical growth—being your own supplier or marketer. Supplying yourself with components, services, or raw materials is a source of potential profit. Setting up your own distribution network outlets can be profitable as well. For example, some utilities have diversified into fields such as coal production and transportation in order to guarantee a source of supply and to reduce the risk associated with fuel cost variations. In this way, vertical integration provides them with additional revenue-producing sources of unregulated profit. Some natural gas utilities sell gas appliances. Being "the gas company" gives them an entry for marketing the appliances. Customers trust a company that provides gas to know which are the best gas appliances.

10. You may want to grow horizontally through product diversification or buying of competitors.

11. You can expand the use of present technologies. The question you should constantly ask is, "What can we do with what we know or what we do best?" How adaptable is the current technology to meet new product innovation or new processes? The opportunity here is to have growth-producing ideas with minimal risks. If you have learned to utilize your technologies efficiently, further endeavors with known technologies generally carry less risk than ventures into new and yet untried technologies.

12. Expand the use of your existing equipment. In-place equipment may not be fully utilized. Increased utilization through subcontracting and selling of time on equipment or process capabilities will better utilize existing capital resources with little additional risk. More use of the fixed-cost base increases efficiency and at the same time produces additional cash flows.

Evaluation of Proposals

After proposals have been generated, one must evaluate competing proposals in a consistent manner to determine which proposals merit further consideration. There are basically four steps in the evaluation process:

1. The most critical step is a qualitative evaluation: Is this proposal consistent with the strategic plan of the business? If not, no future consideration is necessary. If yes, further analysis is indicated. Lots of time, effort, and money can be wasted on things that do not fit the direction you are determined to go in.
2. Define the evaluation process. Set up a system that will be applied consistently for all proposals.
    *   Estimate costs accurately and in the same way for all proposals.
    *   Estimate the benefits consistently.
    *   Use the same time constraints.
    *   Use the same method for calculating the net benefits.
3. Qualify your information sources. When gathering information, you must evaluate the reliability and accuracy of the source of the information. For example:
    *   Engineers often underestimate the time (and costs) necessary.
    *   Salespeople frequently overestimate potential sales.
    You should ask:
    *   Who is providing the information?
    *   How accurate were their last predictions?
    *   How often have I relied on this source before?
    *   Do my competitors use this same source?
4. Install the process. To install the process properly, all affected persons must understand how to use it.
    *   Develop appropriate forms to be used throughout the organization. (Appropriate does not have to mean complex or cumbersome.)
    *   Explain the forms and the evaluation methods to all affected persons.
    *   Use the system consistently to evaluate proposals made by members of the organization.
    *   Provide prompt response to members of the organization as to why their proposals were or were not accepted.

Implementation of a Proposal

In the implementation phase, effective project management requires a firm line of control. First, define responsibility. You need to know who will be responsible at various stages in the proposal's implementation to ensure accountability and control. It is important to consider the time and the talent of the individuals involved and to match their abilities to the needs and responsibilities of each key position in the implementation process. Few things affect the failure or success of a product more than the match or mismatch of key personnel at critical steps in project implementation.

Next, establish checkpoints by setting goals and objectives for milestones at successive stages in the process. You can review your decisions regularly, *before* the next costly step is taken and when progress can be compared with established standards. You may choose to terminate a proposal at some point short of completion if it appears that the project is exceeding cost projections or failing to meet benefit expectations.

It may be necessary to change the budget. This may seem a radical idea. However, if budgets are properly managed, changing a budget is nothing more than considering better data as it flows into the system. Budget changing should not become a self-fulfilling prophecy. Budgets are planning tools and, as such, comparisons between actual performance and projected performance will often show how well or poorly your project is proceeding. Updating budgets for better control is useful in order to improve the quality of the decision making for the project.

When budgets are used for control, regular feedback of information is needed. The establishment of reports is another critical element in the implementation phase. The amount of reporting is a function of balancing the risk of ignorance against the cost of reporting. When reports are generated on a regular basis, you can ensure maintenance of adequate control of the project.

Follow-Up

Neglect near the concluding stages of a project can result in unnecessary delays, increased risk, and higher costs for the discontinuation or normal termination of a product's life cycle. In the follow-up step, you should review the assumptions under which the original project was accepted, determine how well those assumptions have been met, review the evaluation systems that were in place, and, finally, evaluate the implementation of the project. It is at this point that an overall review of a project will show you how well it was planned, how well the budget projected reality, and the necessary areas where improvement in the system will help better evaluate future proposals.

There is really no doubt that all projects will eventually find themselves in the decline phase of Figure 3.1. Predicting when this will occur and planning appropriate actions for when it does can be time- and money-saving.

An important part of the follow-up step is the prediction of discontinuance or normal termination dates for the project. This allows for the timely introduction of proposals for the replacement project. Capital budgeting is cyclical, allowing you to control growth on a continuous basis. The follow-up stage naturally reverts back to proposal generation as each project approaches termination.

To review, the four steps in the capital budgeting cycle are proposal generation, evaluation of those proposals, implementation of selected projects, and follow-up.

Producing Numbers to Get Dollars, the Use of Forms, and Capital Budgeting Model

Risk/Return Relationship

It is axiomatic that the relationship between risk and return should be direct. High-risk ventures should have expectations of high returns; low-risk ventures will be expected to have a lower rate of return. Both must be made attractive to investors.

Figure 3.2 demonstrates the relationship between the risk and return expected for a new line, extending a current line, and the modification or change of a product line or cost reduction programs. From this relationship, a function can be derived to estimate the discount

FIGURE 3.2

Risk Return Relationship

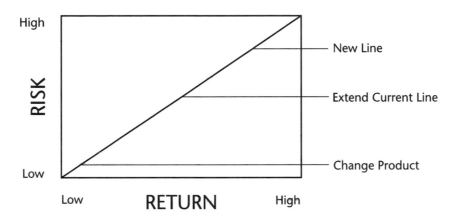

rate. The discount rate, or the necessary return for a project, is equal to the cost of capital plus the risk premium:

Required return = Cost of capital + Risk

The most important criterion in the calculation of a capital budgeting model is the required return. This number can be obtained by subjective estimation or by analytical methods that offer a means of estimating risk. But risk is mostly a perception in the mind of investors.

When considering the cost of capital to be used for the generation of net present value numbers, you should be concerned more with the incremental cost of capital for the project than with the overall cost of obtaining funds. It is the incremental cost of capital—the cost of financing this deal (internally or externally)—with which you are concerned when determining whether a project is cost justified.

Producing Better Numbers for Dollars

Most capital budgeting models use after-tax cash flows as their basis. The following is a capital budgeting cash flow schedule, which will be used to help organize the numbers necessary for the capital budgeting model. Following are some helpful hints for getting the appropriate numbers into the columns of this schedule (see Figure 3.3). The numbers correspond to the columns.

Filling Out the Capital Budgeting Worksheet

1. Column 1 is used to list the estimated net annual cash inflows and outflows.

    Misestimating or underestimating in early years is more damaging than incorrect estimates of amounts in the distant future as

FIGURE 3.3

Capital Budgeting Cash Flow Worksheet

Year	1 Annual Operating Cash Flow	2 Adjustments	3 Depreciation	4 Net Before Tax 1 + 2 + 3	5 Tax	6 After Tax 1 + 2 – 5
0						
1						
2						
3						
4						
5						
6						
7						
8						
9						
10						

a result of the discount factor. Greater significance is placed on cash flows in the beginning periods. The initial outflow will usually be in year zero, which means as of Day 1 of the project period. Therefore, the discount factor is 1.0000 because that is current dollars. (Remember that for most discounting tables, all cash flows are assumed to occur at the end of each year. Although this may be an unrealistic assumption in that carrying costs may be incurred throughout the year, these carrying costs can be calculated and added to the net cash outflows to predict more accurately the total first year cost.)

The initial investment includes not only the usual items, such as plant and equipment, but should also include investments in inventory, accounts receivable, training, product introduction, and the expenses for administrative changes and accounting. A more detailed list of cash flow items to check in the capital budgeting proposals is provided below.

For new products, annual inflows that stay level without fluctuations should usually be suspect because the actual patterns seldom occur this way.

2. In column 2, adjustment to cash should include such items as buildups of accounts receivable and inventories. This allows recognition of the actual cash flows in appropriate years. For example, a new product line may build up $500,000 in inventories in the first year and this investment may not be recovered in cash inflow until the end of the product's life cycle. Taxes and the treatment of expenses and income for tax purposes must be considered and adjusted for in the model. For example, increases in receivables and inventories are examples of adjustments that affect current tax liabilities and must be considered in the calculation of estimated taxes. Inventories require cash in the year purchased but have tax effects when used or sold. Receivables may be taxable in the year sales are made, even though not collected until later periods.

Also, the effect of investment tax credits (when and if Congress has them in place) and other project-related tax deductions should be included for the period in which the cash impact occurs.

3. Depreciation is included solely for the purpose of considering its effect on taxes. The model uses only cash flows and the items

affecting cash flows. Depreciation expense is a noncash item in the current period. If depreciation has already been "expensed" in the operating cash flows of column 1, then an adjustment is necessary to assure that it is not double counted. In the model, the full cost of the investment is made in period 0. Showing the allocation of that cost again through depreciation will count it twice.

4. Column 4 calculates the taxable portion of the inflows. Care must be taken to determine the appropriate tax consequences, as the goal of the model is to determine after-tax cash flows. Because tax consequences change at the whim of Congress, there are no "constant" rules.

5. Column 5 is used for the calculation of tax, which must be subtracted from cash flows. Note that the tax rate may be changed from year to year for sensitivity analysis.

6. Column 6 is the after-tax cash flow to be used in the various capital budgeting models for the evaluation of the proposals.

Ten Cash Flow Items to Check on Capital Budget Proposals

The following list of cash flow items to be considered in evaluating a capital budget proposal is not intended to be exhaustive. However, for every proposal these items should be carefully scrutinized so that a complete evaluation of appropriate costs can be made.

1. Plant and equipment items
2. Installation and debugging of equipment and systems
3. Inventories including consideration of:
   • Raw materials
   • Work-in-process
   • Finished goods
   • Spare parts
4. Market research and introduction
5. Training
6. System changes necessitated by engineering changes and product redesign
7. Accounts receivable
8. Accounts payable

9. Taxes, to include:
   - Income
   - Investment tax credits
   - Property tax
   - Credits
10. Cash and requirements for cash working capital.

Inflation and Cash Flow Estimates

When one estimates cash flows, inflation should be anticipated and taken into account. Often, there is a tendency to assume that the price for the product and the associated costs will remain constant throughout the life of the project. Occasionally, this assumption is made unknowingly, and future cash flows are estimated simply on the basis of existing prices.

If anticipated inflation is embodied in the required return criteria, it is important that it also be reflected in the estimated cash flows from the product over the life of the project. To reflect cash flows properly in later periods, consider adjusting both the expected sales price and the expected costs by reasonable inflation numbers.

You may assume that if all proposals are evaluated without consideration of inflation, the decision matrix will be unchanged. This is not necessarily the case. As in the case for the generation of internal rates of return, inflation will change future cash flows relative to the year in which they occur by the inflation rate specific to that product or industry. Therefore, by not anticipating inflation and assigning values for particular future time periods, the decision model may be biased by not taking into account the different effects on cash inflows and outflows as a result of different rates of inflation. As a result, the project selection may not be optimal.

The Discounted Cash Flow

Because the primary concern is discounted cash flow, we should begin our discussion with the required rate of return. This rate is called by many names, including hurdle rate, cost of capital, interest rate, and discount rate.

Actually, hurdle rate is probably best. It implies a barrier, in terms of the return on investment, which the proposal must clear in order to be considered. The other names arise from the mistaken idea that the cost of capital or interest, which is the cost of some of the capital, is the criterion for judging the investment. A weighted average cost of capital has been suggested; for small businesses, it may not be difficult to calculate because of the limited sources of capital employed. However, neither the marginal cost of capital nor the weighted average cost of capital alone take into account other factors that should be considered in deciding on a required return or hurdle rate to be used, for instance:

- The relative risk of this proposal to other proposals.
- Other opportunities.
- Return on other investments already made.
- The company's loan limit.

There is no magic formula for the evaluation of all the relative factors used in arriving at a correct rate. However, you are encouraged to consider:

- How much return do you usually get?
- How much return can you reasonably expect to receive?
- How much does it cost you to borrow?
- How much should you penalize the proposal for the risk involved?

For many businesses, a simple formula for normal risk projects might be: discount rate = New York bank prime interest rate + 3 points (borrowing premium) + 4 to 6 points risk premium. This is, of course, a very rough rule of thumb and should be used with all appropriate caution.

Capital Budgeting Evaluation Worksheet

Once the cash flows have been determined from the capital budgeting cash flow worksheet (see Figure 3.3), they are listed on the capital budgeting evaluation worksheet (Figure 3.4). Included at the bottom of the capital budgeting evaluation worksheet is an illustra-

FIGURE 3.4

Capital Budgeting Evaluation Worksheet and Present Value Table

1	2	3	4	5	6	7	8
Year	Raw Cash Flow	Trial % No. 1	PV of $1 from Table	PV of Cash Flow (2 × 4)	Trial % No. 2	PV of $1 from Table	PV of Cash Flow (2 × 7)
1	$			$			$
2	$	xxx		$	xxx		$
3	$	xxx		$	xxx		$
4	$	xxx		$	xxx		$
5	$	xxx		$	xxx		$
6	$	xxx		$	xxx		$
7	$	xxx		$	xxx		$
8	$	xxx		$	xxx		$
9	$	xxx		$	xxx		$
10	$	xxx		$	xxx		$
11	$	xxx		$	xxx		$
12	$	xxx		$	xxx		$
13	$	xxx		$	xxx		$
14	$	xxx		$	xxx		$
15	$	xxx		$	xxx		$
		Total			Total		$

(continued)

Figure 3.4 (continued)

							Rate									
Year	.10	.12	.14	.16	.18	.20	.22	.24	.27	.28	.30	.32	.34	.36	.38	.40
1	.9091	.8929	.8772	.8621	.8475	.8333	.8197	.8065	.7937	.7812	.7692	.7576	.7463	.7353	.7246	.7143
2	.8264	.7972	.7695	.7432	.7182	.6944	.6719	.6504	.6299	.6104	.5917	.5739	.5569	.5407	.5251	.5102
3	.7513	.7118	.6750	.6407	.6086	.5787	.5507	.5245	.4999	.4768	.4552	.4348	.4156	.3975	.3805	.3644
4	.6830	.6355	.5921	.5523	.5158	.4823	.4514	.4230	.3968	.3725	.3501	.3294	.3102	.2923	.2757	.2603
5	.6209	.5674	.5194	.4761	.4371	.4019	.3700	.3411	.3149	.2910	.2693	.2495	.2315	.2149	.1998	.1859
6	.5645	.5066	.4556	.4104	.3704	.3349	.3033	.2751	.2499	.2274	.2072	.1890	.1727	.1580	.1448	.1328
7	.5132	.4523	.3996	.3538	.3139	.2791	.2486	.2218	.1983	.1776	.1594	.1432	.1289	.1162	.1049	.0949
8	.4665	.4039	.3506	.3050	.2660	.2326	.2038	.1789	.1574	.1388	.1226	.1085	.0962	.0854	.0760	.0678
9	.4241	.3606	.3075	.2630	.2255	.1938	.1670	.1443	.1249	.1084	.0943	.0822	.0718	.0628	.0551	.0484
10	.3855	.3220	.2697	.2267	.1911	.1615	.1369	.1164	.0992	.0847	.0725	.0623	.0536	.0462	.0399	.0346
11	.3505	.2875	.2366	.1954	.1619	.1346	.1122	.0938	.0787	.0662	.0558	.0472	.0400	.0340	.0289	.0247
12	.3136	.2567	.2076	.1685	.1372	.1122	.0920	.0757	.0625	.0517	.0429	.0357	.0298	.0250	.0210	.0176
13	.2897	.2292	.1821	.1452	.1163	.0935	.0754	.0610	.0496	.0404	.0330	.0271	.0223	.0184	.0152	.0126
14	.2633	.2046	.1597	.1252	.0985	.0779	.0618	.0492	.0393	.0316	.0254	.0205	.0166	.0135	.0110	.0090
15	.2394	.1827	.1401	.1079	.0835	.0649	.0507	.0397	.0312	.0247	.0195	.0155	.0124	.0099	.0080	.0064

tive present value table for 15 years, at rates varying from 10 percent to 40 percent. It is best to keep this table together with the capital budgeting worksheet so that later referral back to the worksheet will not result in questions concerning the origin of the numbers used in the calculation. The use of the evaluation worksheet is straightforward. The cash flows are taken from the cash flow worksheet and are listed in column 2. In column 3, the first trial percentage rate is listed to generate the present value of income flow. Column 4 is read directly from the present value table for the first trial interest rate. Those numbers are filled into the form from the matrix. Column 5 is the multiplication of the cash flow from column 2 by the present value factor from column 4. Column 6 is used for a second trial percentage. Once again the process is repeated and the present value rates are included in column 7 for the second percentage selected. Column 8 is again calculated by the multiplication of the cash flows from column 2 and, this time, the present value numbers in column 7. In this manner, two trials can be made to evaluate the present values of a single cash flow estimate over two different discount rates. Using these worksheets, the cash flows for various proposals may be compared. Examples are included in the appendix to this chapter.

Improving the Estimates

In most cases, the unfortunate truth is that things normally can get only a little bit better but a whole lot worse than expected. Therefore, if the distribution of possible outcomes is considered, it would probably be skewed to the left, in that there is a greater number of unfortunate outcomes than fortunate ones. (See Figure 3.5.)

The possibility of improvement is also limited by the production capabilities. Therefore, the limiting factor on the right side may be plant capacity. Since capacity is normally added in significant increments as opposed to one or two units at a time, there is no continuum of outcome possibilities. Instead, production capacities occur in steps. Without getting into the problem of analyzing additional production quantities, consider the problem of improving the estimates from the standpoint of fixed or limited capacity.

The problem encountered in capital budgeting, as in all other planning, is that a "most likely" figure is normally offered. However, other

FIGURE **3.5**

Distribution of Outcomes

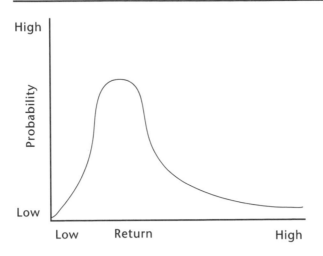

alternatives should be considered. The following situation is not uncommon: "most likely" sales estimate is $300,000; "best case" (limited by capacity) is $400,000; "worst case" sales estimate is $100,000. One way to use this information is to multiply each by some estimated probability. For example, the probable outcome for "most likely" may be estimated as five chances out of ten; "best" is two chances out of ten; and "worst" is three chances out of ten. To calculate the expected outcome, we start by multiplying the "most likely" sales estimate by 5 and repeat this process for each outcome. So:

$$
\begin{array}{rl}
\$3{,}000 \times 5 = & \$1{,}500{,}000 \\
\$400{,}000 \times 2 = & 800{,}000 \\
\$100{,}000 \times 3 = & \underline{300{,}000} \\
\underline{\underline{10}} & \underline{\underline{\$2{,}600{,}000}}
\end{array}
$$

Sum up the probabilities of five, three, and two for a total of ten. Finally, divide the sum of the multiplications by the sum of the probabilities. The expected value is: $2,600,000/10 = $260,000.

The resulting expected value amount of $260,000 is less than the "most likely" figure of $300,000 and reflects the fact that the curve is skewed to the left. While $300,000 is still "most likely" a conservative estimate of $260,000 is also reasonable.

While not impressive statistically, this approach does make use of more information; this would usually justify its inclusion in cash flow projections. Understand that each of the figures—the sales figures and the probabilities associated with each of the three cases—is an estimate. In making these estimates, one should take care to ask a lot of "what if" questions.

When trying to evaluate what is behind the numbers, it is also extremely important to evaluate the information sources. As was mentioned previously, engineers may tend to underestimate time to complete projects and thereby underestimate costs. Marketing and sales personnel may overestimate sales and sales potentials. Ask: "How good are the forecasts of the market, the economic conditions and the expectation of future cash flows?" It is often necessary to question where the numbers came from, who generated them, on what assumptions they were based, and what data were used. It is helpful to know the sources of data, the age of the data, and the method of generation.

Often, sources such as the following are used:

- Government publications, which give useful information on the trends in the economy, consumer spending, and other market information
- Private company publications such as Chase Econometric, Dow Jones, and the like
- Trade publications
- Newspapers

Experience in the industry usually helps provide an understanding about availability and reliability of certain information and data sources.

A major task in capital budgeting is estimating future cash flows. The quality of the final budget and plan is really only as good as the accuracy of the estimates. You should have efficient procedures set up to collect the information necessary for capital budgeting decisions. Try to standardize this information as much as possible for all investment proposals; otherwise, proposals cannot be compared objectively. One of the more difficult capital budgeting problems to evaluate concerns projects associated with environmental protection or safety. It is difficult in those projects to quantify the net cash flows because in most cases the benefit to you is more in the nature of a cost avoidance.

The reason the expected benefits from a particular project are expressed in terms of cash flows rather than in terms of income is that cash is central to all your decisions. You invest cash now in the hopes of receiving cash returns of a greater amount in the future. Only cash receipts can be reinvested or paid to stockholders in the form of dividends. Thus cash, not income, is what is important in capital budgeting.

Miscellaneous Considerations

Another aspect of estimating future cash flows is that the information must be provided on an incremental basis so that the difference between your cash flows may be analyzed with and without the project. This is important in that, if you are contemplating a new product that is likely to compete with existing products, it is not appropriate to express cash flows in terms of estimated sales of the new product without consideration of the effect the new product may have on existing products. You must consider that there probably will be some cannibalization of existing products.

Another assumption often made is that the risk or quality of all investment proposals under consideration is the same as the risk of existing investment projects. Therefore, the acceptance of any proposal or group of investment proposals does not change the relative business risk of the firm. This is not necessarily true; each proposal should be looked at individually relative to its riskiness.

Depreciation

Ordinarily, after-tax cash flows are used for capital budgeting calculations. Usually, depreciation at the maximum allowable method is used for tax purposes. Remember, however, that if depreciation is subtracted other than for calculating taxable income, you are double counting. This occurs because you have already "expensed" (treated the cost as a cash outflow) the investment in year zero. The only reason for being interested in depreciation is for the calculation of expected tax.

Lease-Purchase

Internal rate of return cannot be used for making a decision as to whether to lease or purchase a piece of equipment because a true lease requires no investment. The rate of return, therefore, would be infinite. It is, however, often more profitable to buy. Leasing is usually done because of a lack of, or an attempt to conserve, cash. It is a method of financing and therefore is a part of the second-stage financing decision mentioned at the beginning of this chapter.

Interest

Interest costs on borrowed money should not be included in the calculation of cash flows because the method of financing should not determine the decision as to whether the project is a good deal. Besides, the cash flows will be multiplied by the discount rate, which already includes interest as part of the cost of capital considerations.

Uncertainty

Uncertainty should be included in the discount rate. When trying to quantify uncertainty, you should question the sources of the information: "How old is the information?" and "How reliable is the information?" Always search for alternative sources of information as well as means to accomplish the ends.

There is rarely only one way to accomplish a project. Find other methods and evaluate them. Be suspicious if it appears there is only one way to do the project. Your people may be reluctant to consider alternatives. Ask such questions as: "Are there less expensive ways?" "Are there less risky ways?" "Are there ways that retain more options?"

Product Discontinuance

One of the often overlooked uses of the capital budgeting process is for the determination of product discontinuance. In a highly diversified business, in which large numbers of similar or related products are manufactured, reevaluation of existing product lines should be undertaken on a regular basis using capital budgeting techniques. This is useful to determine whether existing products are optimally utilizing the company's resources.

Checklist of Data

The following is a checklist of the data required to make a decision about maintaining or eliminating a product:

1. An estimate of the variable expenses directly applicable to the production of specific products, including the costs of production and marketing.
2. An indication of the number of units of the product sold during past periods.
3. Total sales revenues generated by each product within each time period.
4. Estimates of sales revenues for competitive products and the price per unit, units sold, and market share of each competitor.
5. Current and past pricing structures for all products including price discount policies and the distribution of order quantities.
6. Inventory turnover ratio for each period of time.
7. Competitive pricing policies, including the average price obtained for a competitor's product.
8. The total company sales volume for past periods.
9. A projection of future sales for each product carried.
10. Estimation of the total overhead costs devoted to each product.

This checklist can be used to detect a warning signal indicating whether a product needs help or should be considered for elimination. The discontinuation of products can result in increased profits through the elimination of marginally profitable or high-cost products and by reducing overdiversification in a business's product mix. Elimination of overdiversification can increase production and marketing efficiencies by concentrating your efforts and resource utilization.

It should be noted, however, that the indications of candidacy for elimination of a product is not simply a go/no-go test established from quantification of the checklist items. Sometimes, healthy products should be eliminated if an analysis shows that your overall goals are better met by product elimination and concentration of efforts. An evaluation of the contributions products make to your objectives will often reveal that the assets dedicated to production of a particular product, if expended on the production of a more profitable item, will create greater returns.

Warning Signals Indicating Product Difficulties

- A decline in absolute sales volume.
- Sales volume decreasing as a percentage of the firm's total sales.
- A decrease in a market share.
- Sales volumes not up to projected amounts.
- Unfavorable future market potential of products.
- Return on investment below minimally acceptable levels.
- Variable cost in excess of actual revenues.
- Costs, as a percentage of sales, consistently increasing.
- An increasingly greater percentage of managerial and executive oversight necessary for the product.
- Price must be lowered repeatedly in order to maintain current or projected sales levels.
- Promotional budgets must be increased in order to maintain sales.

For most of these indicators, a simple graph on a month-by-month basis can quickly show trends. The graph then becomes a simple budget-tracking device.

The key to a successful elimination program is the availability of timely and pertinent information. This is true of all major business decisions. Accounting sources provide the requisite raw data on which you may decide which products to discontinue, which to retain, and which products should be expanded or contracted in your business plan.

Bailout

"What happens if things go sour?" is a question that few people want to think about. Although the answers do not always yield clear-cut decisions, they do provide input to the go/no-go decision. Furthermore, the use of the bailout consideration forces some planning.

To consider bailout, start by asking questions. For example: "What can we bail out with if the project must be shut down after two years?" Then, look at cash flows (discounted, of course) through that period, including salvage. Because a likely reason to bail out may be lack of sales, lowered sales estimates should be substituted for original estimates. All this can be done in the same format previously used to estimate net present value.

An important value of the bailout consideration is that it reminds one that things do not always go as planned. Many people are eternally optimistic and will resist looking at "the dark side." But such considerations can result in much more protection for the remainder of your business should projections not come to pass.

Summary

The necessary steps in the evaluation of capital budgeting decisions include:

1. *Use a discounted payback screen.* A screen is in essence nothing more than a go/no-go test. Think of the device used to screen gravel for size: At each successive stage a keep or reject decision is made and the process continues. Ultimately, the process narrows down the alternatives so that an educated choice can be made.

2. *Use net present value index.* A little more conservative than the net present value in its assumptions, the index therefore will act as a more critical go/no-go decision. The index is the net present value divided by the going-in cost. As an example, if for an initial investment of $300,000 the net present value is $150,000, the NPV index would be .5. For an initial investment of $600,000 and a net present value of $200,000 the NPV index would be .33. If one looked just at the NPV, the $600,000 investment would appear to be the better option, as its NPV is $200,000 instead of $150,000. However, for an investment of $300,000, the NPV index of .5 indicates a better return than does the .33 for the larger investment. Thus the NPV index may give a relative go/no-go test and a better indication than a "NPV only" test. Rank proposals by their internal rate of return (IRR).

3. *Use breakeven in examining alternatives.* It is often helpful in assessing risks as a result of misestimations in sales levels. The breakeven analysis, although a very simple test, shows how varying sales forecasts will affect the period over which we can expect to break even.

4. *Ask "What if" questions and apply some calculations using the bailout consideration.* Bailout is simply an attempt to determine the minimum amount for breakeven on operations.

5. *Relate the size of the decision to the decision maker.* This is merely a reminder that the level in management at which the decision should ultimately be made relates to the significance of that project to your overall objectives.

6. *Keep records.* It is difficult to learn from mistakes if no records exist. Feedback is necessary for improvements. It is a good idea for records be kept from the inception. In order to fully use this information, records should be indexed and retained for future analysis or review. Often, estimates generated for other projects may be very useful in evaluating future projects.

7. *Plan for retirement—not just yours, but the end of each project.* Periodic discontinuance is part of the process. Remember that as each product is discontinued, another product should be ready to take its place to ensure that your growth and prosperity continue. Planning is a cyclical process and the element of discontinuance should herald the introduction of new products.

Appendix: Examples and Comparison of Calculations

The facts are:

A project with an initial cost of $55,000 will return:

	Inflows	Depreciation
Year 1	$ 5,000	$ 5,000
Year 2	25,000	10,000
Year 3	35,000	10,000
Year 4	15,000	10,000
Year 5	20,000	10,000
Year 6	15,000	-0-

The tax rate is 20 percent.

The first calculation example uses the forms developed in the chapter. The second example shows the calculation on an HP12C™ calculator. The third example uses computer spreadsheets.

	18%	20%
Present value of inflows	$58,572.00	$55,480.00
Present value of outflows	55,000.00	55,000.00
Net present value	$ 3,572.00	$ 480.00

The IRR (the discount rate, which causes the NPV to be zero) is very close to 20 percent.

Capital Budgeting Cash Flow Worksheet

Year	Annual Operating Cash Flow (1)	Adjustments (2)	Depreciation (3)	Net Before Tax 1 + 2 + 3 (4)	Tax (5)	After Tax 1 + 2 – 5 (6)
0	<55,000>	0	0	<55,000>	0	<55,000>
1	5,000	0	5,000	0	0	5,000
2	25,000	0	10,000	15,000	3,000	22,000
3	35,000	0	10,000	25,000	5,000	30,000
4	15,000	0	10,000	5,000	1,000	14,000
5	20,000	0	10,000	10,000	2,000	18,000
6	15,000	0	10,000	5,000	1,000	14,000
7						
8						
9						
10						

Capital Budgeting Evaluation Worksheet

1	2	3	4	5	6	7	8
Year	Raw Cash Flow	Trial % No. 1	PV of $1 from Table	PV of Cash Flow (2 × 4)	Trial % No. 2	PV of $1 from Table	PV of Cash Flow (2 × 7)
1	$ 5,000	18%	.8475	$ 4,238	20%	.8333	$ 4,167
2	$ 22,000	xxx	.7182	$ 15,801	xxx	.6944	$ 15,277
3	$ 30,000	xxx	.6086	$ 18,258	xxx	.5787	$ 17,361
4	$ 14,000	xxx	.5158	$ 7,221	xxx	.4823	$ 6,752
5	$ 18,000	xxx	.4371	$ 7,868	xxx	.4019	$ 7,234
6	$ 14,000	xxx	.3704	$ 5,186	xxx	.3349	$ 4,689
7	$	xxx		$	xxx		$
8	$	xxx		$	xxx		$
9	$	xxx		$	xxx		$
10	$	xxx		$	xxx		$
11	$	xxx		$	xxx		$
12	$	xxx		$	xxx		$
13	$	xxx		$	xxx		$
14	$	xxx		$	xxx		$
15	$	xxx		$	xxx		$
			Total	58,572		Total	$ 55,480

Present Value Table

Rate

Year	.10	.12	.14	.16	.18	.20	.22	.24	.27	.28	.30	.32	.34	.36	.38	.40
1	.9091	.8929	.8772	.8621	.8475	.8333	.8197	.8065	.7937	.7812	.7692	.7576	.7463	.7353	.7246	.7143
2	.8264	.7972	.7695	.7432	.7182	.6944	.6719	.6504	.6299	.6104	.5917	.5739	.5569	.5407	.5251	.5102
3	.7513	.7118	.6750	.6407	.6086	.5787	.5507	.5245	.4999	.4768.	.4552	.4348	.4156	.3975	.3805	.3644
4	.6830	.6355	.5921	.5523	.5158	.4823	.4514	.4230	.3968	.3725	.3501	.3294	.3102	.2923	.2757	.2603
5	.6209	.5674	.5194	.4761	.4371	.4019	.3700	.3411	.3149	.2910	.2693	.2495	.2315	.2149	.1998	.1859
6	.5645	.5066	.4556	.4104	.3704	.3349	.3033	.2751	.2499	.2274	.2072	.1890	.1727	.1580	.1448	.1328
7	.5132	.4523	.3996	.3538	.3139	.2791	.2486	.2218	.1983	.1776	.1594	.1432	.1289	.1162	.1049	.0949
8	.4665	.4039	.3506	.3050	.2660	.2326	.2038	.1789	.1574	.1388	.1226	.1085	.0962	.0854	.0760	.0678
9	.4241	.3606	.3075	.2630	.2255	.1938	.1670	.1443	.1249	.1084	.0943	.0822	.0718	.0628	.0551	.0484
10	.3855	.3220	.2697	.2267	.1911	.1615	.1369	.1164	.0992	.0847	.0725	.0623	.0536	.0462	.0399	.0346
11	.3505	.2875	.2366	.1954	.1619	.1346	.1122	.0938	.0787	.0662	.0558	.0472	.0400	.0340	.0289	.0247
12	.3136	.2567	.2076	.1685	.1372	.1122	.0920	.0757	.0625	.0517	.0429	.0357	.0298	.0250	.0210	.0176
13	.2897	.2292	.1821	.1452	.1163	.0935	.0754	.0610	.0496	.0404	.0330	.0271	.0223	.0184	.0152	.0126
14	.2633	.2046	.1597	.1252	.0985	.0779	.0618	.0492	.0393	.0316	.0254	.0205	.0166	.0135	.0110	.0090
15	.2394	.1827	.1401	.1079	.0835	.0649	.0507	.0397	.0312	.0247	.0195	.0155	.0124	.0099	.0080	.0064

Example 1: Hewlett-Packard HP 12C™

Key Strokes			Display
f clear clx			
55,000	CHS	g CFo	–55,000.00
5,000	g	CFj	5,000.00
22,000	g	CFj	22,000.00
30,000	g	CFj	30,000.00
14,000	g	CFj	14,000.00
18,000	g	CFj	18,000.00
14,000	g	CFj	14,000.00
18	i		18.00
f	NPV		3,571.32
f	IRR		20.33
20	i		20.00
f	NPV		479.47

Example 2: Lotus 1-2-3™ Regression Analysis

```
E3:  +B3+C3-D3                                          READY

    A         B         C         D         E      F       G       H

                          Lotus 1-2-3 Example
    Cash Flow  Adjust.  Deprec.  Net B/T  Tax    A/T Cash
    -55000       0         0     -55000
      5000       0      5000
     25000       0     10000
     35000       0     10000
     15000       0     10000
     20000       0     10000
     15000       0         0

 01-Jan-80 01:10 AM    UNDO                        CAPS
```

E11:   READY

A	B	C	D	E	F	G	H

Lotus 1-2-3 Example Chapter 4 Appendix

Cash Flow	Adjust.	Deprec.	Net B/T	Tax	A/T Cash		
-55000	0	0	-55000				
5000	0	5000	0				
25000	0	10000	15000				
35000	0	10000	25000				
15000	0	10000	5000				
20000	0	10000	10000				
15000	0	10000	5000				

28 Mar-90 02:53 PM   UNDO   CAPS

FS: +E5.0.2   READY

A	B	C	D	E	F	G	H

Lotus 1-2-3 Example Chapter 4 Appendix

Cash Flow	Adjust.	Deprec.	Net B/T	Tax	A/T Cash		
-55000	0	0	-55000				
5000	0	5000	0	0			
25000	0	10000	15000	3000			
35000	0	10000	25000	5000			
15000	0	10000	5000	1000			
1000	0	10000	10000	2000			
15000	0	10000	5000	1000			

28 Mar-90 02:56 PM   UNDO   CAPS

```
G4:  +B4+C4-F4
READY

     A          B          C          D          E        F         G         H

              Lotus 1-2-3 Example Chapter 4 Appendix
   Cash Flow  Adjust.  Deprec.  Net B/T  Tax    A/T Cash
    -55000       0         0     -55000           -55000
      5000       0      5000          0      0      5000
     25000       0     10000      15000   3000     22000
     35000       0     10000      25000   5000     30000
     15000       0     10000       5000   1000     14000
      1000       0     10000      10000   2000     18000
     15000       0     10000       5000   1000     14000

28-Mar-90 02:58 PM    UNDO                        CAPS
```

```
G12:  @NPV(0.18,G5..G10)                            READY

     A          B          C          D          E        F         G         H

              Lotus 1-2-3 Example Chapter 4 Appendix
   Cash Flow  Adjust.  Deprec.  Net B/T  Tax    A/T Cash
    -55000       0         0     -55000           -55000
      5000       0      5000          0      0      5000
     25000       0     10000      15000   3000     22000
     35000       0     10000      25000   5000     30000
     15000       0     10000       5000   1000     14000
      1000       0     10000      10000   2000     18000
     15000       0     10000       5000   1000     14000

                                    NPV of Inflows 58571.32

28-Mar-90 03:01 PM    UNDO
```

G13: (F2)+G4+G12   READY

A	B	C	D	E	F	G	H

Lotus 1-2-3 Example Chapter 4 Appendix

Cash Flow	Adjust.	Deprec.	Net B/T	Tax	A/T Cash
-55000	0	0	-55000		-55000
5000	0	5000	0	0	5000
25000	0	10000	15000	3000	22000
35000	0	10000	25000	5000	30000
15000	0	10000	5000	1000	14000
1000	0	10000	10000	2000	18000
15000	0	10000	5000	1000	14000

NPV of Inflows	58571.32
Net Present Value	3571.32

28-Mar-90 03:04 PM   UNDO

G14: @IRR(0.2,G4..G10)   READY

A	B	C	D	E	F	G	H

Lotus 1-2-3 Example Chapter 4 Appendix

Cash Flow	Adjust.	Deprec.	Net B/T	Tax	A/T Cash
-55000	0	0	-55000		-55000
5000	0	5000	0	0	5000
25000	0	10000	15000	3000	22000
35000	0	10000	25000	5000	30000
15000	0	10000	5000	1000	14000
1000	0	10000	10000	2000	18000
15000	0	10000	5000	1000	14000

NPV of Inflows	58571.32
Net Present Value	3571.32
Int. Rate Return	0.203251

28-Mar-90 03:05 PM   UNDO

Comparison of the Internal Rate of Return Method and the Net Present Value Method

When comparing two mutually exclusive proposals using both the net present value method and the internal rate of return method, you will find cases where one project is preferable to the other using one method, and the reverse is true using the other method. It is important to understand how and why this happens. The result is obtained because the two projects will have differing cash flows in different periods. Therefore, the compounding effect of the discount rate and the time value of money will produce different results.

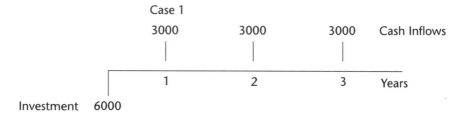

The NPV at 15 percent discount rate is $849.68.
The IRR is 23.5 percent.
The project returns $9,000 total and an undiscounted breakeven in 2 years.

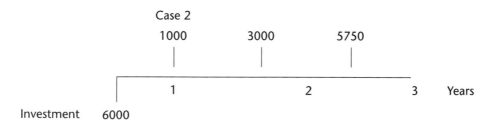

The NPV at 15 percent discount rate is $918.71.
The IRR is 22 percent.
The project returns $9,750 total and a breakeven in 2 years and 4 months.

Which project is a better investment?

This example readily points up how similar cash flows in different periods will affect your decision-making process. Reliance on any one method, therefore, without understanding how it works, may result in a distorted decision-making process.

Some people prefer the net present value method as superior to the IRR on a theoretical basis. The reason for this is that the IRR method implies reinvestment rates that will differ depending upon the cash flow stream for each investment proposal under consideration. With the NPV method, however, the implied reinvestment rate, namely the required rate of return or hurdle rate, is the same for each proposal. In essence, this reinvestment rate presents the minimum return on opportunities available to you. You must employ judgment in evaluating what each model generates as a decision. In order to determine which method is preferable, factors other than the rate of return may alter the decision from one proposal to the other. For instance, long-term tax planning may favor one cash flow projection over the other in order to optimize long-term tax liabilities. Do not accept the decision blindly. Evaluate the expected cash flows and their timing. Question everything!

Capital budgeting in the ongoing system of planning, evaluation, and execution of the business is itself a process. It starts with a determination of where you are, then where you want to be, then how you intend to get there. Even if you do not institute capital budgeting as an ongoing process, simply going through the exercise of trying to set up a process is a valuable endeavor of self-examination. It gets people to think through how prudent investments in capital-intensive projects may help the business grow, diversify, or replace existing plant and equipment.

Capital budgeting is a four-step process of proposal solicitation or generation, evaluation, implementation, and follow-up. In the evaluation step, various alternative proposals have various related returns associated with the investment. With this expected return is a probable risk of loss of all or some part of the invested funds. In any endeavor, the decision must be based upon balancing the return against the associated risk. The problem, of course, is that no certainty, even in the estimates of risk and return, exists. In order to minimize the risk, you should consider the method by which estimates, projections, and other numbers are generated.

You should be cautious when only one solution is proposed because there is seldom a problem without several. When preparing a capital budgeting plan, develop contingency plans and scenarios after asking many "What if" questions. As part of your contingency planning, do not put your "head in the sand." Consider the dark side of the project—"What if it goes sour?" For such a proposition, you should be ready for bailout as a planned withdrawal; you should not be forced into mindless panic in the event that the project faces immediate failure.

Section II

Operating the Business

S ection I was largely devoted to tasks that can and should be accomplished prior to the start of the business (or of the fiscal period for an ongoing business). It focused on planning what you want and intend to make happen.

The two chapters of Section II discuss those areas you must manage when the business period is under way:

- Cash flow concerns
- Financing

Obviously, these also require planning. But they are, to a greater degree, day-to-day management functions, which require constant attention, willingness and ability to adapt, and control.

Day-to-day management should be based on the overall planning discussed in Section I, but changes to the plan may be necessitated by unanticipated occurrences. Therefore, the concepts presented in the following chapters offer a system for adjusting the implementation of the plan in response to new information without changing the basic and underlying desired accomplishments.

Chapter 4

Cash Flow Concerns

Managing working capital is an important function of the business. Contained within working capital are four major elements that you must plan for and consider in order to maintain viability:

- Cash
- Accounts receivable
- Accounts payable
- Inventory

The intent of this chapter is to discuss the management of cash, accounts receivable, and accounts payable.

Cash

Cash is the most liquid of all assets and serves many purposes within the business:

- *Transactions.* Cash is used as a medium for transactional payments. Regardless of the form or nature of the payments, in the final analysis there is normally a transfer of cash.
- *Investment.* Whether made by outside individuals, businesses, banks, or the business investing in itself (reinvestment of excess cash), the transactions ultimately involve cash.

- *Security.* A reasonable level of cash in a liquid account is a measure of security to the business. Depending on the nature and size of the business, the amount of cash necessary may be significant.

When considering the investment of cash, there are four factors most investors consider in determining whether to invest, and if so, how much:

- *Yield.* Yield is in itself composed of two elements: growth and dividends. The *growth* of a business is represented in the market by the market price of its stock or an increase in its valuation, indicating an increase in the equity worth. For example, if your stock is increasing in value in the market at a rate of 12 to 15 percent per year, this could be an adequate expected return, sufficient to attract investors even without cash dividends. If your stock is valued at a relatively constant $10 per share in the market but pays an average annual *dividend* of $1.20 to $1.50, it too is yielding 12 to 15 percent on the investment. In the small or closely held business, the yield is often taken out in the form of higher compensation or "perks" by the owners.
- *Risk.* This element of investing is intangible. Different investors will make different assessments of risk, for example, institutional investors and individual ones looking at the same business. A constant growth business and a steady earnings business, although both have the same return, may be seen as having different risks. If your business demonstrates steady growth and reinvestment of excess earning, it may be seen by bankers as less risky than a business that earns a steady amount and "throws off dividends" to its owners.
- *Liquidity.* Here, the investor is concerned with how quickly the investment can be converted to cash. Liquidity is essentially a timing issue; risk and return will affect liquidity. Real estate may be more risky and have higher returns than Treasury bills but an investor who wants a liquid asset will prefer T-bills because they can be traded with little or no delay. Real estate may tie up the investor's funds for months while he tries to find a buyer, or he may have to discount the price in order to convert the asset quickly.
- *Transactional costs.* Whatever gross yield an investment shows, transactional costs have to be deducted. For the preceding exam-

ple, the steadily growing business shows a gross yield of 12 to 15 percent per year, but the investor realizes no gain until he or she sells the stock and pays brokerage fees and appropriate taxes. In the steady dividend business, the investor realizes his yield periodically through direct payments with no transactional costs except taxes. The transactional costs associated with a real estate sale can be quite significant. Brokerage fees may amount to 6 percent or more. Attorney's fees, recordings, documentary stamps, title search, title insurance, and other factors may amount to an appreciable portion of the gain.

Cash becomes of critical concern when there is too little to meet the immediate needs of the business. However, it is equally important to consider cash when there is an ample supply available. When there is a surplus of cash, many people ignore the significance of this circumstance. Many businesses leave excess cash idle in non–interest-bearing accounts. Optimal cash management requires the investment of idle cash in profitable endeavors. It is easier to earn an income on cash than any other commodity you have. Since it is liquid, cash may be managed or converted without the delay that inhibits the liquidity of other assets.

What to Do with Excess Cash

There are many profitable means available to invest excess cash. Some of the more prominent, convenient, and well-known opportunities will be discussed here.

Interest Accounts

Cash flows into and out of the business on a daily basis. Unfortunately for most businesses, large and small, the inflows and outflows are neither steady nor all predictable within an acceptable degree of certainty. The business may be cash-rich or -poor at different times during the month.

Because of this uncertainty, you must always have adequate cash on hand or in liquid accounts to meet the demands as they are returned for payment. You should be equally concerned that no idle excess cash is sitting in a non–interest-bearing checking account. If the buffer of cash is excessive, you are losing the opportunity to earn on that money.

Investigate the options available at your bank for earning interest on checking or for keeping cash in an interest-bearing account, with provisions for automatic transfers when checking balances are below a certain level.

Another option is the deposit of cash in money market accounts. This is a liquid, higher-yield form of savings account. Often, these accounts may be used in conjunction with a form of checking, with restrictions as to minimum balances in the accounts and as to the maximum number of transactions per period.

Idle cash represents an opportunity easy to capture; the returns can be worth the effort expended in finding a solution.

Treasury Securities

U.S. Treasury obligations constitute the largest segment of the money market. The principal securities issued are bills, tax anticipation bills, notes, and bonds. Treasury bills are auctioned weekly by the Treasury Department, with maturities of 91 days and 182 days. In addition, nine-month and one-year bills are sold periodically. Treasury bills carry no coupon but are sold on a discount basis. These securities are extremely popular with companies, large or small, as short-term investments. In part because of the large amount outstanding, the market is very active and the transaction costs involved in the sale of Treasury bills in the secondary market are small. Very often, in some of the more sophisticated financial models, Treasury bills are considered risk-free, interest-bearing notes. They are used as the basis on which to place risk premiums in such financial models as the capital asset pricing model taught in most business schools.

Agency Securities

Obligations of various agencies of the federal government are guaranteed by the agency issuing the security and not usually by the Treasury. The principal agencies issuing securities are the Federal Housing

Administration and the Government National Mortgage Association. These obligations are not guaranteed by the Treasury; however, there is an implied backing of the government. It would be hard to imagine the federal Treasury allowing an agency to fail. Major government-sponsored agencies that issue securities include the federal home loan banks, federal land banks, and the Federal National Mortgage Association. The securities provided by these agencies return a modest yield advantage over treasury securities of the same maturity. These securities have a high degree of marketability and are sold in the secondary market through the same security dealers as the Treasury securities.

Banker's Acceptances

Banker's acceptances are drafts accepted by banks and used in financing foreign and domestic trade. The creditworthiness of banker's acceptances is judged relative to the bank accepting the draft rather than the drawer. Acceptances generally have maturities of less than 180 days and are of very high quality. They are traded in an over-the-counter market dominated by a few dealers. The rates on banker's acceptances tend to be slightly higher than rates on Treasury bills of similar maturity.

Commercial Paper

Commercial paper consists of short-term unsecured promissory notes issued by finance companies and certain industrial concerns. Commercial paper can be purchased either directly or through dealers. Among the companies selling commercial paper on this basis are CIT Financial Corporation, Ford Motor Credit Company, General Motors Acceptance Corporation, and Sears Roebuck Acceptance Corporation.

Negotiable Certificates of Deposit

Negotiable time certificates of deposit (CDs) are time-certain investments. The CD is evidence of the deposit of funds at a commercial bank for a specified period of time and at a specified rate of interest. Money market banks quote rates on CDs that are changed periodically in keeping with changes in other money market rates. Yields on CDs are greater than on T-bills but are about the same as on banker's acceptances and commercial paper.

Cash Flows

Before dealing with the problem of insufficient cash, we should consider the sources of cash inflow. There are four sources of cash inflow to the business:

- New investment
- New debt
- Sale of fixed assets
- Operating revenues (including collection of accounts receivable)

Each of these sources has important limitations on it; there are, in fact, no other sources of cash. The only source that can be relied on in an ongoing way is operating profits. That is what makes profit planning such an important activity for any business. When the business experiences continued profitable operations, *accompanied by a positive cash inflow,* it can grow most efficiently.

Inflows

The inflows, or the receipt of payment from customers for product or services, is the lifeblood of any business. The obvious rule with inflows is to get customers to pay as promptly as possible. For example, many doctors and lawyers now demand cash on receipt of service for routine office visits.

It is obvious that the efficiency of cash management improves with the acceleration of customers' payments. The fast food industry illustrates how, by sticking strictly to a cash-only business, an extremely low current ratio can be maintained. Contrasted to cash payments, payments by check have an inherent delay associated with the time it takes for a check to clear the bank. During this period, the funds are not available for use by the business. The objective should be to reduce the delay in receiving payment and the clearing time necessary for the transfers of funds. In addition to federal legislation concerning maximum times for banks to clear checks, several methods have been developed to decrease the float (i.e., the speed of realizing actual cash receipt).

- *Concentration banking.* If your business is large enough to have broad market coverage, you may consider using banks at various locations within your market areas to speed the clearance of checks. Using banks in areas where sales occur allows for the processing of local checks. These generally clear faster, and funds can be more quickly concentrated for wire transfer to a central bank.

- *Lockboxes.* Businesses may use a lockbox system for collections. To do so, rent a post office box, centrally located in a market, and authorize your bank to open the box and directly credit payments to your account, similar to direct deposit for Social Security. This has advantages and disadvantages. The obvious disadvantage is the loss of control over the physical receipt of funds and the direct monitoring of clients' payment habits. You do not have the ability to process receipts before the bank gets them. This elimination of handling saves you time but the bank does charge a fee for the service.

- *Elimination of unnecessary accounts.* Having an account in each local bank where you do business or have some operations creates goodwill and a sense of presence. However, by maintaining many separate and diverse accounts, you are dispersing money that could be used more effectively if it was concentrated. By concentrating cash, you can probably reduce cash reserves and still function efficiently.

- *Zero balance accounts.* If a company wants to retain a number of checking accounts, it is wastefully keeping cash in each of those accounts that is earning either zero or very little interest income. A better approach is to keep it in a single, central account that earns the highest possible rate of interest, because the company has concentrated its funds in one place and can now access higher-earning investments that require a higher minimum investment. To make this cash centralization system work while still retaining several checking accounts, a company can use a zero balance account. This is a checking account that contains a zero cash balance at all times, but which pulls funds from another account, such as the investment account, when checks clear. The only disadvantage to this approach is that the bank reconciliation is made more difficult, because the reconciliation of all checks now flows through a single account, which results in a large amount of check volume to sort through.

- *Controlled disbursements.* It is also possible to retain cash through the accounts payable function without suppliers realizing that cash is being withheld from them for an extra day or two. This approach is called controlled disbursements, and involves the payment of checks from banks that are so isolated that it takes longer for checks to clear through them. This additional float period is minor but does allow a company to retain its cash for slightly longer than normal, so that it can keep the funds in short-term investments and earn slightly more interest income than would otherwise be the case. This approach can also be expanded to include the mailing of checks from company locations that are furthest from supplier locations, in order to take advantage of a few days of additional mail float. However, this delaying tactic is more obvious to suppliers and tends to meet with stiff disapproval by them.

An item that was mentioned at the beginning of this section was the sale of fixed assets as a source of cash flows. Selling assets is a task that most companies address only sporadically, resulting in assets' losing value over time while they lie ignored in odd corners of the company. However, if dealt with in a systematic manner, the periodic review of fixed assets will result in the prompt identification of unused assets and continuing attention to their disposal, which results in the highest possible sale prices for the assets, thereby contributing to cash flows. The basic process is to schedule a periodic asset review, certainly no less than annually, in which the management team reviews the list of fixed assets to determine which items can be sold off at once. One person should be in charge of this process, so that the system will not be dropped for lack of attention. Also, this person should be required to regularly report to the management team regarding the progress of those asset sales. This simple system will ensure that a company realizes the greatest possible cash flow from the sale of its unused assets.

Outflows

The largest volume of cash outflows is generally referred to on the income statement as expenses, although some "accrued" expenses may not yet have been paid in cash. Other non–cash flow expenses shown on income statements are such things as depreciation. Another item to be added to "other expenses" is the principal portion of loan payments, which, although not an expense item, is still a use of cash.

The business must be concerned with the timing and nature of the demands made on its cash. The timing of cash inflows and the importance of shortening the "float" were discussed earlier. For cash outflows, the corollary is that you want to ride the float or use the delay in cash transfers to your advantage. Some businesses capitalize on the float by writing checks on accounts without sufficient funds available to cover those checks. They may in fact have adequate reserves of cash maintained in high-yield accounts until needed to meet a draw. In this way, the business is maximizing its return by using the float to its advantage. Extreme care must be exercised to avoid "kiting," an illegal act.

How does one plan for the use of float? A reasonable float pattern to study is that of paychecks. Some employees have automatic deposits to credit unions; others deposit their checks immediately, some even in the employer's bank; some employees will hold their checks for several days; and a few hardy souls may hold their checks for a week or more. To determine the necessary balances, you should gather some data:

- Collect the number of checks and the amount presented for payment on each day after the payday.
- Calculate the amount presented by day.
- Repeat the process for successive pay periods.
- Construct a frequency distribution of funds demanded by day.

From this frequency distribution, you can plan for having the appropriate amount of cash in your account at the right time. In order to ensure that you are not embarrassed by insufficient funds, maintain a safety margin in the account. (Even this safety margin can be determined statistically if there is sufficient data to determine variations in returned checks.) If the payroll is significant, holding portions of that payroll even for a day or two in a high-yield account amounts to significant returns. In the case of automatic deposits, you can determine with certainty the delay in funds transfer and can earn extra interest on this systematic float. You should probably have an agreement with your bank either to notify you if your account is underfunded, to make automatic transfers from another account, or to "cover" you with a line of credit.

Introduction to Cash Flow Budgets

Before you attempt a cash flow budget for the business, it is useful to do a cash flow analysis. Preparing a cash flow analysis often gives managers a much better understanding of the operation of their business. It is particularly important for some small businesses to get an understanding of cash flows because they are especially vulnerable to problems dealing with cash. Smaller businesses tend to operate with inadequate cash reserves or none at all.

Perhaps the most critical element to be considered is the timing of cash flows. If all of the cash outflows occur in the first six months and most of the cash inflows occur during the second six-month period, the business may fail before it has an opportunity to receive sufficient cash inflows to sustain itself. Timing of flows is critical.

Indications of Cash Flow Problems

Many businesses never achieve cash flow control. These businesses are always in trouble, chronically overdrawn and slow in paying bills. Many eventually fail. Some could survive if managers would take the necessary planning steps to create a cash flow budget and manage their cash flows as they manage other portions of the business.

- *Decreased liquidity.* Running out of working capital. Some symptoms include too little inventory to meet demand and stretching payables.

- *Excessive turning.* Turning inventories over more than other businesses of comparable size in the industry. This can be an indication of good management, but in extreme cases may be caused by too little working capital to support adequate inventories.
- *Excess reliance on short-term debt.* Here, you may be rolling over short-term debt to raise needed working capital. Contrary to popular belief and most finance books, not all working capital is short-term. In most businesses, there is a level of working capital required for the reasonable operation and growth of the business. We call this *fixed working capital.*
- *Dropped discounts.* Past-term payments and failure to take advantage of timely payment discounts could indicate poor management of payables or the lack of cash necessary to pay in a timely way.
- *Slow collections.* A high percentage of old receivables probably indicates poor management of receivables. It certainly indicates a potential cash problem.

These problems may be caused by insufficient cash, or the insufficient cash may be the result of poor management. In some cases, low cash balances might even indicate a planned result. For example, rapid inventory turns may be advantageous. In the grocery business, with a low margin per sale, the more frequently sales are made and inventory is turned over, the more profit is earned. Indicators of cash flow problems may signal nothing more than that further investigation may be necessary; but they always show that at least investigation is warranted.

Managing Cash

The control of cash is not mysterious, nor is the process itself complex. What is required is a systematic and organized approach. A few simple guidelines, set out in the following eight steps, help organize the process and make for an efficient handling of cash.

1. Identify all your sources of cash inflows: operations, debt, sale of assets, and investment.
2. List the uses to which you put the cash.

3. Identify the timing of cash flows, both in and out.
4. Calculate the difference between cash inflows and cash outflows. It is important here to identify time delays in receiving cash.
5. Identify any bottlenecks to getting cash in quickly and determine how to open up the inflow.
6. Enumerate any constraints on the use of cash, such as bank loan covenants.
7. Identify those cash inflows and outflows that can be rescheduled or whose timings may be changed.
8. Most important, establish a plan for positive cash flows. This step cannot be accomplished until the other seven steps have been completed and analyzed. Each of these steps will require your time and effort to complete. However, like most planning, the rewards in the long run significantly outweigh the costs to gather and analyze the information. It may save your business.

In order to effectively carry out the design and implementation of a cash flow analysis, a flowchart of how cash flows through the business is helpful. For the development of a cash flow budget we have constructed the flowchart shown in Figure 4.1 as an aid, with an analysis of each step contained in it.

Step 1. Identify all sources of cash inflow.
- New investments and debt are sources of cash. However, they are infrequent and cannot be relied on as continuing sources of cash.
- The sales of fixed assets are like new investments. The sale of fixed assets is not a source of recurring cash. You can sell the asset only once legally. While these sources cannot be ignored, they are secondary to operating profits. Consequently, it is important to focus on operating profits as your main source of cash. It should be noted, however, that operating profits will probably not be the source of capital for major plant expansions.
- Operating profits, unlike new investments or debt, are ongoing and also harder to track. They must be constantly monitored and controlled. Even growing businesses, with increasingly larger amounts of cash inflows, must review the budget and related variances periodically and maintain control or they may suffer from shortages of cash. As your business grows, you will often suffer

Figure 4.1

Cash Budgeting Flowchart

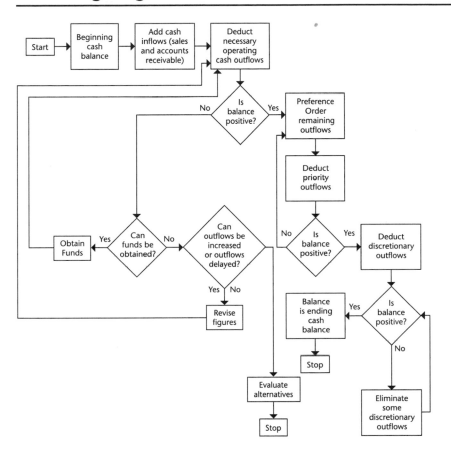

© E. J. Burton. Used by permission.

from liquidity problems. Such problems may cause your business to fail to meet its short-term obligations even when it is quite viable and profitable.

As you advance through the business or product life cycle, cash demands will vary with the stages of the cycle. Typically, a company's life-cycle graph will look like that in Figure 4.2.

For example, in periods of fast growth, the business will probably need growing inventories, receivables, and transactions cash. These

FIGURE 4.2

Life-Cycle Graph

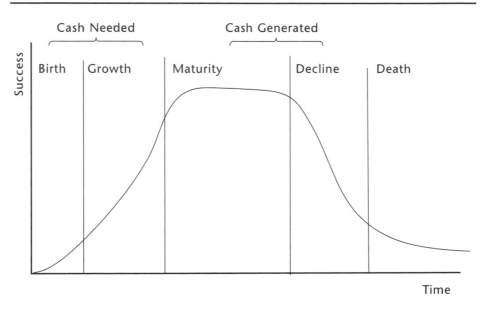

inventory growth periods demand the commitment of large amounts of working capital, much as would be the case for adding to a building. This we call the fixed working capital problem.

Figure 4.3 may help explain this unusual (at least as far as calling it "fixed") problem.

Notice that inventory turn is shown as improving as more sales produce faster turn. Also notice that receivables turn degenerates as sales are made to marginal customers and staff is not available to perform proper credit checks and follow-up. Unfortunately, these are typical scenarios. Assume that these numbers are indicative of trends in many businesses and could apply to you.

On sales of $1 million with profits at, say, 15 percent of sales, you generate $150,000 to contribute to your working capital needs. On sales of $2 million (assuming you have to "deal" to get the other sales), your average profit percentage drops to 13 percent, so you generate $260,000. Your working capital needs increased by $280,000 ($490,000 − 210,000) while your profit contribution increased by only $110,000. How do you finance this growth?

FIGURE **4.3**

Typical Growth Company

Sales Level	Inventory Turn	Inventory Amount	Receivables Turn	Receivables Amount	Transactions Cash	Working Capital
$1,000,000	6.0	$100,000	10	$100,000	$10,000	$210,000
1,250,000	6.2	121,000	9	139,000	12,500	272,500
1,500,000	6.5	138,500	8	187,500	15,000	341,000
1,750,000	7.0	161,500	7	250,000	17,500	429,000
2,000,000	7.0	185,000	7	285,000	20,000	490,000

The "fixed" working capital issue is that there is some minimum amount of investment in working capital that is required and should be financed as a long-term asset, not on a short-term basis. In our illustration, if base sales stay around $1.5 million with peaks and valleys, then the "fixed" component of working capital is about $340,000.

The period of rapid growth, rather than being a source of net cash inflow, may be a problem period. In periods of fast growth, inventory, receivables, and so on might not only consume all of your profits but might also require debt financing.

Part of the problem might result from offering extended payment terms to customers while at the same time being required to pay material suppliers on short terms. This difference between the time when you must pay suppliers and when you receive payment from your purchasers could mean the difference between continuing to operate and having the business fail.

The problems just outlined in regard to the increase in working capital that are associated with rapid growth may also arise in a company that is not growing at all, but for different reasons. For example, a company's investment in inventory will increase if the purchasing staff is buying parts in excessively large quantities, if finished goods are not being sold, or if the engineering staff has made a number of parts obsolete by switching to new parts on existing products. Similarly, a more liberal customer credit granting policy or a weakened collections effort will increase the investment in accounts receivable, whereas taking early payment discounts will reduce the amount of accounts payable outstanding. Since any of these issues can arise at any time, no matter what the growth stage of a company, it is best to constantly monitor changes in the balances of all working capital items on a weekly basis, and immediately investigate the reasons for sudden jumps in the investment in this category. Otherwise, a company may find itself in need of far more cash than its cash flow forecast would lead it to expect.

Step 2.   List cash outflows or uses.

A good place to start considering cash outflows is the cash journal or, if you don't have one, the checkbook. The important activity for this step in the process is to determine where the cash is going.

Many businesses experience lengthy delays between the time they pay for goods for resale and when they actually receive cash from the sale. To some extent, the delay is unavoidable. By analyzing the delay, however, you can plan for the amount of cash necessary to sustain this short-term investment in inventory and receivables. A representative (but hypothetical) example of the analysis of delay is shown in Figure 4.4.

In Figure 4.4, you paid for the item of inventory but do not receive payment from the customer until 95 days later. Built into the system

FIGURE 4.4

Analysis of Delay

is some unavoidable delay. But the problem can become worse. In this example, you sold the item before you had to pay for it. If the item sits on the shelf for a month or more, the problem gets worse.

All expenditures of cash should be listed and carefully considered. Then, the effort must be made to determine whether all of those cash expenditures are necessary. Pertinent questions are:

- Can we get along without it?
- Can we postpone this expenditure?
- Is the timing proper?
- Would it make more sense to pay for it earlier or later?
- Can it be done less expensively?

We often get into the rut of believing there are only two ways of doing something: our way and the wrong way. People typically act according to habit simply because it takes less mental effort than to think out every action in the day. The way to be innovative is to ask *why*.

When addressed to business activities, probing questions might uncover areas in which significant savings can be realized. For the computer system dealer in Figure 4.4, several questions can be asked:

- Why do we have a 45-day acceptance period?
- Why do we have a 30-day credit period after acceptance?
- Why does it take so long to deliver the product?
- Why do we carry this item in inventory?

The answers to these questions may save both expense and cash immediately. If you cannot determine where the cash is going, it may be necessary to consult your accountant and get help establishing controls. However, for many small businesses, a checkbook can provide adequate daily records of cash disbursements.

Step 3. Identify when cash is received and expended.

The most useful tool in identifying cash inflows and outflows is a calendar. Because most businesses deal in a cyclical variation, a year is generally a useful period for which to examine expenditures and receipts of cash. To begin with, a list should be made of those outflows that have fixed dates:

- Paydays
- Tax deposits
- Bank debt repayments
- Insurance payments
- Other periodic obligations

Continue to list those items for which cash is expended until you are sure that you have accounted for all of the periodic expenditures that occur in an annual period.

Once the cash outflows are listed, you may begin listing inflows. In doing so, you must consider the delays in receiving accounts receivable payments and your seasonal and periodic sales fluctuations. It may be necessary to consider mean or average receipt times for some of these items.

Step 4.   Examine the timing of cash inflows minus cash outflows.

A positive cash flow period is one in which the inflows of cash exceed the outflows of cash. This may not happen in all circumstances. However, it should average out over the year. In the event that the business is experiencing a negative cash flow period, then, for any operating period in which this occurs, funds must be obtained from some other source.

Negative cash flow periods will occasionally occur—for example, during growth spurts. Many businesses experience sales rhythms. If you are experiencing such a rhythm, look to see if it is typical for the industry. In such cases, you must understand the rhythm and time-discretionary cash inflows in order to properly plan for those periods in which you may experience a negative cash flow period. Understanding the phenomenon of delayed cash inflow as a result of growth will help to determine how fast the business can afford to grow. It may be better to sustain a slower growth rate in order to avoid significant negative cash flow problems.

By looking at the timing of cash inflows and cash outflows, you may find ways to improve profitability by both cutting costs and increasing your opportunities.

Step 5. What effect does the current cash flow have on the business?

Plan payments so as to maximize the utilization of cash. That is, consider extending payments for as long as practical without incurring adverse consequences from the creditors.

Everyone in business knows that the way to improve cash flow is to slow down the outflow of cash while speeding up the inflow. This is particularly true in a tightening economy. However, before blindly following this path, one should consider the consequences of slowing down payment to vendors. In business, terms for payment are still commonplace. In fact, 2/10, N/30 is a commonly offered discount. In order to monitor discounts taken and discounts missed, you should establish a regular reporting mechanism to control this process.

The chart in Figure 4.5 can be expanded or redesigned to meet the specific discounts available and the payment schedules you use. In this way, you can effectively monitor performance.

The intent of discounts is to encourage early payment. But what are the consequences of not taking the discount? Let's assume a 2/10, N/30 discount. For one thing, if you wait the full 30 days to pay, you are still incurring, in essence, a 36.9 percent annualized interest rate on that money. Even if the payment period is extended for a full 50 days without adverse consequences from the vendor, you have merely cut the interest rate to 18 percent. This is derived from the following relationship: Under the 2/10, N/30, you receive a 2 percent discount on the money due if you pay within the first 10 days. However, in the event you wait the full 30 days to pay the bill you

Figure 4.5

Annualized Interest Equivalent Cost
of Not Taking a Cash Discount

If Paid In:	1/10, N/30	2/10, N/30
Day 10	0%	0%
Day 20	36.9%	73.8%
Day 30	18.5%	36.9%
Day 40	12.3%	24.6%

incur interest of 2 percent of the amount due for holding the money for an additional 20 days. Because there are approximately 18 such 20-day periods per year, the annualized interest rate of 2 percent per 20 days amounts to an annual interest rate of 36 percent. This is hardly an equitable interest rate to incur for borrowing money for such a short period. Even if you extend the period for a full 50 days, you are, in a sense, borrowing at 2 percent for 40 days. Since there are approximately 9 such 40-day periods per year, the 2 percent for each of these periods amounts to 18 percent per annum. Most businesses can afford to borrow from a bank at less than 18 percent interest rate.

Other consequences may result from delaying payment for up to 50 days. The creditor may institute proceedings for collection. But even if it doesn't, you will not become a favored customer by holding the vendor's money for a 50-day period. In times of tightening economics or shortage of the materials provided by this vendor, the slow-paying customer will not sit high on the list of "most favored customers." You may find shortages of necessary materials or none at all coming from that vendor, if you are more costly to do business with than other customers.

In managing accounts payable, there are four rules to be considered:

1. Do not buy necessary material too early; buy no unnecessary materials at all. Manage your purchases using the procedures set forth in the chapter on inventories.
2. Plan buying so as to balance needs with some measure of safety stock.
3. Pay so that unnecessary costs are not incurred. In doing so, consider vendor relationships and the interest rates associated with early payment discounts.
4. Set up an accounting system to monitor discounts lost or not taken. Most accounting systems list discounts taken. While this has some benefits, you will fail to take advantage of the opportunity costs. These lost opportunities may, in the long run, be more important than those discounts taken. Since it should be policy to take discounts, exception reporting would dictate capturing discounts lost.

Step 6. Identify which cash inflows or outflows cannot be changed.

Many payments made periodically by the business may not be rescheduled. In addition, collection policies might fail to achieve their objectives. Identify the extent to which payments and receipts are inflexible. Consider methods intended to speed up cash inflows. It is possible to identify particular clients who are for the most part reliable in payment and others who are dilatory. It may prove to be true that it is more profitable to discontinue sales to purchasers with late payment records than to continue to provide them with goods. Remember, in shipping goods to a purchaser, you are in effect loaning that purchaser money. Those goods represent a cash investment by you and can be considered a loan to that purchaser.

An important consideration here is to establish a credit policy. Having a credit policy and exercising that policy consistently is a major point of control. Before extending credit, you have the maximum leverage on a particular purchaser. Once credit has been extended, much of that leverage is lost. Although there is legal recourse against the purchaser, that will not improve the cash flow in the short run.

The following are four rules for credit extensions:

1. Have a written credit policy.
2. Have a business collection policy that everyone understands.
3. Know your legal rights when it comes to collections.
4. Know the legal restraints and conditions when offering credit.

It is important to maintain an aged accounts receivable file. Knowing which accounts to either collect or receive payment from and in what period of time is very important for estimating cash inflows. Remember the following points about aged accounts receivables:

- The older the account gets without payment or collection, the less likely you are to receive payment or make collection. The age of the account has a direct effect on the efforts that must be made in collecting.
- You may want to establish rules for termination of further shipments based on the age of receivables.

When establishing a collection policy, consider the following:

- Know the steps you wish to take in making a collection. This may include "first letters," first phone calls, referral of the collection to the legal department, and so on.
- Set the steps. Make a conscious effort to determine the order in which they will be taken.
- Do not establish fixed time frames for advancing from step to step. If the time frames are known, many customers will wait to pay until the last possible moment before you move on to the next collection step.
- Don't be predictable in collection efforts. Once your collection efforts become normalized, debtors will behave accordingly.

Step 7. Identify those cash inflows and cash outflows that can be rescheduled.

By identifying those cash inflows and outflows that can be rescheduled, you may be able to balance payments and receipts so as to avoid unnecessary negative cash flow situations. Sometimes, talking with your creditors and working out payment schedules that meet your needs and theirs can be an effective compromise. A surprising number of banks and large companies are willing to work out such payment schedules, because a smaller payment that can be expected with some degree of certainty is preferable to uncertainty or no payment at all. Also, creditors, if they know that there may be a nonpayment period, are able to work out their own cash flow requirements so as not to be adversely affected.

Very often, businesses get into trouble with their accounts payable. You may end up spending more time talking with the people to whom you owe money than you spend in producing the money to pay your bills. This can become a cycle that gets you deeper into trouble. The solution to this problem may be to sort through all the creditors and identify all the small bills under some particular cutoff. Creditors of less than the cutoff can prompt as many phone calls as the large creditors. Often, it is less expensive to borrow an amount of money and pay off all of the small creditors than to try to pay off each one separately. In this way, time becomes available to get back to the business of earning money. The bank may be able to help you out of short-term financial problems. Often, grouping together many small bills into one large bill with a fixed payment period may resolve some of the intermediate cash flow problems. Be careful about lumping nonrevolving payments (due upon billing) into revolving or longer-term, periodic payments in order to avoid the following:

- Building in an interest payment (perhaps lower than the penalty or interest due on all the small bills).
- Paying off many nonrevolving accounts. This may encourage the incurring of further liabilities on these accounts. In doing so, you simply restart the cycle.

Trade associations and trade organizations may be good sources of information on how to improve the business's cash outflow and inflow picture. Other businesses in the same industry may have had similar experience with collections and have ready advice on how to improve collections.

Step 8. Plan for positive cash flow.

A major tool available for planning cash flow is a cash budget. Cash budgets involve projections of future cash needs as well as cash receipts. This budget reveals the timing and amount of expected cash inflows and outflows over a particular period. For example, most businesses use a one-year business cycle. You may want to consider a two-year cash budget with modifications to the second year's budget after significant experience in the first year. The cash flow budget should take into account seasonal variations in sales and cash outflows. If cash flows are extremely volatile, short time period increments should be used in the budgeting process. If the budgeting shows a more stable period, the time periods may be longer depending on the stability of the data. Remember that the farther into the future you try to predict cash flows, the more uncertain the forecast is. The cash budget is only as useful as the accuracy of the forecast that is used to make the predictions. If your cash flows are subject to high levels of uncertainty, you should provide for either a cash cushion, ready borrowing, or both.

Preparation of the Cash Budget

A key to the accuracy of most cash budgeting is a forecast of sales. When using an internal approach for the generation of a sales forecast, the salesmen must be asked to project sales for the forthcoming periods. The product sales manager or other appropriate person gathers these estimates and consolidates them into a sales estimate for a particular product line, thereby building up data into useful information. Often, however, internally generated sales forecasts may be too narrow in scope and overly optimistic. They may miss important trends in the economy and the industry generally. For these reasons, many companies use externally generated sales forecasts. Advisory or consulting businesses are available that use econometric modeling techniques to approximate future industry and economy conditions. These businesses may be helpful only to larger, multi-operational, multiproduct, multisectional companies.

Given the basic predictions of business conditions and industrial sales, the next step is to estimate market share by individual product, price, and the expected customer reception of the new products. These estimates should be made in conjunction with the business's marketing managers. By using a consolidated approach with the sales forecast generated in conjunction with internal and external marketing personnel, a more accurate projection may be realized. The importance of the accuracy of sales forecasts cannot be overstated, as most of the other budgets, projections, and forecasts are based on expected sales.

The next step in generating a cash budget is to determine the cash receipts from the expected sales. Consider your past history of cash and credit sales to determine offsetting factors and time delays associated with each. Some probabilities may be applied to projected sales in order to generate expected receipts. In this way, you are considering the credit terms used and offsetting the timing of receipt of those sales dollars.

Disbursements

Given a sales forecast, another important body of information to be generated is a production schedule. Decisions must be made whether to gear production closely to sales or to produce at a relatively constant rate over time, ignoring the periodic fluctuations in demand. Remember that with a level production schedule, inventory carrying costs are generally higher than when the business tends to match production to sales. However, level production is generally more efficient than fluctuating production. Therefore, it is important to consider the trade-off in inventory carrying costs versus the efficiencies that can be realized in various production schedules.

Another important consideration is whether you intend to produce just enough to meet demand or to commit the resources to build inventory levels. The sales forecast is a valuable tool in determining expected future production needs. You should consider the generation of a production forecast based upon some strategy for meeting this expected need. Almost all strategies will require a commitment of resources. Even production tailored to meet demand exactly requires a commitment of cash and other resources before you expect to receive cash inflows. If you plan to build a buffer inventory, you must expect an even greater delay in receipt of compensating cash inflows.

Once a production schedule has been established, estimates can be made concerning the necessary materials to be purchased, the labor required for that production, and any additional fixed assets you may need to meet the demand. From the production schedule you can evaluate the expected cash outflows and even the timing of those outflows. There is a lag between the time a sale is made and the time of actual cash payment.

Wages are assumed to increase with the amount of production. Another factor of wages is the trade-off of overtime versus increased production staff. Very often, production peaks can be taken care of more cost effectively by using overtime rather than incurring the cost of hiring new employees. Establish a policy concerning the amount of overtime you will tolerate before hiring additional employees. This can be calculated on a cost basis. For example, if the cost to the business for overtime is 2.5 times the cost of regular time (adding in overtime benefits, wages, premiums, etc.), how many hours of additional labor justify the addition of another employee?

$$\text{Breakeven for new employee} = \frac{40 \text{ hrs/wk}}{2.5} = 16 \text{ hours of overtime}$$

If your business sustains more than 16 hours of overtime for a particular function, it may be cheaper to hire another employee.

In calculating the trade-off between overtime hours and the decision to hire additional labor, we have simplified the problem for example purposes only. The problem is more complex. In the example, we have considered only the variable cost component of adding an additional employee. There are still fixed and semivariable components. When you decide to add a new employee, you will incur additional costs associated with recruitment, training, insurance, administrative processing, health examinations, and other factors. In making the overtime versus hire decision, consider the costs of additional overtime hours against these fixed and semivariable cost components as well. Obviously, this is only a first approximation. You must also consider the duration of the need and the learning time for new employees to become productive.

In addition, you will have other demands on cash. Included in other expenses are general administrative and selling expenses; property taxes; interest expenses; power, light, and heat expenses; and maintenance expenses. These expenses tend to be reasonably predictable over the short run.

You must also take into account capital expenditures, dividends, federal taxes, and other cash outflows. As shown in Chapter 3, a business should plan as far in advance as possible for its capital expenditures. These forecasted expenditures should be predictable for the short-termed cash budget. Dividend payments, if appropriate, for most companies are discretionary and are paid on specific dates. Estimation of federal income taxes can be based on projected profits, which a cost accountant or bookkeeper can readily generate. These cash outlays must be combined with the total cash expenditures in order to obtain a schedule of total cash disbursements. The four most critical categories to be included in the schedule of cash disbursements are:

- Total cash expenses.
- Capital expenditures.

• Dividend payments.
• Income taxes.

These should be listed on a month-by-month basis for the fiscal year.

Many accounting software packages include a report that itemizes short-term future cash flows based on the billing and payment information already entered into the system. These systems review the open accounts receivable and determine the most likely cash receipt dates from customers, based on the dates when these invoices are due for payment. The systems also analyze open accounts payable in a similar manner, to determine the dates when supplier invoices must be paid. The information is usually presented in weekly time buckets for as far into the future as there is available information in the system to add to the forecast. Although this information is based on detailed underlying information and should be quite accurate, there are several reasons why it must be heavily supplemented by manual adjustments:

• *Missing accounts payable.* Many companies do not enter their accounts payable into the computer system until shortly before they are due for payment, because the accounting staff prefers to match supplier invoices to supporting purchasing and receiving documentation prior to making any computer entries. Because this information is not included in the computer, there will be an insufficient amount of accounts payable forecasted for payment by the computer.
• *Missing capital expenditure payments.* The accounts payable system may not include payments for capital expenditures, since many of these purchases require either cash in advance or cash on delivery, or several periodic payments; in all these cases, the payments may not be entered into the system until the day they are due for payment, which does not allow the system to include them in forecasted cash flows.
• *Accounts receivable timing.* The actual dates on which payments arrive from customers will vary significantly from the scheduled dates itemized by the computer because there is always a mix of late payments caused by a variety of factors that delays cash receipts. Also, there are always delayed cash receipts coming in

from earlier billings, the receipt of which the computer had already predicted in some earlier period, which will impact the forecasted cash flow in a positive manner.

- *Does not include payroll.* Many companies use outside payroll services or payroll software that is not integrated into the remainder of their accounting systems. For these reasons, the accounting software cannot access any information about cash outflows to pay for employee salaries and wages.

For these reasons, it is best to use the computer-generated cash forecast as a tool in constructing a more accurate manual forecast. If there is a detailed version of the report that itemizes the specific timing of individual accounts payable and receivable, then this may be of use in verifying the cash forecast that is being derived manually.

Net Cash Flow and Cash Balances

An enterprise must carefully review its schedules in order to ensure that it has taken into account all foreseeable cash inflows and outflows. By combining the cash receipts and the cash disbursements schedules, you can obtain the net cash inflow or outflow for each period. Once you have identified the months in which you will have difficulty in meeting your cash needs, means must be found to address the cash deficiencies and to plan for them. This is further discussed in Chapter 5. Before seeking additional cash to meet these demands, you may be able to delay your capital expenditures or your payments for purchases in order to prevent the negative cash flow months from occurring. Knowing what the cash position will be in each month allows you to consider such options as when to make capital investments, investments of excess funds in marketable securities, and other forms of cash planning.

Exceptions to Expected Cash Flows

A cash budget merely represents an estimate of future cash flows. Depending on the care devoted to preparing the budget, the volatility of the market, and the accuracy of the data used, there may be considerable deviation between the actual cash flows and the expected cash flows. When considering such uncertainty, it is necessary to provide information about the range of possible outcomes. Considering cash flows using only one set of assumptions may result in a faulty perspective of the future and misinformation for planning purposes.

In order to consider deviations from expected cash flows, it may be important to work out additional cash budgets using different forecasted sales levels. Such cash budget scenarios help you plan for contingencies. In addition, you may want to generate budgets for best-case, most likely, and worst-case scenarios.

One of the benefits of discussing the cash budget within the business is that management is better able to plan contingencies for possible consequences and probable events. These discussions tend to sharpen the perspective of management on the future. Finally, management will be encouraged to realize the magnitude and impact of various occurrences on the profitability of the business.

Computers may be of some assistance in evaluating different scenarios. An example of such a computer-generated budget is included in the appendix to this chapter. Very often, the cash budget can be designed in such a manner that you may substitute different probabilities for outcomes, thus generating a probable cash budget more rapidly and with more flexibility than by trying to adjust by hand for all the alternatives. In addition, you may change the assumptions dealing with some occurrences. In this manner, cases may be rerun on a computer allowing extensive analysis of the sensitivity of your decisions. Using this information, you can more accurately gauge minimum cash balances, the maturity structure of needed debt, the borrowing power of the business, and the ability of the business to adjust to deviations in expected outcome. For example, questions such as the following may be asked:

- How flexible are expenses?
- What can be cut or eliminated?
- How much can be eliminated?
- How quickly can we respond?
- How much effort should be devoted to the collection of receivables?

- What additional purchases will be required for unexpected increases in business?
- Can labor be expanded and at what cost?
- Can the present plant handle the additional demand?
- How much money will be needed in order to finance buildup?

The answers to these and other questions will show the efficiency and flexibility of the business under varying conditions. By relying on numerous budgets with different ranges of possible outcomes, you have the option to consider and be prepared for many more contingencies. It is important to be truthful to yourself in the preparation of these budgets. Do not fall prey to extreme optimism or pessimism but rather examine numerous possibilities.

Summary

Your working capital is principally composed of cash, accounts receivable inventory, accounts payable, and other short-term payables.

Cash serves many functions within the business and actually is the medium of exchange for all transactions. The investment of excess or temporarily idle cash should be made with a consideration for the expected yield, the associated risk, the liquidity of the investment, and the transactional costs associated with the exchange of investment with cash. There are many ways to invest excess cash, each of which has a risk-and-return relationship and other conditions and constraints. Many of the constraints deal with liquidity and transactional cost considerations.

A business selling its product in a large geographic area has to be concerned with the time delays associated with the physical transfers of payment (cash). This delay, or float, costs the business money. Many methods have been developed to minimize the delay and to speed up the receipt of cash—concentration banking, lockboxes, and others. The other side of the coin, of course, is the delay in making cash outflows. You can analyze these cash flows and take advantage of them for earning interest.

You should have a cash flow budget. Determining how cash flows within the business may best be envisioned as an actual flow of dollars for each transaction. Cash management should consider how things are being done and question all cash expenditures: Can we get along without it? Can we postpone it? Can it be done more cheaply?

As with cash, you can profit from managing your accounts receivable. One of the easiest methods of gaining an understanding of how well collections are being made is to establish a frequency distribution of the age of the receivables. It may be more profitable to discontinue sales to delinquent customers than to continue to advance credit, tying up valuable assets. An unpaid account receivable is an outstanding loan.

The other side is your policy about paying your bills. Another simple tool is a chart showing discounts taken and, more important, discounts not taken. A common discount, 2/10, N/30, means that it costs you 2 percent of the invoice amount to extend payment for 20 days. This can be equated to a 37 percent per annum interest rate. Discounts lost can have serious cost implications.

Timing is all-important in transactions. Many businesses experience cycles that affect the cash status. Planning for these timing variations may allow you to earn during periods of excess cash while having enough cash available in times of poor cash flow to avoid cash borrowing.

Appendix: Cash Flow Example

In this appendix, we review a typical cash forecasting model that uses a series of assumptions to arrive at a monthly prediction of cash inflow and outflow. The model begins with assumptions regarding sales levels, collection periods, and debt interest rates in the sections entitled "Sheet 1.1" and "Sheet 1.2." These assumptions are then used to arrive at predicted cash receipts and cash disbursements by month, as noted in the sections entitled "Sheet 2.1" and "Sheet 3.1." We bring this information together in "Sheet 4.1" to arrive at a net cash change per month. The final section, "Sheet 5.1," notes the amount of cash the company expects to invest in its working capital and other key accounts over the course of the year. This format is short and easily readable, so managers can quickly grasp the reasons for changes in cash flows.

We will note the reasons for using each line item in the cash forecast, as well as how the information is derived. This line-by-line explanation gives the reader a thorough understanding of the model, allowing one to easily duplicate it. The line item descriptions are as follows:

Sheet 1.1

- *Total dollar sales.* This information comes from the sales department's forecast and is extremely important—the sales figures are used later in the cash forecast to determine the timing of cash receipts and the amount of likely cash expenditures. Because it affects so much of the cash forecast, a company must be sure to enter the most accurate information possible into this line.
- *Collections, cash sales.* This is a percentage and is multiplied by the total dollar sales figure in the preceding line to derive the "cash sales" figure that is listed under the *Cash Receipts Detail* section. This figure represents the cash inflow that has no timing delay, since customers pay at the time of product receipt.
- *Collections, collect in 30 days.* This is a percentage and is multiplied by the total dollar sales figure in the first line of this section to derive a portion of the "Collections of Receivables" figure that is listed under the *Cash Receipts Detail* section. This figure represents the proportion of cash inflow that has a delay of approximately 30 days in arriving, and represents that portion of accounts receivable that arrives on time. Those businesses using different payment terms on their billings should use their stated number of payment days instead of the 30 days used in this example.
- *Collections, collect in 60 days.* This is a percentage and is identical to the preceding one in its usage, except that it represents the proportion of accounts receivable that are collected later than normal. This figure tends to fluctuate with the looseness of a company's credit granting policy and in inverse proportion to the aggressiveness of its overdue accounts receivable collection efforts.
- *Collections on November sales.* The sample cash forecast we are reviewing begins with December, so any late cash receipts from preceding months must be entered in this line. Based on the dollar quantities entered in the example, we can estimate that the sales in November were $100,000, since the standard proportion

collected in 30 days is 40 percent, and $40,000 is entered as having been received in December.

- *Average gross margin percentage.* This is a percentage and represents the average cost of sales in each month. In this model, it is used to derive the Total Purchases on Credit, which is the first line in the *Assumptions* section. For example, by multiplying the February sales figure of $140,000 by 70 percent, we arrive at total purchases for the month of $98,000, to which we add an inventory buildup for the month of $94,000 (as noted in the Inventory line in the *Balances in Key Accounts* section). When added together, this equals total purchases of $192,000, which is the number listed under February in the Total Purchases on Credit line in the *Assumptions* section.

Sheet 1.2: Assumptions

- *Total purchases on credit.* The derivation of the amounts in this line were described for the Average Gross Margin Percentage in the *Sheet 1.1* section. The total purchases number is later used in the Payment for Purchases on Credit line in the *Cash Disbursements Detail* section, with a delay of one month (since we assume supplier payment terms of 30 days). This is the chief component of the cash disbursements total.
- *Line-of-credit interest rate.* This is a percentage, and is used later in the *Cash Disbursements Detail* section to determine the interest payment on the line of credit, which is a cash disbursement.
- *Line-of-credit balance in December.* The last line of the cash forecast includes a calculation of the balance in the line of credit; however, this figure will be incorrect unless the model already contains the balance from the previous year. Therefore, we include this preliminary debt figure.
- *Long-term debt interest rate.* This is a percentage and is used later in the *Cash Disbursements Detail* section to determine the interest payment on the long-term debt, which is a cash disbursement. Unlike the interest rate for the line of credit, there is only a single entry for this amount, rather than an entry in every month of the year; the reason for the difference is that most long-term debt is fixed at the beginning of the debt agreement, so there is no need to adjust the rate over the course of the year.

- *Long-term debt balance in December.* The *Cash Disbursements Detail* section includes line items for the interest and principal payments on long-term debt. Those payments are derived from the December debt balance, since it reveals the total amount that the company still has left to pay on its debt.
- *Long-term debt payment schedule.* This line item lists the grand total payment to lenders each month that is required to fulfill debt payment obligations on the long-term debt total that was listed in the last line item. If there are debt balloon payments, they should be entered in the correct month in this line.
- *Minimum acceptable cash balance.* This figure is the minimum amount of cash that the management team has decided must be kept on hand at all times, perhaps to meet short-term cash needs. This figure is needed to calculate the Cash Needs Comparison line in the *Analysis of Cash Requirements* section.
- The figure also appears in the Ending Cash Balance line of the same section, where we have borrowed enough funds through the line of credit to ensure that the cash balance never drops below the minimum acceptable cash balance.

Sheet 2.1: Cash Receipts Detail

- *Cash sales.* The numbers in this line denote the total amount of cash received from cash payments for sales. These cash receipts have no timing delay, since they come from customers as immediate payment for sales to them. The numbers are derived by multiplying the sales figure in the Total Dollar Sales line in *Sheet 1.1* times the cash sales percentage in the same section, and for the same month.
- *Collections of receivables.* This line is a calculation that summarizes the delayed cash receipts from sales in the past two months. Specifically in this model, it is 50 percent of the sales from two months ago, plus 40 percent of the sales from the preceding month (these collection percentages were listed in the *Sheet 1.1* section).
- *Other.* There are always miscellaneous cash receipts that can come in from a variety of sources, such as tax rebates or proceeds from asset sales. These figures are manually entered in this line.

- *Total cash receipts.* This line summarizes all the cash receipts previously noted in this section.

Sheet 3.1: Cash Disbursements Detail

- *Payment for purchases on credit.* The numbers in this line are drawn directly from the Total Purchases on Credit line in the *Assumptions* section. However, their timing is moved forward one month, since we are assuming that purchases made in the preceding month have payment terms of 30 days, and so must be paid in the following month. For example, purchases made in July of $90,000 do not appear in the cash forecast as payments until August.
- *Operating expenses.* The numbers in this line are entered from the annual budget, and contain the salaries, facility expenses, and other miscellaneous administrative costs associated with running the business.
- *Long-term debt interest.* This line item and the next one, Principal, are based on an electronic spreadsheet command. The command is derived from the debt payment amount listed in the Long-Term Debt Payment Schedule line and the Long-Term Debt Interest Rate line, both located in the *Assumptions* section. One can use the IPMT command in Microsoft Excel to determine the proportion of the monthly debt payment that is ascribed to interest expense, while one can subtract the interest expense from the total debt payment to derive the principal payment that is listed in the next line. These two lines can be merged if management is not interested in the interest and principal components that comprise a debt payment.
- *Principal.* See the preceding Long-Term Debt Interest line item.
- *Interest payment on line of credit.* This line item is a calculation that is based on the month-end line-of-credit balance from the preceding month, multiplied by the interest rate for the month, which results in the interest payment due to the lender during the current month. For example, the February interest payment is derived by multiplying the January debt total of $58,250 by the interest rate of 15 % (reduced to one-twelfth, since this is a single-month payment), which results in an interest expense of $728.

- *Income taxes.* This line contains the estimated income tax payments for each quarter of the year, and is usually inputted directly from the annual budget.
- *Other.* There are always additional cash payments that do not fall into the standard categories previously noted in this section. This line item is used for manual entries of these extra cash outflows.
- *Total cash disbursements.* This line summarizes all of the cash disbursements previously noted in this section.

Sheet 4.1: Analysis of Cash Requirements

- *Net cash generated this period.* The numbers in this line are calculated by subtracting the amounts in the Total Cash Disbursements line in the preceding section from the amounts in the Total Cash Receipts line in the *Cash Receipts Detail* section.
- *Beginning cash balance.* This figure comes from the Ending Cash Balance line at the end of this section, but for the preceding month. It is netted against the Net Cash Generated This Period line to arrive at the Cash Balance Before Borrowings line, which follows.
- *Cash balance before borrowings.* As just noted, this line is derived by netting the Net Cash Generated This Period line against the Cash Balance Before Borrowings line. As the description states, the resulting numbers show the cash inflow or outflow resulting from operations.
- *Cash needs comparison.* This line compares the Cash Balance before Borrowings line to the Minimum Acceptable Cash Balance in the *Assumptions* section to arrive at a total amount of borrowings needed or cash available for an additional debt payment. For example, in the month of April, we have a preliminary cash need of $32,450, but then increase it by $20,000, since we require an internal cash balance of $20,000, resulting in a total cash need of $52,450.
- *Current period short-term borrowings.* This line is a calculation that is essentially the inverse of the preceding line. It itemizes a borrowing requirement that exactly matches the cash need we have just calculated in the Cash Needs Comparison line. However, note that the amount of debt paid down in August is lower than the amount of cash spun off by operations. This is because we are paying off the line of credit in August and have surplus cash left over.

- *Total short-term borrowings.* The numbers in this line are cumulative from month to month. For example, the total short-term borrowings at the end of January are $58,250 but are increased by $47,478 in February (see the Current Period Short-Term Borrowings line), resulting in a total borrowings figure of $105,728.
- *Ending cash balance.* The numbers in this line are based on a minimum cash balance of $20,000 (as noted earlier in the Minimum Acceptable Cash Balance line in the *Assumptions* section), or a higher cash balance, if the line of credit has been paid off. For example, the ending cash balance in July is $20,000, but this increases to $67,404 in August, because the line of credit has been paid off, leaving an extra $47,404 to add to the beginning cash balance for the next month.

Sheet 5.1: Balances in Key Accounts

- *Cash.* The numbers in this line are drawn directly from the Ending Cash Balance line in the preceding section. Its purpose in this section is to be part of the summary of key accounts that most affect monthly cash flows.
- *Accounts receivable.* The numbers in this line are derived from the sales and collection figures at the top of the *Sheet 1.1* section. For example, the December accounts receivable figure is composed of two calculations. The first is 90 percent of the current month's sales, which is derived by assuming that only 10 percent of sales are paid for in cash (as noted in the Cash Sales line in the *Sheet 1.1* section). The remaining amount comes from previous month sales, which in this example are 40 percent of the November sales. After adding the two calculations together, we arrive at an estimated accounts receivable balance of $152,900.
- *Inventory.* The numbers in this line are manually derived, and are normally input from the production or inventory budget page in the annual budget. Many manufacturing companies will build inventory levels prior to the commencement of their main selling seasons, and so the inventory level will not necessarily bear a direct relationship to sales levels each month. This line item is part of the calculation for the Payment for Purchases on Credit line in the *Cash Disbursements Detail* section, as explained earlier in the bullet for that line.

- *Accounts payable.* The numbers in this line are drawn directly from the Total Purchases on Credit line in the *Assumptions* section and represent the total source of funds from suppliers that will offset cash used by the other line items in this section (e.g., accounts receivable and inventory).
- *Line of credit.* The numbers in this line are drawn directly from the Total Short-Term Borrowings line in the preceding section. Its purpose in this section is to be part of the summary of key accounts that most affect monthly cash flows.

The reader should review the following cash flow example in detail, consulting the explanations section to clarify any points of uncertainty, for as long as it takes to obtain a thorough understanding of how a cash flow forecast works. We highly recommend that every company create a cash flow forecast and update and consult it regularly, because cash flow is the lifeblood of a business and can rapidly lead to a cash flow coronary that results in a business heart attack.

Sheet 1.1

	Dec	Jan	Feb	Mar	Apr	May	Jun	Jul	Aug	Sep	Oct	Nov	Dec
Total Dollar Sales	110,000	120,000	140,000	180,000	240,000	242,000	187,000	154,000	121,000	110,000	110,000	110,000	121,000
Collections: Cash Sales	10	10	10	10	10	10	10	10	10	10	10	10	10
as Percent Collect in 30 Days	40	40	40	40	40	40	40	40	40	40	40	40	40
of Sales Collect in 60 Days	50	50	50	50	50	50	50	50	50	50	50	50	50
Collections on November Sales	40,000	50,000											
Average Gross Margin Percentage	70	70	70	70	70	70	70	70	70	70	70	70	70

Assumptions   Sheet 1.2

	Dec	Jan	Feb	Mar	Apr	May	Jun	July	Aug	Sep	Oct	Nov	Dec
Total Purchases on Credit	112,000	144,000	192,000	198,000	153,000	126,000	99,000	90,000	81,000	90,000	90,000	90,000	117,000
Line-of-Credit Interest Rate:	14	14	15	17	18	16	16	16	16	16	15	14	12
Line-of-Credit Balance in December:	0												
Long-Term Debt Interest Rate:	14												
Long-Term Debt Balance in December:	100,000												
Long-Term Debt Payment Schedule:	2,500	2,500	2,500	2,500	2,500	2,500	2,500	2,500	2,500	2,500	2,500	2,500	2,500
Minimum Acceptable Cash Balance:	20,000	20,000	20,000	20,000	20,000	20,000	20,000	20,000	20,000	20,000	20,000	20,000	20,000

Cash Receipts Detail   Sheet 2.1

	Jan	Feb	Mar	Apr	May	Jun	Jul	Aug	Sep	Oct	Nov	Dec
Cash Sales	12,000	14,000	18,000	24,000	24,200	18,700	15,400	12,100	11,000	11,000	11,000	12,100
Collections of Receivables	44,500	103,000	116,000	142,000	186,000	216,800	195,800	155,100	125,400	104,500	99,000	99,000
Other												
Total Cash Receipts	56,500	117,000	134,000	166,000	210,200	235,500	211,200	167,200	136,400	115,500	110,000	111,100

Cash Disbursements

Detail — Sheet 3.1	Jan	Feb	Mar	Apr	May	Jun	Jul	Aug	Sep	Oct	Nov	Dec
Payment for Purchases on Credit	112,000	144,000	192,000	198,000	153,000	126,000	99,000	90,000	81,000	90,000	90,000	90,000
Operating Expenses	12,250	12,250	12,250	12,250	12,250	12,250	12,250	12,250	12,250	12,250	12,250	12,250
Long-Term Debt Interest	1,167	1,151	1,135	1,119	1,103	1,087	1,071	1,054	1,037	1,020	1,003	985
Principal	1,333	1,349	1,365	1,381	1,397	1,413	1,429	1,446	1,463	1,480	1,497	1,515
Interest Payment on Line of Credit	0	728	1,498	2,700	3,099	2,601	1,372	198	0	0	0	0
Income Taxes	3,000	0	0	3,000	0	0	3,000	0	0	3,000	0	0
Other	0	5,000	0	0	2,000	0	5,000	0	2,000	0	25,000	0
Total Cash Disbursements	129,750	164,478	208,248	218,450	172,849	143,351	123,122	104,948	97,750	107,750	129,750	104,750

Analysis of Cash Requirements

Requirements — Sheet 4.1	Dec	Jan	Feb	Mar	Apr	May	Jun	Jul	Aug	Sep	Oct	Nov	Dec
Net Cash Generated This Period		−73,250	−47,478	−74,248	−52,450	37,351	92,149	88,078	62,252	38,650	7,750	−19,750	6,350
Beginning Cash Balance		35,000	20,000	20,000	20,000	20,000	20,000	20,000	20,000	67,404	106,054	113,804	94,054
Cash Balance Before Borrowings		−38,250	−27,478	−54,248	−32,450	57,351	112,149	108,078	82,252	106,054	113,804	94,054	100,404
Cash Needs Comparison		−58,250	−47,478	−74,248	−52,450	37,351	92,149	88,078	62,252	86,054	93,804	74,054	80,404
Current Period Short-Term Borrowings	0	58,250	47,478	74,248	52,450	−37,351	−92,149	−88,078	−14,848	0	0	0	0
Total Short-Term Borrowings	0	58,250	105,728	179,976	232,426	195,075	102,926	14,848	0	0	0	0	0
Ending Cash Balance	35,000	20,000	20,000	20,000	20,000	20,000	20,000	20,000	67,404	106,054	113,804	94,054	100,404

Balances in Key Accounts

Accounts — Sheet 5.1	Dec	Jan	Feb	Mar	Apr	May	Jun	Jul	Aug	Sep	Oct	Nov	Dec
Cash	35,000	20,000	20,000	20,000	20,000	20,000	20,000	20,000	67,404	106,054	113,804	94,054	100,404
Accounts Receivable	99,500	152,000	174,000	218,000	288,000	313,800	265,100	213,400	170,500	147,400	143,000	143,000	152,900
Inventory	35,000	95,000	189,000	261,000	246,000	202,600	170,700	152,900	149,200	162,200	175,200	188,200	220,500
Accounts Payable		144,000	192,000	198,000	153,000	126,000	99,000	90,000	81,000	90,000	90,000	90,000	117,000
Line of Credit	0	58,250	105,728	179,976	232,426	195,075	102,926	14,848	0	0	0	0	0
		64,750	85,272	121,024	168,574	215,325	253,874	281,452	306,104	325,654	342,004	335,254	356,804

Chapter 5

Financing

When considering business financing, it is important to distinguish between businesses just beginning their life cycle and those that have an established business record on which to build.

New Businesses

Many new businesses begin operations using "stolen funds," which means funds diverted from other normal financial activities unrelated to the project. With the inception of a new business, the capital for start-up will often come from personal resources. Even in larger businesses, start-up funds may come from stolen funds. As such, they may appear in another budget, not directly earmarked for the project to which they are applied.

Another source of stolen funds may be personal loans advanced by individuals using homes and items of personal property as collateral. Finally, an ultimate source of venture capital for a small business may be funds invested by, or loaned from, friends or family.

In all events, these funds represent a source not to be counted on for long-term or continued financing. As businesses start to grow, additional funds from these sources probably will not be available for continuing operations and growth. Additional resources and capital will be needed for inventory, equipment, operations, and to support accounts receivable. Many people with new businesses are surprised to learn the amount of money needed to support accounts receivable. As the business grows, accounts receivable may seem to eat money.

Later in the chapter, we will discuss sources of equity capital. At this point, however, it is important to mention that, in many circumstances, it is better to borrow money than to seek money from outside equity sources. Equity sources often dilute entrepreneurial control—a significant potential problem for smaller businesses.

Debt may be the best form of financing for at least two reasons:

1. It is sometimes cheap. Interest payments on debt are made in before-tax dollars. Dividends paid on equity are in after-tax dollars. However, interest payments are mandatory, and dividends can be discretionary.
2. Debt has an amplifying effect on earnings. Provided the business is profitable "after debt service," as the percentage of debt to equity increases, the earnings available to stockholders increase for a given amount of earnings. That is, once debt is serviced, the additional earnings on that capital go to the stockholders, not the creditors.

Zero Working Capital and Zero Fixed Assets

Before we delve into the various forms of financing, it may perhaps be worthwhile to note several approaches for avoiding the need for financing. One of the best is the concept of zero working capital, which is a state in which the sum of a company's investments in accounts receivable, inventory, and accounts payable nets out to zero. This is made possible by using different management techniques for each of the following elements of working capital:

- *Accounts receivable.* The goal in managing accounts receivable is to shorten the time needed for customers to pay the company. This can be done through several approaches. One is to use a very aggressive collections team to contact customers about overdue payments and ensure that payments are made on time. Another approach is to tighten the credit granting process, so that potential customers with even slightly shaky credit histories are kept on a very short credit leash or granted no credit at all. A final approach that has the best results is to drastically shorten the standard customer payment terms, which can even go so far as requiring cash payments in advance.

- *Inventory.* The goal in managing inventory is to reduce it to the bare minimum, which can be achieved in two ways. One is to outsource the entire production operation and have the production supplier drop ship deliveries directly to the company's customers, so that the company never has to fund any inventory—the company never has to purchase raw materials or work-in-process. Instead, it pays the supplier when finished goods are delivered to its customers. A different approach is to use a manufacturing planning system, such as just-in-time (JIT). Under this concept, the inventory levels needed to maintain a proper flow of inventory are reduced to the bare minimum through a number of techniques, such as many small supplier deliveries straight to the production line, kanban cards to control the flow of parts, and building to specific customer orders.

- *Accounts payable.* The goal in managing accounts payable is to not pay suppliers for as long as possible. One way to do this is to stretch out payments, irrespective of whatever the supplier payment terms may be. However, this will rapidly irritate suppliers, who may cut off the credit of any company that consistently abuses its designated payment terms. A better approach is to formally negotiate longer payment terms with them, perhaps in exchange for slightly higher prices. For example, terms of 30 days at a price point of $1.00 per unit may be altered to terms of 60 days and a new price of $1.02 per unit, which covers the supplier's cost of the money that has essentially been lent to the company. Although there is a cost associated with lengthening supplier terms, this may be a good deal for a company that has few other sources of funds.

Forcing longer payment terms on one's suppliers is much easier if a company knows that it comprises a large part of its suppliers' sales, which gives it considerable negotiating power over them. The same situation exists with a company's customers if it has a unique product or service that they cannot readily find elsewhere, so that they must agree to abide by the short payment terms. If a company does not have theses advantages, or competitive pressures do not allow it to make use of them, the best option left is the reduction of inventory, since this is an internal issue that is not dependent on the vagaries of suppliers and customers.

Dell Computer Company has achieved a *negative* working capital position, which means it makes money from its working capital. It does this by keeping only a day or two of inventory on hand, and orders more from its suppliers only when it has specific orders in hand from its customers. In addition, it pays its suppliers on longer terms than the terms it allows its customers, many of whom pay by credit card. The result is an enviable situation in which this rapidly growing company can not only ignore the cash demands that normally go along with growth, but actually take in cash from it.

Working capital is not the only drain on cash that a company will experience. It must also invest in fixed assets, such as office equipment for its staff, production machinery for the manufacturing operation, and warehouses and trucks for the logistics department. Though these may seem like unavoidable requirements that are an inherent part of doing business, there are a few ways to mitigate or even completely avoid these investments:

- *Centralize operations.* If a company adds branch offices or extra distribution warehouses, it must invest in fixed assets for each one. This is a particular concern when extra distribution warehouses are added, since a company must absorb not only the cost of the building, but also the cost of the inventory inside it. A better approach for a cash-strapped company is to centralize virtually all operations, even if there is a cost associated with *not* decentralizing. For example, shifting to a central warehouse will eliminate the cost of a subsidiary warehouse, but will increase the cost of deliveries from the central warehouse, assuming that shipments must now travel a further distance.
- *Rent or lease facilities and equipment.* With so many leasing companies in the market today, as well as manufacturers financing the lease of their own equipment, a company has a wealth of financing choices that allow it to avoid the purchase of its facilities and

equipment. These arrangements can be a straight rental, wherein the company has no ownership interest in the assets it uses (also very similar to an operating lease), or a capital lease, in which the terms of the lease agreement assume that the company will take possession of the asset being leased at the end of the payment term. In either of these cases, the total of the rental or lease payments will exceed the cost of the asset if a company chose to purchase the asset; this is due to the maintenance and interest costs of the lease supplier, as well as its profit. The main advantage is that there is no large lump-sum payment required at the time of asset acquisition.

- *Outsource operations.* Some portion of every department can be outsourced to a supplier. Though the main reasons for doing so are related more to strategic and operational issues, one can also make a strong case for outsourcing because it reduces the need for fixed assets. By using outsourcing to avoid the hiring of clerical staff, a company no longer has to invest in the office space, furniture, or computer systems that they would otherwise require. Also, shifting the distribution function to a supplier can completely eliminate a company's investment in trucking and warehouse equipment, whereas outsourcing production will eliminate the massive fixed asset investment that is common for most manufacturing facilities. Similarly, shifting a company's computer operations to the data processing center of a supplier will eliminate its investment in its own data processing center, which may be considerable. By using outsourcing, a company will not only avoid an initial investment in fixed assets, but also the update and replacement of those same items. However, outsourcing is expensive, because suppliers must absorb the cost of purchasing the assets that the company would otherwise have purchased.

- *Use partnerships.* If a company can enter into a partnership with another company, it may be possible to use the other company's assets to transact business. For example, if a drug research company has a new drug to market, it should enter into a partnership with an established drug manufacturing firm, so that the research firm does not have to invest in its own production plant. This arrangement works well for both parties: The research company can avoid additional cash investments in fixed assets, while the other company can more fully utilize its existing assets. If a company brings a particularly valuable patent or process to a partnership, it can use this to extract a large share of the forthcoming partnership profits, too.

In the preceding list, there were many cases in which fixed assets could be eliminated, but at the cost of increased variable costs. Examples of this were heightened distribution costs in exchange for eliminating an outlying distribution warehouse, renting equipment rather than buying it, and outsourcing services rather than attempting to operate them in-house. These are acceptable approaches for many companies, and for several reasons. One is that avoiding the fixed costs associated with a fixed-asset purchase will keep a company's total fixed costs lower than would otherwise be the case, which allows it to have a lower break-even point, so that it can still turn a profit if sales take a turn for the worse. Another reason is that, if there are few and meager funding sources, the added variable costs will not seem like much of a problem when weighed against the amount of cash that a company has just avoided investing in fixed assets. Finally, the centralization of operations and use of outsourcing will reduce the amount of management attention that would otherwise be wasted on the outlying locations that are now no longer there, or the departments that have been shifted to a supplier. In smaller companies with a dearth of managers, this is a major advantage. Consequently, the increased variable cost of some of the fixed-asset reduction options presented here should not be considered a significant reason for not implementing them.

Types of Financing

Typically, businesses are financed using either or both of two forms of capital investment: debt and equity. Within these two general classifications, there is an array of alternatives as diverse and creative as human imagination. Probably the only thing more complex than the means of financing available is the tax code that is intended to finance the country. The first and most common form of financing is debt.

Debt

Debt—borrowing—can be structured with repayment in the short, intermediate, or long term. It can be unsecured or (as is more commonly the case) secured by the assets of the business and/or owners. It typically has conditions or covenants that define the terms of the commitment and repayment of the loan.

Short-term debt is generally intended to be self-liquidating in that the asset purchased with that loan will generate sufficient cash flows to pay off that loan within one year. It is often used to finance inventory buildups and seasonal increases in accounts receivable. Trade credit, lines of credit, and commercial paper (for the large firm) are sources of short-term, unsecured financing. With some forms of short-term, unsecured financing, some extra compensation is required. For example, for a line of credit, a bank may require a compensating balance to be deposited. If you wish to establish a line of credit for $200,000, many banks require you to maintain a balance of, say, 15 percent, or $30,000, in a demand-deposit account during the year. If the compensating balance is above the amount you would ordinarily have on deposit, the cost of the incremental amount represents an additional cost of borrowing. In the above example, if you wish to borrow $200,000 and the bank rate is 12 percent, with the compensating balance of $30,000 *more* than you ordinarily have on deposit, you would net only $170,000 to use. The nominal annual dollar cost is 12 percent of $200,000, or $24,000. The actual cost of the loan as a percentage is:

$$\frac{\$24,000}{\$170,000} = 14.11\%$$

The use of compensating balances is falling with the advent of variable interest rates. Some banks are charging higher interest rates more in line with their incremental cost of money and deemphasizing compensating balances.

Another method used by banks to improve their return is discounting. For example, under a "regular" loan, a bank lends $20,000 for one year at 14 percent simple interest. At the end of the year, the borrower repays the $20,000 plus $2,800 in interest. If the loan is discounted, the bank collects its interest at the time of lending. The borrower receives a net loan of $17,200. At the end of the year, when the borrower repays the loan of $20,000, the actual effective interest rate is higher. It computes to:

$$\frac{\$2,800}{\$17,200} = 16.28\%$$

Secured Loans and Intermediate Financing.   Many new firms cannot obtain credit on an unsecured agreement because they have no proven track record. First, banks look to your cash flow ability. Failing that, the security of the collateral pledged to insure payment must be considered. The lender will seek collateral in excess of the loan value to guarantee a margin of safety. The greater the margin of safety, the more liquid the collateral, because the asset can be discounted further (and still realize full repayment) and sold more quickly to meet the call on the debt.

One method that may be employed to secure the debt is borrowing against accounts receivable. The collateral to the lender is the debt owed the borrower on goods or services provided to customers. From the lender's standpoint, there is a cost to process the collateral and there is a risk of fraud and default. Therefore, this may be an expensive method of borrowing.

A loan against accounts receivable is generally made through a commercial bank because the interest rate is lower than that offered by finance companies. The lender discounts the face value of the receivables and may even reject from consideration some that have low credit ratings, are unrated, or are slow to pay.

Another factor of concern to the lender is the size or amount of each receivable. There is a trade-off: the larger the amount of the receivable, the larger the amount of potential default. But, with fewer accounts to keep track of, the cost of administration is less. A large number of small accounts have higher administrative costs, but any single default has less overall impact.

Accounts receivable financing is a continuous financing arrangement because as new accounts are added and assigned, additional security is added to the base. New receivables replace old, and the amount of the loan may fluctuate with each change in the base. This form of financing is advantageous to growing companies that have growing receivables.

Selling or factoring receivables is another form of financing. When receivables are sold (with notification), the purchaser steps into the place of the seller and the customers pay the purchaser of the receivables. The sale of receivables may be with or without recourse against the seller. When the sale of receivables is without recourse, the discounting will be much higher than when the buyer of the receivable still may see recovery from the seller. Sometimes receivables are sold "without notification." In this case, customers continue to pay the goods or service provider who acts as agent for the purchaser.

The problem with selling accounts receivable is that it is often done by companies that are in financial trouble. If you are not in financial trouble and you attempt to sell accounts receivable, you may send a signal that will be incorrectly interpreted by both the customers and your lending institutions. This may have a detrimental effect despite the offsetting benefits received from the sale. You may lose customers as a result of selling their accounts. Sometimes firms that purchase accounts receivable do not have the same equitable treatment of customers in mind when they undertake collection policies. Their rigidity in collection is based upon one and only one premise—collecting their money. Your interest in collecting from your customer includes maintaining the good customers for a long time. The goals of the collection department of the receivables purchasers are not congruent with your goals.

As was stated earlier, accounts receivable financing is expensive. And selling or factoring receivables is quite expensive for the following reasons:

- The firm purchasing receivables incurs substantial costs in collecting.
- It also incurs front-end costs in analyzing the worth of the receivables. This analysis cost has to be recovered somewhere, and that somewhere is in the discount rate for the receivables.
- The collection firm stands the risk of noncollections. Because there is a risk associated with noncollections, the purchasing firm will additionally discount the receivables to compensate for the percentage of potential bad debt.

- The purchasing firm might not purchase high-risk-of-default accounts, leaving the selling firm with the "worst" receivables still on its books.

Inventory Loans.   Inventories, as discussed in Chapter 4 dealing with working capital, represent a significant investment. The lender making a loan secured by inventory generally discounts the market value of the inventory based on a perception of the ease of liquidation. The advance on an inventory secured loan may be as high as 90 percent. However, lenders do not want to be in the sales business and prefer to have the loan repaid rather than have to seek foreclosure on the stock. These loans can be ongoing and variable in amount depending on the size of the inventory.

Long-Term Financing.   Long-term financing is generally considered an equity-based investment. Acquiring such investment often requires the services of investment bankers who act as middlemen between a firm issuing securities and sources of funds wishing to invest those funds. Investment bankers take some of the risks associated with the selling of a company's offering. Investment banking firms are used because of their expertise.

Investment banks use two methods of obtaining offerings: bidding and negotiation. In either case, the investment banker makes a margin in the issue between the selling price and the price at which the banker purchases the offering. This margin may be small—often less than 1 percent of the offering price. This function is called underwriting and relieves the offering company of the risk of selling the issue.

Convertible Debt.   The firm may issue bonds that are convertible to common stock at a given ratio. One of the arguments against convertible debt is that it may lead to further stock dilution. Other conversion options are available to corporations besides conversion of long-term debt to common stock. For example, short-term debt may be converted to long-term debt or vice versa. This later conversion can have dangerous consequences but is really no different from a creditor's accelerating payments as a result of failure to meet a loan covenant.

Common Stock

Common stock represents an ownership right in the firm issued to investors in return for the input of capital. Common stock has two statements of value: that which the stock certificate says and that which the market says. The stock certificate may indicate a par value, a stated value, or that the stock is issued without par or stated value. Ideally, the par or stated value should approximate the market value at date of issuance. That need not be the case. In any event, these values have legal ramifications as to the required legal capital in the company. Because various state laws govern in these cases, a competent corporate attorney should be consulted concerning state requirements.

The truly important value is the market value. Simply, that is what someone will pay to acquire a share of the stock. This is the perception of worth that governs how much ownership percentage you may have to surrender to acquire sufficient money to make the business go.

Investors buy common stock for cash dividends and/or appreciation in stock prices. The reason common stock is sold is to raise money. The advantage of common stock is that there is no obligation for the corporation to pay dividends in any given year. Dividends are declared at the discretion of the board of directors, assuming the company is profitable and there are sufficient additional dollars to pay the dividend.

Unlike debt, there is no maturity date on a stock. Therefore, common stock is a financial cushion for the firm (and the creditors). The common stockholders are the ones who absorb the bad times and enjoy the profit in the good times. Common stock ownership is considered residual ownership and should be considered a risky investment.

Companies can have approximately the same yields but different dividends and growths. A formula for yield or cost of stock equity (depending on whether you are a buyer or seller) is:

$$\text{Yield, or cost of stock equity} = \frac{\text{Annual dividend}}{\text{Stock price}} + \text{Growth}$$

Thus, the real cost of common stock cannot be measured by the dividend alone; consideration should be given to the growth rate in the stock's value as well.

When a company issues more stock, it is in effect selling ownership interests in the business. The problem with the sale of new stock is that it dilutes the percentage ownership of existing stockholders. For example, take a company that has three stockholders who own respective interests:

Shareholder	Percentage	Dollars	Shares (@ $100/share)
A	23%	$23,000	230
B	41%	41,000	410
C	36%	36,000	360
Total	100%	$100,000	1,000

If 300 additional shares are sold at $100 per share to D, the resulting ownership looks like:

Shareholder	Percentage	Shares
A	17.7%	230
B	31.5%	410
C	27.7%	360
D	23.1%	300
	100%	1,300

By selling 300 new shares of common stock to D, the percentages of ownership for A, B, and C have been reduced. Sometimes, the price of the stock will also drop to reflect the additional stock selling on the market. This reaction is caused by the perception (or misperception) that the total value of the business has not changed, but is just being spread over more shares. This dilution in value may give existing stockholders certain legal rights. In the preceding example, if the market believes the business is worth $100,000, by selling 300 additional shares the price might drop from $100 per share to, say, $77. This happens because the business is perceived to be worth $100,000/1,300 shares. The value of each shareholder's interest would then be:

Shareholder	Shares	Value	Change in Value
A	230	$17,692	(5,308)
B	410	31,537	(9,463)
C	360	27,692	(8,309)

The initial stockholders may file a lawsuit against the company for these losses through a proceeding called a *derivative suit.* They can claim a real loss in value as a result of a sale of additional stock by the company. For example, stockholder A claims a loss of $5,308 because the firm sold 300 shares of new issue. To protect against such a suit, the company could offer the option to purchase a pro rata share (usually this preemptive right is granted to shareholders by covenant) of the new issue to existing stockholders. In this example, the following would be offered:

A: 23% of 300 shares, or 69 shares
B: 41% of 300 shares, or 123 shares
C: 36% of 300 shares, or 108 shares

In this way, their ownership percentages could be maintained, but the value per share may still decline. One of the governing criteria of the market price (or price per share) will be the use to which the additional funds are put and whether the value of the business appears to increase in the eyes of the market. It comes down to what the potential buyers *believe* the value of the business is. The decision to sell additional stock should be carefully considered and planned for in advance of issue. One should consider an information release indicating what plans the company has for the funds. The intent is to let the market know that the value will increase with the new issue.

Common stockholders are the last to receive a return when times get difficult. Because there is no legal obligation to pay dividends, the business may choose not to pay them. Also, when the business is forced to liquidate assets to capital contributors, common stock owners are the last in line to share in the asset distribution.

The question, then, might be: "Why not always use debt financing?"

- The stockholder may lose the expectation of future returns if new debt capitalization is added. Additional debt increases the debt service against gross profits and decreases earnings, which translates directly into a risk of reduced dividends.
- There may be a decrease in the amount of managerial freedom. Debt reduces the amount of unaccounted-for profits by increasing debt service and the fixed obligations of interest payments. This may also reduce the operating latitude of management because of the covenants to which management agrees when accepting the debt.
- As a company issues more debt, it approaches its debt capacity. As it nears this limit, it reduces the margin of safety available to issue more debt if it needs additional capital, particularly if it needs capital quickly. The company has reduced its financial flexibility.

Preferred Stock

Often called a compromise investment, preferred stock has some of the attributes of common stock and some of the features of debt. Usually, a company's interest in selling preferred stock increases under the following conditions:

- The company cannot issue further debt but wants to use further leverage.
- The company does not want to dilute the interests of current common stockholders but wants more stock equity.

In either case, the company may wish to sell preferred stock. These are some of the distinguishing characteristics of preferred stock:

- While it may have a fixed rate of return (like debt), the dividend is optional and paid only when declared by the directors (but the dividend may be "cumulative" and therefore payable before any common stock dividends are paid).
- Preferred stock may have sinking funds provisions for the repurchase of the stock.

- Debt holders have a superior claim to assets in case of liquidation and have first claim to earnings. However, preferred stockholders' claims are superior to common stockholders'.

Taxes affect the amount of earnings needed to meet debt service and preferred stock dividends. However, because they receive different tax treatment, they affect earnings differently.

Suppose that both debt and preferred stock command a return of 12 percent and the applicable corporate tax rate is 46 percent. To pay the 12 percent interest rate on debt, the firm has to earn 12 percent before taxes. Interest on debt is paid in before-tax dollars. To pay the 12 percent dividend for preferred stock, the firm has to earn 12 percent in after-tax dollars.

For a 12 percent earnings after taxes, 22.2 percent—12 percent/ (1 − .46)—is required in before-tax dollars. Because dividends are paid in after-tax dollars, the firm has to earn more to pay a dividend of comparable worth to an investor than it has to earn for interest.

The tax rate the company pays will have a great deal to do with the amount of dividend paid for two reasons:

- The lower the company's real tax rate, the more disposable cash it will have to reinvest and pay dividends.
- The lower the company's tax rate, the more flexibility it can have in designing dividend policies to be attractive to investors and enhance the goodwill and value of the firm.

How to Obtain a Bank Loan

A businessperson making a first-time loan application has greater reporting responsibilities and requirements than does a borrower who has been dealing on a continuing basis with a bank for short-term financing. Once a bank has had good experience with a borrower, a loan request is much simpler. Usually the borrower need only provide updated information for an application that is on file.

Bankers are also interested in information that is not always reflected in the financial statements. For example, they like to be informed about the borrower's management capability, organizational strength, experience, and reputation. However, in addition to this reputation information, the bank will generally require completion of certain standardized reporting forms in order to evaluate the creditworthiness of the borrower. Some of these filing requirements will be discussed next.

Projected Cash Flow Statements

One of the most effective tools to determine the amount of the loan needed and its repayment date is the projected cash flow statement. The projections should disclose the significant assumptions used by management in preparing the cash forecast. Generally, past performances will serve as the basis for preparation, but it should be adjusted to reflect current trends. Two ways of making these adjustments are (1) pro forma and (2) an attrition allowance. Pro forma adjustments reflect changes in a company's projected cash flow that are nonrecurring; an attrition adjustment can be used to reflect recurring changes and expenses. For example, if the company has an agreement with labor for an annual increase of 7 percent, this would be treated as an additional allowance and grouped together with other recurring costs as an overall percentage adjustment to expenses. Nonrecurring expenses can be treated as one-item adjustments to individual expenses. An example of a typical nonrecurring item may be the payment of damages due to a loss in a personal injury lawsuit. It is not anticipated that in any succeeding period the company will lose a similar lawsuit. If it does, it should be treated as an attrition allowance.

The cash flow statement should show a monthly estimate of receipts from all sources, such as cash sales, accounts receivable, miscellaneous income, and loans. The estimated expenditures should include capital improvement, accounts payable, taxes, payroll, other operating expenses, and repayment of loans. Many bankers request projected income statements and balance sheets as well as cash flow statements.

Financial Trends

When bankers look at a company's figures or ratios, they are concerned not only with cash flow but also with other financial trends. The question may not be what the ratios are for the year, but rather how they compare with those of the previous years. The question that will be asked is: How does your financial picture (past, present, and projected) relate to the general economy and to the borrower's industry? Banks generally keep a record of clients' financial trends by periodically transcribing all of the vital balance sheet and operating statistics to a worksheet.

The following are some of the key financial factors that banks may calculate:

- Profitability
- Net working capital
- Working capital or current ratio
- Net quick ratio
- Ratio of debt to net worth
- Number of days of sales in accounts receivable
- Number of days of purchases in accounts payable
- Number of days of supply of inventory (related to cost of sales)

These are discussed in Chapter 6, but the relevant ones will be defined and briefly discussed here.

Profitability.   Profitability is a measure of how well the business has been doing. At least three ratios generate meaningful potential measures of a firm's profitability:

1. Net profit to net sales
2. Gross profit to sales
3. Net profit to net worth

It is important that a company be able to earn profits in a manner consistent with the capital invested and the expected growth. When the company shows that it has a high net profit, it not only shows that it has debt-paying dollars but also that it has fresh capital to reinvest and support its own growth. These are indications of good management. A bank will be interested in looking at year-to-year profitability and noting any trends in ratios.

Bankers will also want to see if the company's flow of net profits into its working capital is growing. They will be interested in whether profits must constantly be reinvested in fixed assets. Also, a company that pays out all of its profits in dividends and salaries will be unable to show growth in net worth from this source.

Bankers will usually add back noncash items, such as depreciation to the net profit of the company to arrive at the cash flow or debt-servicing dollars available from profit. Caution must be emphasized here, for what the bank might be doing is looking to funds that are earmarked as a "reserve" for equipment replacement. While the bank may be interested in the potential use of those funds for debt servicing in the worst case, enlightened bankers will also care about replacement of worn-out assets. The best bankers are concerned with the long-term needs of the business as well as protecting their own interests.

Net Working Capital.   The net working capital of the company is defined as the excess of the current assets over the current liabilities and is a significant factor to be considered for credit purposes. A bank expects a company to provide enough of its own normal working capital to carry its inventory, accounts receivable, and other current assets at prudent levels. The company should be able to meet these obligations during nonpeak sales periods of the year. Thus, even during slow times, the bank expects the company to cover its current liabilities within the customary terms of trade.

Working Capital or Current Ratio.   This is the ratio of current assets to current liabilities. It is even more significant in the bank's appraisal than in the working capital budget. For example, company A has current assets of $200,000, current liabilities of $100,000, and net working capital of $100,000. The working capital ratio is $200,000 to $100,000, or 2 to 1. Company B has current assets of $500,000, current liabilities of $400,000, and net working capital of $100,000. The working capital ratio is $500,000 to $400,000, or 1.25 to 1.

Both firms show the same net working capital of $100,000, yet the first company is in a more favorable position in that it has $2.00 in current assets from which to pay for each $1.00 in current liabilities in the event that it must liquidate assets. The second company, on the other hand, has only a $1.25 to meet its current liabilities of $1.00. Therefore, based upon this ratio, company A would be considered to be in a much stronger financial position.

Net Quick Ratio. Another indicator used by bankers to determine the ability of a company to pay its bills is the net quick ratio. This ratio is generally determined by taking the total of cash, short-term marketable securities, and net receivables, and dividing it by the total of current liabilities. This is a simple measure of the firm's liquidity or the ability of the company to pay its debts. Again, a bank will be more concerned with the trend established by several years of net quick ratios. This will show the bank whether the company is increasing or decreasing its liquidity and hence its ability to meet its debt. Since cash and accounts receivables are far more current than inventory, this ratio is a good indicator of the relative short-term liquidity risk of the company.

Ratio of Debt to Net Worth. Another test of the adequacy of the company's net worth is the ratio of total debt, including current liabilities, to net worth. Banks will, again, generally rely more on the trend in the ratio than in the specific number itself.

Other debt ratios are discussed in Chapter 6.

Number of Days of Sales in Accounts Receivable. In calculating this number, the following assumptions are made:

- An even flow of sales.
- A uniformity in collecting accounts receivable.

The question here is the average number of days it takes the company to collect its accounts as compared with other firms within the same industry. The banks will factor in the number of days normal for the terms of the sale and those of the industry. For example: Assume a firm has average daily credit sales of $20,000 and accounts receivable are $1.8 million. The terms of the sale are 30 days. The first step is to divide the accounts receivable of $1.8 million by 20,000, the average daily credit sales. This indicates that 90 days of sales are still in accounts receivable and that the accounts receivable are taking longer to collect than the normal 30-day terms. In fact, on average, this company is collecting its accounts receivables 60 days after the expiration of the due date. This is 60 days more than the pricing policy allows; it is probably having considerable financial effects on cash flow.

This also indicates that management may not be doing a good job of managing its accounts receivable. However, this may also be typical for the industry. If this is your situation, you should take some steps to try to improve your accounts receivables collection policy. You are loaning money to your customers for *an average* of 60 days *more* than you intended when you set your terms of sale. This has significant cost consequences.

Number of Days of Purchases in Accounts Payable. This figure is computed by dividing the average daily purchases into the accounts payable. If, for example, the average daily purchases are $5,000 and the accounts payable are $150,000, the number of days purchases in accounts payable is 30 days. This number tells a banker quickly if the company is paying its bills promptly. Significant variations from normal trade terms must be explained. If the company is on a net 30-day cycle, then it is meeting its obligations and perhaps obtaining all of the discounts it is entitled to under the terms of its purchase agreements. That question requires further examination. The ratio is helpful, but one should also be concerned with those accounts payable for which discounts were lost and not only the average payments.

The company should be examining its aging of payables and monitoring discounts lost.

Number of Days of Supply of Inventory. This number is computed by dividing the *cost* of the inventory by the average daily cost of sales, assuming an even flow of sales. The answer gives the banker the average number of days it takes the company to turn over inventory. The abuse that the bank is looking for here is excess inventory. This ratio will vary substantially from business to business. Supermarkets generally have very short inventory cycles, whereas automobile dealers have longer cycles.

Other Supplemental Data. Other information that should be considered for submission in the loan request presentation includes:

- A summary of insurance coverage.
- An analysis of profitability by product line, if available and applicable.
- Unusual events, historical or prospective, affecting the company.

- Concentration, if any, of sales within a small number of customers. This shows the bank the reliance on a few select customers. If sales are concentrated in very few buyers, as in the aerospace industry, the risk associated with that industry may be considered to be somewhat higher.
- Analysis of the effect of special situations on the company, such as a last-in, first-out (LIFO) method of inventory evaluation.

Letters of Credit

A company may not want to borrow any money from a bank; however, a prospective subcontractor or provider of raw materials may be unsure as to the company's creditworthiness. A method for improving assumed creditworthiness that may be available at low cost is the purchasing of a letter of credit.

If the company is new or is experimenting with a new product or product line, some vendors will refuse to sell it materials on a trade accounts payable basis. They would instead prefer to have the company establish creditworthiness by showing good payment records. A possible way around this problem is to obtain a letter of credit and, in effect, to use the good credit standing of a bank. By obtaining a letter of credit, the company is saying: "If we fail to pay you, the bank will pay you." The bank then has recourse to the company for its money.

In this way, the company is advancing the bank's creditworthiness. Typically, letters of credit cost 1 percent of the amount the company wishes to advance, and the letter of credit is normally good for one year. The real cost of a letter of credit depends on how frequently the company wishes to purchase using the letter of credit as a guarantee of payment.

For example, suppose a supplier of raw materials wants his money net 30 days, but is willing to extend credit for 90 days if the company provides a letter of credit. Also, suppose that the letter of credit costs 1 percent. Since the company is having money advanced for two additional months for the cost of 1 percent, this is the same as borrowing money at 6 percent per annum, assuming the letter of credit and the materials purchased are the same amount. However, each time the company uses the guarantee of the letter of credit during the year, it is still taking advantage of that one-time payment of 1 percent. The more the firm uses the letter of credit, the cheaper (on a cost-per-transaction basis) the cost of the guarantee.

The company may consider joint ventures. Joint ventures are, essentially, a technique whereby a company changes its organizational structure. However, this is still a form of financing whereby the financial creditworthiness of a collective entity is used to improve the market appearance to lenders and investors. The financial strength of two or more entities is put behind the joint venture entity.

Sources of Debt Financing

A business may consider a number of financial institutions as possible lenders. The large and popular ones include:

- *Banks.* Both commercial banks and savings and loan associations grant a significant portion of all the available credit they have on hand to businesses.
- *Commercial finance companies.* Most commercial finance companies have a specialty, such as discounting accounts receivable. Interest rates are generally higher with finance companies because as a financing source they seem to be institutions of last resort. Companies that are unable to find other means of financing may resort to commercial finance companies.
- *Insurance companies.* Many large insurance companies participate in investment banking both directly and indirectly. Typically, insurance companies loan substantial blocks of money. Because of this, the typical insurance company borrower is a large company. They do not as often or as readily extend credit to smaller companies. Insurance companies prefer transactions of $1 million or more. Some insurance companies are interested only in transactions greater than $5 million.
- *Brokerage houses.* Many stock brokerage houses offer or arrange financing that ranges from bonds and commercial paper to private loans from individual investors. Brokerage houses do just as their name suggests: They broker money from sources to ultimate users.
- *Investment bankers.* Investment banking may be a function of any of the previously named lenders. They generally facilitate the sale

of security issues, through either a bidding process or a contractual arrangement. For a fee, they use their expertise and market contacts to sell securities.

In some financing agreements, the lender takes an equity position in connection with a loan or takes an option or warrant to buy stock in the event that the company grows. This is known as a "kicker" or "sweetener" and is generally viewed by borrowers as giving up some possible future control over the business in exchange for controlling current costs. Many investors wish to have some financial or managerial say over the direction and nature of the business. Typically, when substantial funds are loaned to a business, it has to give up some measure of control.

- *Venture capitalists.* Venture capitalists may be investment bankers when they invest capital, make loans, and give management advice intended to assist the company to achieve significant growth. Many companies financed by venture capitalists convert from closely held corporations to public corporations during the course of their growth.
- *Government loans and grants.* A wide variety of loan programs are offered by the federal government. Some are direct loans, others are government-sponsored or guaranteed loans channeled through banks. Small Business Administration loans are available to smaller businesses. Additionally, the federal government has a program for small business innovation research grants. These grants are intended to assist small businesses in obtaining financing for the development of specific ideas.
- *Federal tax laws.* The federal tax code provides some options for deferring taxes. This is essentially an interest-free loan. Many large corporations, by taking advantage of deferred taxes, have in effect put off the payment of taxes for many years.

Types of Loan Arrangements

Several types of loans are possible. Some of these are:

- *Commercial loans.* The terms of a commercial loan are designed to repay the loan on the basis of specific assets or business-cycle activities. These loans may take the form of either short-term or long-term commitments.

- *Leases.* Many lending institutions offer a choice between debt and a lease. Leases are obligations for the specific assets, and are generally fixed as to rate and payment. In addition, most offer a purchase option. Some caution must be exercised in selecting between leasing and outright purchase with a mortgage. Very often, under the terms of the lease, significantly higher costs are incurred over the costs of the outright purchase of the item.

- *Mortgages.* A mortgage secures a loan by pledging an asset as collateral, with an associated repayment schedule. Amortization schedules of repayment show the principal and interest payments over the life of the mortgage.

- *Balloon loans.* Balloon loans are very similar to mortgages except that the maturity date occurs before the end of amortized schedule. The repayment terms are based on a long-term commitment. However, an unpaid balance or balloon payment is due and payable after a specified time. A typical example of a balloon payment is a 20-year mortgage with a requirement that after five years of payment on the mortgage the unpaid balance of the principal is due. The advantage to a lender of a balloon mortgage is that it obtains significant interest payments during the early years of the mortgage. It is during this period that the interest constitutes the bulk of the payment. The benefit to borrowers is that they expect to pay off the principal without incurring further interest liabilities after a few years of operation. In addition, these interest payments represent significant deductions for tax purposes. Remember that if the firm is paying taxes at the rate of 46 percent on profits, the federal government is returning $.46 on *each* dollar of interest paid. Very often, these loans provide for refinancing in the event that the balloon payment cannot be met.

- *Leverage-financed loans.* These loans are used to acquire businesses. The largest percentage of funds used to acquire a business is supplied by a lender, who secures all assets. These loans ostensibly are attractive to borrowers because if a firm is heavily leveraged a smaller increment of profit yields a much higher percentage return on equity. For example, compare: Firm A makes $100,000 profit (after taxes) and is capitalized for $1 million. It has 50 percent debt and 50 percent equity. The firm realizes a return on equity of:

$$\frac{\$100,000}{50\% \times \$1,000,000} \text{ or } \frac{\$100,000}{\$500,000} \text{ or } 20\%$$

- Firm B makes $100,000 profits (after taxes) and is capitalized for $1 million. It has 80 percent debt and 20 percent equity. The firm realizes a return on equity of:

$$\frac{\$100,000}{20\% \times \$1,000,000} \text{ or } \frac{\$100,000}{\$200,000} \text{ or } 50\%$$

- For the same level of after-tax profits, for the same size firms, the higher the leverage the greater the percentage return on equity. The fallacy in the cited example is that firm B would have to pay interest on the additional $300,000 of debt.
- The greater the debt to equity ratio the greater the risk, because the fixed obligation to pay debt service increases. However, this relationship to risk may be incorrect if one can show substantial cash flow ability to service the debt. Therefore, the debt to equity ratio can be misleading without additional information.
- *Bonds.* Bonds represent debt sold to lenders either privately or through public underwriting. Usually, a business needs to be fairly substantial in size to float a bond issue. Bonds typically are not available to small businesses except in some special cases, where they are backed by local governmental units.
- *Commercial paper.* Commercial paper is offered by large, stable companies intent on raising working capital for short periods of time. Commercial paper generally is sold in a public market and is in the form of short-term, unsecured promissory notes. The usual denominations are $25,000 and over.
- *Small Business Administration (SBA) loans.* The SBA generally guarantees a bank loan, thereby lowering the risk and interest cost for the borrower. These loans are intended for businesspeople who

can qualify based on certain profiles. Usually, these loans are offered only after a firm has been turned down by two banks but otherwise qualifies for an SBA loan. These loans may be based on needs such as a business in a hardship area or areas where unemployment is high. Occasionally, these loans are extended for areas in which a natural disaster has occurred.

- *Economic Development Authority (EDA) loans.* EDA loans generally relate to social goals promoted by the authority, such as increasing minority employment or employment in depressed areas. These loans are made and administered through state agencies. The nature of these loans is to obtain working capital allowances and not generally to purchase specific assets.

- *Industrial revenue bonds (IRBs).* IRBs are issued through governmental agencies and are intended for use in the acquisition of real estate and equipment. The governmental agency issues the bonds, which are then purchased by investors, often banks. Because they are governmental bonds, they are tax exempt. As such, the prevailing interest rate on IRBs is lower than the prevailing market rate. A great deal of criticism has been leveled against IRBs because some businesses, which compete with others that get IRBs, complain they are unable to acquire similar low-interest money and thus are less able to compete.

- *Research and development (R&D) financing arrangements.* Often, companies and private investors have entered into creative financing arrangements in order to raise necessary funds to pay for research and development. These have taken the shape of limited partnerships in recent years. Typically, the sponsoring company contributes the right to a product in a limited partnership, in exchange for an interest in the partnership, often as the general partner. Capital contributions by limited partners usually provide funds for R&D that may be subcontracted to the sponsoring company or even to other entities. The limited partners expect to receive income in the form of royalties from the sale and development of the product. They may also receive income tax breaks in the form of capital gains rates. The major advantage to the sponsor is that in the event that the project fails, no repayment of the loan is required and there is no liability for interest cost.

Restrictions on Loans

When an institution is considering making substantial loans to a company, it often requires, as part of the loan, agreements to control the business activities and obtain reports about the current status of the firm. Typically, these arrangements include:

- *Limitations on the purchase of new assets.* Some lenders have a policy to keep additional expenditures low after a loan has been made. This has the effect of slowing or stopping growth. Negotiate with the lender to ensure that this is not an absolute limitation on acquisition of new assets. Be sure that additional new assets can be purchased on a regular basis if there is provable growth associated with the need for those purchases. Show the lender that through planned growth, the risk of default is lessened. Planned growth can be accomplished only by the acquisition of additional assets based on a schedule and a good business plan.
- *Limitations on additional debt.* Once again, a lender may try to restrict the incurring of additional debt. This too has the detrimental effect of limiting growth. When negotiating with the lender, make it clear that additional debt may have to be incurred in order to sustain regular growth. An adequate business plan will certainly help as bargaining leverage for the execution of the appropriate terms in the lending agreement. The selling point to the lender is that additional debt supports additional income through growth. As the company grows, so does the lender's security of repayment.
- *Salary restrictions.* Because salaries of chief executives and other executives are a direct expense, lenders will typically want some restriction on these salaries so they do not skyrocket. Large increases in these salaries will dig into the profits of the firm, sometimes radically increasing expenses. Counter with a reasonable alternative, which may include tying the increases to profitability, earnings, or the general growth in the gross income of the firm. This also has the beneficial effect of motivating management.
- *Dividend restrictions.* If the company pays dividends, one should attempt to negotiate a reasonable formula for payment. The company is confronted with the competing interests of debt holders

and holders of equity. The lender may try to put an absolute prohibition on the payment of any dividends. This allows for the additional retained earnings to be used for debt servicing. But it may have a chilling effect on the raising of additional equity capital. A company's attraction as an equity investment opportunity is based on two factors: its absolute growth in net worth and the income stream of dividends. A "no dividends" policy reduces the attractiveness of an equity investment possibility.

Typically, firms will be required to provide lenders with regular financial reports. Lenders will generally require financial statements accompanied by a certified public accountant's (CPA's) report. Audited reports certified by CPAs are costly and time-consuming documents to prepare. Look to reduce the requirement to a cheaper alternative such as a review or even a compilation.

Some people think that when they incorporate, they absolve themselves of any personal liability for the debt incurred by the business in its operation. Legally, that might be true. However, lenders too have learned that people try to limit their personal liability by incorporating and often require certain personal guarantees by the business owner. Some banks may want one to sign a general guarantee of the business loan as a sign of "good faith" or as a "personal commitment" to the business. That kind of guarantee can be dangerous because it typically has no limits.

- *Specific personal assets.* As a rule it is not wise to risk everything you own. If a pledge of "good faith" is required by the lender, pick one particular asset to risk. Do not risk more than you are willing to lose in any situation.
- *The value of business collateral already offered.* Typically, lenders will require as much collateral as they can reasonably get. They may even seek collateral that is unreasonable. In such cases, it may be beneficial to prepare reports showing the extent and valuation of those assets pledged to secure the loan. Often, appraisals by independent groups as to the value of real estate and other assets tend to dissuade the bank from seeking further collateral.
- *Stock in the business as collateral.* If the business has some attractiveness and a reasonably high probability of success, the lender

may take back some stock as collateral. Be wary that you are not giving up so much stock that you lose control of your business.

Conditions That a Borrower Should Seek

The success of the business depends on you. Too much reliance on the lending institution to help run the business may prove disastrous. There should, therefore, be flexibility in the agreement to let the business grow and be successful. Advice and help from the lender should not be overlooked. It may be a lifesaver. Lenders may have had experience with other similar businesses, and you can profit from that experience. As a borrower, you should request the following considerations in the lending agreement:

- *There should be an option available to you to refinance at any time.* Often, the lender will qualify this provision to permit refinancing only after a certain period of time or with a prepayment penalty. You may need this provision in order to take advantage of lower prevailing interest rates should they occur.
- *A conversion agreement should allow for more favorable loan conditions once certain "growth forecasts" have been met.* You should require that this provision take into consideration the fact that as your business grows, its risks may decrease. Because interest rates should be tied to perceived risk, as you prove your viability and success, you are entitled to pay less of a loan premium; arguably, your riskiness has been reduced.
- *Agree on no prepayment penalty.* Changing financial conditions may provide you with sufficient cash to prepay the loan. This may be done to realize significant tax benefits, as a requirement for the obtaining of additional financing, or to put you in a better business posture. Prepayment generally will work no hardship on the lender other than to take away the guarantee of expected future earnings. There would be nothing to stop the lender from reloaning this money to other individuals and thus recovering the future earnings from someone else. The lender's risk is that the money cannot be reloaned at equal or better rates.

- *Request limitation on interest rates.* Currently, the vogue is variable interest rate. The federal government has placed certain requirements on capping the variability of some interest rates. You should be aware of limitations or caps on rates and make this a major consideration in determining whether to enter into the financing agreement.
- *Agree on the possibility of an increased loan based on meeting certain tests.* Often, if you are successful and the business is growing within certain predictable ranges, additional debt financing may be necessary to continue the growth pattern. As such, you may want the loan agreement to provide for additional advances of debt to aid in sustaining that growth. A lender should consider itself an ongoing business partner in these agreements. As you grow, so does the income of the lender. Some loans have an absolute upper credit limit, and one may borrow up to that limit without further formal application.
- *The agreement should specify identifiable assets that are pledged as collateral.*
- *Seek a loan "grace" period of 30 to 60 days for noncompliance with debt arrangements.* Very often this provision will require a notification by you to the lender in advance that you will use the provision. There will probably be a limit on how frequently this can be done. Lenders may be more willing to permit minimum defaults when there is a plan submitted showing how you will make it up after appropriate notice to the lender. The worst thing you can do is surprise your lender. In most cases, they would rather work out a mutually agreeable accommodation than seek legal redress.

Summary

Financing is in some respects similar to the operational side of the business. They each have associated risks and returns. Each has strategic consequences for a firm.

There are two fundamental sources of financing: debt and equity. Each has certain consequences. Debt, either secured by property or unsecured, is the most common form of financing. It has fixed repayment requirements for both principal and interest. Failure to make interest payments, unless otherwise provided for, generally results in default. Additionally, interest payments are made with before-tax dollars. As such, depending on the tax rate, interest payments are in effect discounted by federal tax liability. The relative amount of debt financing has a multiplying effect on earnings. The greater the percentage of debt to equity for a fixed amount of profits, the greater the percentage return on equity.

A company may seek to raise capital through the sale of ownership. This is done through the issuance and sale of stock. There are two forms of certificates that businesses generally sell: common and preferred stock. Common stock carries with it no obligation to pay a dividend. Preferred stock, however, may have a fixed rate, as does debt, but payment is optional if no dividends are declared. Dividends on preferred stock (sometimes cumulative over a period of years) have to be met *before* payment can be made to common stockholders.

Obtaining financing is a matter of convincing conservative lenders or investors to part with their money. As in all selling, it is a process of convincing these people that risks are low and that reasonable returns will compensate them for taking the risk. The best method of selling is through the use of a good business plan showing good ratios and a sound financial picture. One of the chief objectives should be to build a lasting, sound financial relationship with these sources.

Remember that many of the terms of a financial agreement are negotiable. Therefore, when approaching any such situation, try to be prepared to negotiate from strength. The more preliminary work that is done in getting ready to deal with lenders and investors, the greater the likelihood of a favorable financial agreement.

Evaluating the Operations of the Business

The first two sections addressed the tasks to be accomplished before the business, or operating period, begins, and those that are ongoing during the operating period. Naturally, there is a close connection between what you determine to do—your plan—and what you actually do.

In this section, we discuss what happens when the operating period is completed. This may be an intermediate time—not necessarily the end of a complete fiscal year. For example, some of what is discussed in these final five chapters is equally appropriate to monthly or quarterly considerations.

As Sections I and II were closely related, so Section III is closely linked to both of them. The topics to be covered here include:

- Reporting
- Ratios
- Taxes and insurance

These flow directly out of your intended accomplishments as well as actual ones during the fiscal period.

Chapter 6

Ratios

Ratios, like many of the tools discussed earlier, can be used to make rational decisions in keeping with a company's objectives. Ratios are analytical tools used by outside suppliers of capital, creditors and investors, and by the company itself to evaluate how well it is doing. Ratios may also be used to evaluate how the business appears to the investor. The type of analysis undertaken varies according to the specific interest that the party seeks to satisfy.

- A trade creditor who has supplied goods, services, or raw materials would generally be interested in liquidity—the company's ability to pay bills.
- A bondholder is more interested in long-term financial stability. As such, he or she would be interested in cash flow and the company's ability to service its debt.
- The present and expected future earnings and the stability of these earnings may be primary concerns to an investor in common stock.

Depending on the planning horizon of each person interested in the ratios, the value of trend analysis may be greater than any point-in-time or present ratios. How well the company has done over time and is expected to do in the future are pieces of information necessary to make reasoned decisions.

Finally, the company too should be concerned with the trend depicted through ratios. In order to bargain more effectively for outside funds, one should be aware of all of the aspects of financial analysis that outsiders use in evaluating the business. Financial and operating ratios can also be effective tools for managing and controlling the business.

There are two broad categories of ratios that will be of concern in this chapter. The first set is financial ratios. Financial ratios were discussed briefly in Chapter 5. Therefore, we will not endeavor to repeat that material, but rather only supplement it here. The second set of ratios, which one should consider in setting up controls, are the operating ratios. Operating ratios can be designed to meet specific needs of the user. These ratios are intended as a tool for analysis and control of business operations.

Financial Ratios

Some unit of measure is necessary to evaluate the financial condition or the performance of the business. A system frequently used is a ratio, or index, which connects two pieces of financial or operational information. Interpreting a ratio correctly gives the analyst an understanding of the financial condition and performance of the firm, which may not be readily apparent from the traditional forms of reporting. It is important to remember that a single ratio in itself may not be a particularly meaningful piece of information. Often, a trend showing past historical ratios will indicate more than will the current individual ratio alone. When financial ratios are listed on a spreadsheet for a period of years, a study of the composite change will quickly indicate whether there has been an improvement or deterioration in the financial condition over time. In addition, the productivity, profitability, or performance of the firm relative to past performances is easily demonstrated. For example, by arraying the last five years of current ratios—that is, the ratio of current assets to current liabilities—one can compare the ability of the business to pay its bills and determine if that is improving or deteriorating.

The second comparison method involves evaluating the ratio of one company against others similarly situated for the same period. Such a comparison, if properly done, will give some insight into the relative financial condition of the company. If improperly done, the information derived from this study may be worse than meaningless—it may be harmful. The primary problem is comparability.

Avoid using "rules of thumb" indiscriminately. The comparison of your financial ratios with the ratios published by major sources may be inaccurate. For example, you may have multiple product lines and may not have the same product mix as other companies in the industry. You may be differently diversified, crossing industry boundaries. It is preferable to build comparable numbers over time for your own business rather than seek comparisons with others. However, sometimes outside comparisons, properly used, can be helpful. A rule of thumb, if it is to be used, should be from your industry. Trade associations can be a source of good financial ratio information.

For example, the standard rule of thumb for the current ratio—that is, the ratio of current assets to current liabilities—is 2:1. It is considered advisable for a small business to maintain a current ratio of at least 2:1 for the sake of sound cash flow and healthy financial condition. Remember, however, that rules of thumb are averages. As such, there may be as many companies above the average as below it. To show how this rule of thumb may be misapplied, take the example of a fast food outlet. It may have a current ratio of 1:2 or even 1:3. Comparing this current ratio with the rule of thumb, one quickly concludes that the business has a liquidity problem and may not have sufficient liquid assets available to meet all of the debts falling due. However, this is probably not the case. A typical fast food outlet has:

- *Receivables.* There are generally no credit sales and no delayed payments at a fast food store.
- *Inventory levels.* Fast food stores generally carry very small inventories and deliveries are small, frequent, and fresh.
- *Normal or extended trade payables.* Some profitable franchises can delay payments to local suppliers for longer than is normal because of their volume of business.

Fast food outlets, therefore, turn over inventory at a tremendous rate and generate continuous streams of cash. At any one point, the company may not have large amounts of cash on hand if it is using cash to retire longer-term debt or to acquire additional fixed assets. By comparing the company's own historic trend in the current ratio, and examining those ratios with other fast food outlets, one can perhaps see that a 1:4 ratio may be even better than a 1:2 ratio. The traditional rule of thumb may not be applicable or representative of the fast food industry. The point of this example is that one should consider those ratios that make sense for the business, give usable management information, and can be obtained on a timely basis.

It is often important to have the financial information generated by ratios on a more timely basis than can be generated from full-blown financial statements. In some cases, by the time the financial statements are prepared, it may be too late to take corrective action. In determining how timely the information should be, the trade-off between timeliness and accuracy must be considered. Full-blown financial statements may produce extremely accurate, audited information. However, it will likely be too late for many important decisions.

"Per book" ratios may be generated monthly by a company's bookkeeper or accountant. Although this information may not be as accurate as a fully audited financial statement, generating the data on a monthly basis provides periodic, consistent reports that may point out problems long before the audit is even undertaken.

Figure 6.1 shows a balance sheet and statement of earnings that will be used to demonstrate the financial ratios.

Types of Financial Ratios

Liquidity Ratios

Liquidity ratios give an indication of a company's ability to meet short-term obligations. These ratios give some insight into the present cash solvency and are a measure of the company's ability to meet adversity. Generally, liquidity ratios look at the short-term assets or resources and the short-term debts and obligations.

Current Ratio. As discussed in Chapter 5, the current ratio is the ratio of:

$$\frac{\text{Current assets}}{\text{Current liabilities}}$$

FIGURE 6.1

Sample Balance Sheet and Statement of Earnings

Fruit Crate Mfg. Co., Inc.
Assets

	2001	2000
Current Assets		
Cash and marketable securities	$ 21,285	$ 20,860
Accounts receivables	83,473	91,155
Inventories	164,482	157,698
Prepaid expenses	2,554	2,049
Accumulated prepaid tax	4,261	3,475
Current assets	$276,055	$275,237
Fixed Assets		
Fixed assets	$198,760	$192,666
Less: Accumulated depreciation	107,330	99,030
Net fixed assets	$ 91,430	$ 93,636
Long-term investment	$ 8,229	$ -0-
Other Assets		
Goodwill	$ 23,839	$ 23,839
Debenture discount	751	833
Other assets	$ 24,590	$ 24,672
Total Assets	$400,304	$393,545

Liabilities and Net Worth

	2001	2000
Current Liabilities		
Bank loans and notes payables	$ 53,638	$ 42,544
Accounts payable	17,560	16,271
Accrued taxes	4,321	15,186
Other accrued liabilities	22,775	19,608
Current liabilities	$ 98,294	$ 93,609
Long-term debt	$ 75,562	$ 74,262
Stockholders' equity		
Common stock @ $1 par value	$ 50,420	$ 50,420
Capital surplus	43,179	43,016
Retained earnings	132,849	132,238
Total stockholders' equity	$226,448	$225,674
Total Liabilities and Net Worth	$400,304	$393,545

(continued)

FIGURE 6.1   (*continued*)

Fruit Crate Mfg. Co., Inc.
Statement of Earnings

	2001	2000
Net sales	$492,374	$464,383
Cost of goods sold	$330,383	$311,601
Selling, general and administration expense	98,475	90,555
Depreciation	13,786	14,396
Interest expense	10,340	8,823
Expenses	$452,984	$425,375
Earnings before taxes	$ 39,390	$ 39,008
Less: Income taxes	18,907	19,114
Earnings after taxes	$ 20,483	$ 19,894
Less: Cash dividend	12,495	12,732
Retained earnings	$ 7,988	$ 7,162

For Fruit Crate Manufacturing Co., Inc., the current ratio for 2001 is:

$$\frac{\$276,055}{\$98,294} = 2.81:1$$

Supposedly, the higher the ratio, the better the company's ability to pay bills. However, the ratio does not take into account how liquid the "current" assets really are. For example, if the current assets are mostly cash and current receivables, these are more liquid than if most of the current assets are in inventories. To refine the ratio as a measure, we eliminate the effect of inventories, prepaid expenses, and prepaid tax.

Acid Test Ratio

$$\frac{\text{Current assets} - (\text{Inventories} + \text{Prepaids})}{\text{Current liabilities}}$$

For Fruit Crate Manufacturing Co., Inc.:

$$\frac{\$276,055 - 171,297}{\$98,294} = 1.066{:}1$$

The acid test ratio eliminates the least liquid components of the current assets and therefore focuses on the assets most easily converted to debt payment.

Liquidity of Receivables. Analyzing the current assets by components enables the company to detect problems in its liquidity. One thing that can be examined is how current are the receivables. Receivables are a liquid asset only if they can be collected in a reasonable time. The first of two ratios that examine receivables is *average collection period ratio:*

$$\frac{\text{Receivables} \times \text{Days in year}}{\text{Annual credit sales}}$$

For Fruit Crate Manufacturing Co., Inc., the average collection period rate for 2001 is (assuming all sales are credit sales):

$$\frac{83,473 \times 365}{492,374} = 62 \text{ days}$$

This tells that the average collection period receivables are outstanding, in other words, how long, on average, the company waits to convert receivables to cash.

The second basic receivable ratio is the *receivable turnover ratio:*

$$\frac{\text{Annual credit sales}}{\text{Average receivables}}$$

For Fruit Crate Manufacturing Co., Inc., the receivables turnover ratio is:

$$\frac{\$492,374}{\$83,473} = 5.90 \text{ times}$$

If there is no figure for the amount of credit sales, one must resort to the total sales figure. Care should be taken to analyze all ratios, especially receivables ratios. Often, the numbers available are year-end numbers, which may not recognize seasonal fluctuations or significant, steady growth. If there are significant seasonal sales, the average of the monthly closing balances may be a more appropriate figure to use. If the company is experiencing a steady growth in sales, the year-end receivables will not match accurately with the annual sales figure. If this is the case, the number may be calculated based on the annualized sales from the last six months and the end-of-year level of receivables.

Some questions to ask when analyzing these ratios are:

- How does the average collection period compare with the sales terms? For Fruit Crate Manufacturing Co., Inc., the credit terms are 2/10, n/60. The bulk of the collections are made around the due date.
- How does the collection period compare with others in the industry? This can give some insight into the investment in receivables.
- Is the average collection period so low that it may be inhibiting sales? The firm may have an excessively restrictive credit policy.
- How old are the receivables? Here, one must ask "What does the average tell us?" Fruit Crate Manufacturing Co., Inc., had 433 accounts and found the average collection period ratio was 62 days. But when it grouped the accounts by age it discovered the following statistics:

Number of Accounts	Paid in How Many Days?
110 (25%)	10
80 (18%)	30
170 (39%)	60
73 (18%)	180 days

Eighty-two percent of the receivables are collected before or by the due date, and only 18 percent extend beyond the due date. But the late receivables are *really* late: averaging six months after shipment of goods and four months after payment was due.

Adding an aging of receivables provides more usable information than the average collection period ratio alone. This tells:

- Where collection efforts need to be concentrated.
- How much investment the company has in receivables.
- Accounts that may require discontinuation of service.
- Whether the terms are speeding up the recovery of receivables.

Another question the aging would raise is "Are the good accounts paying in the 10–30 period taking the cash discounts even though they have no right to it?" If the answer is yes, the cash discount terms are really 2/30, n/60.

Debt Ratios

Up to now, we have been concerned with short-term liquidity measures. Depending on the use, certain long-term solvency ratios may be of interest to a company and its investors. These ratios give an indication of the company's ability to meet long-term obligations.

Debt to Net Worth.   This ratio is computed by dividing the total debt, including current liabilities, by the net worth (total stockholders' equity). For Fruit Crate Manufacturing Co., Inc.:

$$\frac{\text{Total debt}}{\text{Net worth}} = \frac{\$98,294 + 75,562}{\$226,448} = \frac{\$173,856}{\$226,448} = .77{:}1$$

Frequently, intangible assets, if relatively large, are deducted from net worth to obtain the tangible net worth. Note that for the liquidity ratios discussed earlier, we used assets divided by liabilities. Here, we are creating debt ratios—putting liabilities over other measures. For liquidity, the higher the number, the "better" the ratio. For debt ratios, the reverse is true: The lower the number, the "better" the ratio. Sometimes in computing this ratio, preferred stock is included with debt instead of net worth. This acknowledges that preferred stock represents a claim superior to the claim of common stockholders. It also points out that when using "comparable ratios" one must be certain that the calculations are truly comparable; that is, one must compare the definitions of the ratios.

The debt to net worth ratio varies from industry to industry. One factor often contributing to this variation is the volatility of cash flows. The more stable and predictable the cash flow, the greater the debt one may be able to service consistently. Because this ratio is a good measure of ability to pay debts over time, it is sometimes used as a measure for approximating financial risk.

Debt to Total Capital. Another useful debt ratio is the ratio of total debt to total capital. In this ratio, only the long-term capitalization of the firm is considered.

$$\frac{\text{Long-term debt}}{\text{Total capitalization}}$$

The total capitalization is composed of long-term debt and net worth. For Fruit Crate Manufacturing Co., Inc.:

$$\frac{\$75,562}{\$75,562 + 226,448} = \frac{\$75,562}{\$302,010} = .25{:}1$$

This ratio shows the importance of long-term debt financing relative to other financing in the capital structure. When computing this ratio, it may be more informative to use market values instead of book values for the stock components. (Book values were used in the preceding calculation.) If market values of stock are available, this computation may indicate a very different leverage factor.

Coverage Ratios

Coverage ratios are used to examine the relationship between finance charges and a company's ability to service them. One of the traditional coverage ratios is the interest coverage ratio. To compute this ratio for a given period, divide the annual earnings before interest and taxes by the interest charges for the period.

Different coverage ratios use different interest charges in the denominator. For example: the overall coverage method considers all fixed interest regardless of the seniority of the claim. By ignoring the seniority of some debt, the implication is that senior debt obligations are only as secure as the ability to meet all debt servicing. A method that gives some consideration to the seniority of debt is the cumulative deduction method.

For cumulative deduction methods, assume the following hypothetical data: Fruit Crate Manufacturing Co., Inc., has:

$49,730 = earnings before interest and taxes ($39,390 + 10,340)
$4,210 = interest on 7% senior notes.
$6,130 = interest on 9% junior notes.

The coverage on the senior notes would be:

$$\frac{\$49,730}{\$4,210} = 11.81 \text{ times}$$

The coverage on the junior notes, after the senior debt has been covered, is:

$$\frac{\$49,730 - 4,210}{\$10,340} = 4.40 \text{ times}$$

Using this method, the coverage ratio on the junior notes takes into consideration the fact that there are outstanding senior obligations.

Both of these methods ignore the fact that the payment of interest is only part of the obligation covered by debt service. Debt service includes payment of both interest and principal. And because these payments are made from cash, a more appropriate ratio may be the cash-flow coverage ratio. One adjustment should be made in computing this ratio. Interest payments are accounted for before taxes, whereas principal payments are treated as after-tax dollars. To adjust for the tax effect you must adjust the principal by the factor $[1/(1-t)]$, where t is the effective tax rate. So:

$$\text{Cash flow coverage ratio} = \frac{\text{Annual cash flow before interest and taxes}}{\text{Interest and principal } [1/(1-t)]}$$

If you had a $10,000/year principal payment and a 46 percent tax rate, it would require:

$$\$10,000 \times [1/(1 - .46)] \text{ or}$$

$10,000 × (1.85), or $18,500 in before-tax dollars
to meet that principal obligation

This type of analysis can, in some cases, be expanded to consider other fixed obligations like dividends on preferred stock, lease payments, and long-term essential capital expenditures.

Debt ratios or coverage ratios may not give an accurate picture of the company's ability to meet obligations. Because of the timing of the payment of debt obligations, the average interest rates, and other factors, one may wish to calculate other ratios showing the relationship of profitability to sales or to investment.

Profitability Ratios

When the profitability on sales ratio and the profitability on investment ratios are considered, they can give an indication of your efficiency of operation. The first such ratio is the *gross profit margin.*

For Fruit Crate Manufacturing Co., Inc., the gross profit margin is:

$$\frac{\$492,374 - 330,383}{\$492,374} = \frac{\$161,991}{\$492,374} = 33\%$$

This ratio gives the percentage of profit relative to the sales after deducting the cost of goods sold. A more reflective ratio of profitability is the *net profit margin:*

$$\frac{\text{Net profit (after taxes)}}{\text{Sales}}$$

For Fruit Crate Manufacturing Co., Inc., the net profit margin is:

$$\frac{\$20,483}{\$492,374} = 4.2\%$$

This ratio gives a measure of overall efficiency after taking into consideration expenses and taxes but not extraordinary charges. With these two ratios one can, over time, evaluate operational changes. For example, if the gross profit margin remained relatively constant over time, but the net profit margin declined, it shows that either the tax rate has changed or selling and administrative expenses have increased. The relative change between these ratios can identify areas where management attention may be necessary.

As another example, if the gross profit margin declines, the cost of goods sold has increased. This could signal several things:

- The firm may have had to lower price to be competitive.
- Cost of labor, materials, or purchased components may have increased.
- Overall efficiency may have declined.

Another group of profitability ratios relate profits to investment. For example, *rate of return on common stock equity:*

$$\frac{\text{Net profit after taxes} - \text{Preferred stock dividend}}{\text{Net worth} - \text{Par value of preferred stock}}$$

For Fruit Crate Manufacturing Co., Inc. (no preferred stock involved):

$$\frac{\$20,483}{\$226,448} = 0.90 \text{ or } 9\%$$

This ratio gives an indication of the earning power on the book investment of the shareholders' interest. A more general ratio used to analyze profitability is the *return on assets ratio.* To calculate this ratio:

$$\frac{\text{Net profits (after taxes)}}{\text{Total assets (tangible)}}$$

For Fruit Crate Manufacturing Co., Inc.:

$$\frac{\$20,483}{\$375,714} = 5.5\%$$

Profits are considered after interest is paid to creditors; to some extent this ratio may be inappropriate because some of these same creditors provide the means by which part of the assets are supported. When the finance charges are large, it may be better for comparative purposes to calculate a different ratio. An arguably more appropriate ratio may be the *net operating profit rate of return*. It is calculated from:

$$\frac{\text{Earnings before interest and taxes}}{\text{Total assets (tangible)}}$$

For Fruit Crate Manufacturing Co., Inc.:

$$\frac{\$49,730}{\$375,714} = 13.24\%$$

Turnover and Earning Power Ratios

The asset turnover ratio relates total sales to total tangible assets. Like many of the ratios discussed before, the meaningfulness of this ratio lies in the trend the company establishes and how it compares with similarly situated, comparable businesses in the same industry. The ratio is used as a measure or indicator of how well the company uses its resources to generate output.

The *asset turnover ratio* is calculated as:

$$\frac{\text{Sales}}{\text{Total tangible assets}}$$

For Fruit Crate Manufacturing Co., Inc., the asset turnover ratio is:

$$\frac{\$492,374}{\$375,714} = 1.31$$

A shortcoming of this ratio is that it puts a premium on businesses that have more fully depreciated equipment than on more new investment. This ratio may distort efficiency. New equipment should be producing goods at lower per-unit costs than older, out-of-date equipment. As a consequence, this ratio should be used in conjunction with other ratios.

The earning power ratio on total assets is obtained when the asset turnover is multiplied by the net profit margin, generating the *earning power percentage:*

$$\text{Earning power} = \frac{\text{Sales}}{\text{Total assets (tangible)}} \times \frac{\text{Net profit (after taxes)}}{\text{Sales}}$$

$$= \frac{\text{Net profits (after taxes)}}{\text{Total assets (tangible)}}$$

Because the net profit margin ignores the asset utilization and the turnover ratio does not consider profitability, each by itself is an inadequate measure of operating efficiency. The earning power ratio resolves these shortcomings. From this ratio, it is clear that earning power will increase if there is an increase in turnover, net profit margin, or both.

Using Ratios for Predictions

Any ratio calculation is based on historical information, which may have no bearing whatsoever on future results. For example, the profitability ratio for a Christmas ornaments company may look awful for the first two-thirds of a year, leading one to assume a continuing pattern of losses, only to see a late-season surge in sales volume that completely overturns all assumptions based on previously calculated ratios. Because of their historical foundation, does this mean that ratios are useless for predicting the future? Not at all. However, the results they show must be tempered by one's knowledge of the business, as well as a comparison to a variety of other performance measures. For example, if the current ratio suddenly drops from 2:1 to 1:1, this may signify that a company is rapidly using up its available resources to pay its liabilities, which is a clear preliminary signal of bankruptcy. However, the ratio can also be completely misleading, because a company may have simply chosen to use much of its current assets to pay off a long-term debt in advance of its scheduled payment date. The correct interpretation would have required either a complete knowledge of the subject company's financial transactions (which is not always easy to come by) or a more comprehensive view of other ratios. For example, if the current ratio had been supplemented by the debt-to-equity ratio, then it would have been an easy matter to see the drop in the current ratio being offset by the improvement in the debt-to-equity ratio. Thus, ratio analysis must be supplemented by other information before it can be used as a predictive tool.

For prediction purposes, the ratio format shown in Figure 6.2 can be of considerable use. Having just noted that a number of measures, combined together, are superior to a single ratio for predictive purposes, we have created a mix of ratios that tell a more comprehensive story of a company's financial condition. The measures are described in month-to-month format, so that the observer can see a clear trend line of financial performance. Figure 6.2 uses a mix of ratios and percentages, as well as the monthly sales figure, to determine what is happening to Company XYZ.

In Figure 6.2, the trend line of sales has gone up substantially, as Company XYZ has clearly obtained much new business, beginning in the month of May. The trouble is that this sales increase is coincident with a marked drop in profitability, probably because the company has increased its incremental sales by selling at too low a margin, thereby converting itself from a low-volume, high-margin company into the reverse—a high-volume, low-margin company. Further, to meet the demands of the company's sales growth, note that the return on assets has dropped markedly, probably due to the purchase of new fixed assets that are needed to produce the added volume. The turnover ratios for both accounts receivable and inventory have also dropped, implying that the company's working capital investment has increased, probably due in part to worsening credit problems with its new customers. The increase in assets and working capital have contributed to a shortage of cash, as evidenced by the worsening current ratio, not to mention the increase in debt, as revealed by the debt-to-equity ratio. To make matters worse, the added expenses and reduced margins associated with these extra sales have resulted in a much higher break-even point, so that the company must maintain a very

Figure 6.2

Predictive Ratio and Margin Analysis

Measurement	Jan	Feb	Mar	Apr	May	Jun	Jul	Aug	Sep	Oct	Nov	Dec
						Low-Margin Sales Added Here						
Sales (000s)	$550	$560	$565	$570	$800	$950	$1,150	$1,300	$1,500	$1,780	$2,000	$2,125
Breakeven (000s)	$450	$450	$450	$450	$600	$850	$950	1,150	$1,350	$1,550	$1,800	$1,950
Current Ratio	2.5:1	2.5:1	2.5:1	2.5:1	2.0:1	1.7:1	1.5:1	1.2:1	1.0:1	.8:1	.7:1	.6:1
Receivable Turnover	8	8	8	8	8	6	6	6	5	5	5	5
Inventory Turnover	7	7	7	7	7	6	6	6	6	6	5	5
Debt/Equity	.2:1	.2:1	.2:1	.2:1	.2:1	.4:1	.6:1	.8:1	1:1	1.3:1	1.5:1	1.7:1
Gross Margin	25%	26%	26%	26%	27%	24%	23%	22%	21%	21%	21%	21%
Net Margin	6%	7%	7%	7%	8%	5%	4%	3%	2%	2%	2%	2%
Times Interest Earned	3.0x	3.0x	3.0x	3.0x	2.7x	2.5x	2.4x	2.1x	1.9x	1.7x	1.3x	1.0x
Return on Assets	18%	20%	20%	20%	22%	16%	14%	12%	10%	8%	6%	4%

high sales level in order to cover its costs. This type of more comprehensive analysis, when set up in a multiperiod format, is much more revealing for prediction purposes than a single-ratio examined for a single period. From this wider range of information, we can easily determine the course of a company's future finances, as well as possible reasons for the current situation, and suggestions for further improvements. To use the example in Figure 6.2, we can predict a speedy demise for this company, because its cash requirements for working capital and fixed assets vastly exceed the ability of operations to spin off substantial cash. Our recommendation, based on the analysis, would be to eliminate the new customers and return to the smaller sales levels that also resulted in higher margins.

Only by creating a complete picture of a company's financial condition, which requires a mix of ratios, percentages, and other calculations, can one have a firm basis on which to predict future financial performance.

Operating Ratios

Operating ratios may be even more useful than financial ratios because of the timely nature of their calculation and the decision-specific nature of their use. While these ratios are in keeping with the thinking of most engineers and managers of sales, service *and* manufacturing can also use the principles of operating ratios effectively.

Comparison of Financial and Operating Ratios

Similarities

- Both financial and operating ratios are most useful when the information generated by the ratio is timely. Ratios are like other tools; they are beneficial only if you have them when you need them.
- As with financial ratios, operating ratios can be generated for any two numbers, for example, the number of salespeople and the dollars of sales per month. These two numbers will generate an average sales per salesperson, against which there may be a relative

performance index. Also like financial ratios, unless there is a relationship, the resulting ratio is meaningless.

- Like financial ratios, operating ratios should not be accepted at face value. For the sales per person ratio, assume we find the average to be 17 sales per salesperson per day in an automobile dealership. Two of the salespeople make 43 and 53 sales per day, respectively, and the remaining five salespeople make three sales, six sales, five sales, five sales, and four sales, respectively. It would appear that you could replace the five salespersons with one aggressive person and be better off. However, additional information may reveal that the low-volume employees are automobile showroom salespeople, and the other two are in the parts department. The parts room accounts for only 17 percent of the revenues but has 28.6 percent of the sales force. Several more ratios can be generated that would help in determining whether the sales force is well managed, efficient, and economical. Standing alone, no one ratio is as useful as a series of related ratios.

- Ratios for operations, like financial ratios, can be more effective if they are "trended." Taking the salesroom salespeople's past 12 months average ratio of sales per day, we observe the following data:

Jan.	3.6	July	4.9
Feb.	4.2	Aug.	2.1
Mar.	5.4	Sept.	4.7
Apr.	6.1	Oct.	7.0
May	7.7	Nov.	6.3
June	6.3	Dec.	4.1

From this we see a two-peak cycle of automobile sales. The dealership can plan when it should order more cars to increase the inventory in anticipation of seasonal sales. It also may help plan for sales incentives, promotional advertising, vacation schedules, and other operational elements.

- The cost of generating the data necessary for any ratio should not exceed the benefit derived from the information produced from the data. As with any tool, a ratio should itself have a favorable cost–benefit relationship. In other words, the benefits should outweigh the costs.

- Ratios are useless if they do not meet a need. Looking back, the ratio of average sales per salesperson per period was designed to measure the relative performance of sales personnel. It did not adequately do that. It failed to inform management what the meaningful performance was for automobiles versus parts sales personnel.

- Properly structured, an operating ratio or series of ratios can be used for planning and control. As an example, some of the financial ratios mentioned can be used to evaluate credit policy. The same is true for operating ratios. If we monitor how well auto sales personnel are doing individually, compared to the monthly historical figures, we have a quantitative measure of individual performance. If we look at the aggregate sales figures of average sales per person per day against the historical average, we have a measure of how well the business is doing compared with past performance.

Dissimilarities

- Financial ratios relate to numbers from the balance sheet and income statement, whereas operational ratios are oriented more toward production, service, and sales—figures that may not be accumulated in the accounting system. Because of this, standard financial ratios are more likely to be routinely prepared, whereas operating ratios are more often tailored to meet particular needs. There is a greater tendency to compare financial ratios among businesses almost indiscriminately—resulting in bad comparisons among dissimilar businesses. Since operating ratios may be tailored, there is less of a tendency for misapplication and greater reliance on historical trends.

- Operating ratios can often be calculated very quickly from obvious data. For the example of average sales per salesperson, management can have an accurate number for the previous day's sales for each member of the sales force at the start of each workday. It is often more difficult to compile and verify the financial data.

Use of Operating Ratios

Operating ratios can be used to evaluate any function. There may be a very large number of data-gathering efforts necessary to compile the needed input for ratio generation. Data gathering is costly and time consuming. It represents an investment that should have an expectation of a return to justify the expenditure. Therefore, one should first implement the use of ratios that have the greatest return or control. The ability to improve control through ratio generation and evaluation should be directed at critical steps in the process.

Breakdowns at critical steps may halt all production. For example, in a law firm specializing in appeals, time constraints are externally generated by rules of court with limited opportunities for extensions of time or deviations. Operationally, research is accomplished using sophisticated terminals connected to national data banks. Writing and editing is done on electronic word processing equipment. All work flows through personnel highly skilled in the use of word processors. A breakdown in the word processor/printer could be very serious for the meeting of critical deadlines. Typing a draft into the machine may be a critical function or a potential bottleneck. Often, the speed of input into the word processor is slower than dictation. Therefore, the ratio of skilled typists to writers may be critical. Ratio analysis can play a key role in determining a proper relationship.

There is a general five-step process for designing and implementing a control system based on ratio analysis. These five steps may not all be necessary if the system is not complex. More steps may have to be added if the process or system is very complicated. This five-step system is a good outline of an analysis control system.

The five steps are:

1. Analyze the process or system: Write out a step-by-step description of the process.
2. Look for and identify critical steps: Is there any one step through which most or all work flows?
3. Analyze the critical step: Is it a potential bottleneck or constriction? Why is it a bottleneck?
4. Set a target performance ratio: Determine from past historical data how well you have done and ask, "How much better can we do?"
5. Evaluate performance and feedback: How well are you now doing? How do you improve the system? What is the justification?

Applications

Operating ratios can be applied to any business. The following case study applies a ratio analysis to a service company (a law firm). Other suggestions will be given for a retail store and a manufacturing firm.

The firm of Simmer, Braize, and Broyle, P.A., is a Midwest law firm composed of six partners and 11 associate attorneys. They represent three large automobile insurance companies in defense litigation. The firm's business is basically steady, with two small seasonal variations. The firm has a sophisticated word processing system with satellite terminals; one draft, high-speed printer; one letter-quality printer; and a new laser printer. The firm has two senior secretaries, two junior secretaries, and one clerk-typist/receptionist. As the case load has grown, one senior secretary spends almost all her time setting up new case files.

The firm noticed that the secretaries were putting in more overtime and the senior partner was concerned that things were getting done only just in time. Ratio analysis was undertaken by an associate who had an undergraduate degree in business.

1. She analyzed the flow of paper from the receipt of a complaint through the final order of the trial court. She prepared a flow chart of what work was done, when, and by whom.
2. She discovered two critical steps:
   (a) All work product passed through the two junior secretaries and one senior secretary as they input, edited, and printed out lawyers' work products.
   (b) The reproduction and mailing of letters, pleadings, and briefs.
3. (a) The technical word processing function was on the verge of becoming a bottleneck. The work just seemed to take too long to process.
   (b) The reproduction facility was a disaster. The equipment was always breaking down; when it worked, people were constantly seen walking back to work without copies because "the line was too long" or "a long critical job was on the machine."
4. (a) After studying the number of words processed by each of the three secretaries, she found an average of 52 words per minute. Not to be fooled by averages, she looked at the distribu-

tion. The two junior secretaries typed at 38 and 42 words per minute each and the senior secretary typed at 75. The other senior secretary, who only set up files, could type at 81 words per minute. The associate, told that this secretary had been hired because of her typing speed, calculated that if the senior secretary switched roles with the junior secretary, the firm could target word input at 67 words per minute, average, without changing personnel (a 29 percent increase). The junior secretary and the receptionist would be able to prepare all the files as they came in. The associate found that the senior secretary had started or updated 61 files per day. She set a target of 45 files for the junior secretary and 20 for the receptionist (because of her other duties).

(b) She ran a study of the copier by asking each user to log in the number of copies made of each original and the number of originals. From this, she learned several things. There were only two basic types of copying requirements: (1) long runs (many copies of large jobs with many originals) and, (2) short runs (few originals, few copies). The long runs, on average, consumed 6 hours a day total time, and the short runs 1.5 hours. The average short run took less than 30 seconds, but the average long run took 17 minutes. Twenty-one long runs and about 200 short runs were run each day. With the machine breakdowns considered, the copier (owned by the firm), worked properly on average 8.2 hours each 9-hour day. Often, copies were run through lunch hour on a staggered secretarial shift.

5. From these ratios, the associate made the following recommendations: Buy a highly reliable, small copier and dedicate it to short runs. Hire a clerk to do the copying. As justification, she made the following findings based on ratio analysis:

(a) On average, each secretary saved up five small runs or one long run before going to the machine.

(b) On average, the machine was tied up doing long runs or broken down 6.8 hours out of every 9 hours, roughly 75 percent of the time. On three out of every four trips to the machine, a secretary found it occupied by a long run. Because the secretaries made 40 successful trips to the copier per day

(200 short runs/5 runs per trip), they were making approximately 120 unsuccessful trips to the machine. If they waited for a long run to finish rather than returning to their desk, they waited 8½ minutes (17/2).

(c) By assigning a clerk to copying, all unsuccessful trips were eliminated. Even though an unsuccessful trip to the copier took only 45 seconds, 1.5 hours of secretarial time was saved (120 trips × 45 seconds).

(d) By reducing the demand on the copier, the breakdown rate was expected to improve.

(e) The biggest bonus to the firm was the actual freeing up of 7.5 hours of secretarial time. Simply to do the copying, a secretary stood at the machine for 6 hours a day for long runs and 1.5 hours per day for short runs. This, coupled with the 1.5 hours of time saved on unsuccessful trips, amounted to enough savings in dollars of overtime to pay for the small-run copier in nine months and still pay the salary and benefits of the clerk.

Ratio analysis improved the operation of the firm, gave it quantifiable measures of performance and got some control over the operation.

Other Ratios

The following is a list of other operating ratios a firm might generate; it is not meant to be complete.

1. For the law firm, other ratios were considered:
   - Total hours worked to hours spent on task for which hired
   - Clerical hours to professional hours
   - Billable hours to hours worked
   - Billable hours brought to firm (new clients, new or repeat work) to hours billed
2. For a retail store:
   - Number of customers making purchases to the number of customers coming through door

• Number of sales to number of customers waited on (by each salesperson)
• Number of sales per hour of the day
• Dollars of sales per dollars of inventory (by product or product type)
• Number of sales to number of salespersons

3. For a manufacturing firm:

Lower Management

• Hours of set-up time to hours of run time
• Hours of downtime to available hours
• Hours of downtime to run time
• Hours of sick time to hours worked
• Labor hours per product produced
• Hours of rework to hours of production
• Number of quality control steps or inspections to hours to produce or steps to produce
• Work area per employee

Middle Management

• Number of supervisors to direct laborers
• Number of indirect laborers to direct laborers
• Scrapped product to good finished goods
• Number of returns to goods sold

Upper Management

• Dollars of profit to cost to produce
• Number of products back-ordered to number delivered
• Dollars of sales to number of employees
• Lost time accidents to hours worked
• Number of service employees to manufacturing employees
• Number of units shipped per day

Each manager or supervisor concerned with the operations of the firm or store should monitor at least two or three critical ratios on a continuous basis. This information may be plotted on a daily basis to accumulate historical information that could be used for planning, control, and budgeting. Often, this information will point up areas of critical concern before it has a fatal effect. Therefore, ratios, if properly structured and monitored, can be powerful management tools.

The Balanced Scorecard

Too often, a company focuses exclusively on its financial results. By doing so, it may be forcing attention away from other key measures that ultimately have a strong impact on financial performance and enhance that performance in the long run. To counteract this problem, Robert Kaplan and David Norton published *The Balanced Scorecard* (Harvard Business School Press, 1996). In this book, the authors make a strong case in favor of splitting up a company's key performance measurements into four areas—the financial, customer, internal business processes, and learning and growth areas. These areas are designed to build on each other, so that a proper level of attention to the three nonfinancial measurement areas will result in an improved set of financial measurements, as well. An example of this measurement system is shown in Figure 6.3. In it, we see that the learning and growth measurements, shown in the lower left-hand corner, are designed to improve the performance of employees through training as well as reduced turnover (on the grounds that fewer employee departures results in fewer new employees, hence a more experienced staff). Measurements for the last month are compared to those from previous periods, so that employees can see trends in the measurements. Success in the learning and growth area should result in an improvement in the company's internal business processes, which are itemized in the lower right corner of the figure. In this area, increased employee training has led to improved processing time for customer orders, as well as the near completion of a just-in-time manufacturing system. These process changes should result in improved customer-related measurements, which are noted in the upper right corner. With improved product quality, on-time shipments, and customer satisfaction, we assume that financial per-

FIGURE 6.3

The Balanced Scorecard

XYZ Company
Balanced Scorecard

Goal: To spin off enough cash flow to build new facilities and acquire competitors.

Financial:	Actual	Goal
Net profits		**6%**
This Month	4.5%	
This Quarter	3.4%	
Last Year	2.6%	
Inventory Turns		**20%**
This Month	16.0%	
This Quarter	12.5%	
Last Year	12.0%	
Receivable Turns		**9.0%**
This Month	8.2%	
This Quarter	7.6%	
Last Year	8.1%	

Customer:	Actual	Goal
Customer Satisfaction		**95%**
This Month	59.5%	
This Quarter	54.0%	
Last Year	50.0%	
On-Time Shipments		**98%**
This Month	71.0%	
This Quarter	68.0%	
Last Year	42.0%	
Quality Percentage		**99.5%**
This Month	94.5%	
This Quarter	91.3%	
Last Year	89.2%	

Learning & Growth:	Actual	Goal
Employee Turnover		**10%**
This Month	19.0%	
This Quarter	21.0%	
Last Year	38.0%	
Training Hours per		
Employee Annualized		**40**
This Month	29	
This Quarter	25	
Last Year	21	

Internal Business Processes:	Actual	Goal
Just-in-Time System		
Percentage Complete		**100%**
This Month	65%	
This Quarter	45%	
Last Year	20%	
Average Time to		
Process Orders		**2 Days**
This Month	2.9 Days	
This Quarter	3.2 Days	
Last Year	3.5 Days	

formance will improve, which will be reflected in the final box in the upper left corner. In this area, the financial measures are closely tied to the corporate goal, which is listed at the top of the page—to spin off enough cash from operations to fund new facilities and acquire competitors. Thus, the balanced scorecard reporting system results in a coherent set of interlocking measurements that are directly tied to a company's goals.

The balanced scorecard must be individualized for each company that uses it, since each one operates within a unique set of constraints. The measurements used in the example are designed for a manufacturing facility, and so would be inappropriate for use by a service company. To obtain the correct set of measurements for a balanced scorecard, a company's senior management group should compile a short list of the most appropriate measures, possibly with the assistance of a trained facilitator who can keep the discussion on track. Once everyone has agreed on the most appropriate measures, there must be further agreement on how each one should be calculated, as well as when the measures will be sent back to the management team for periodic review. These up-front decisions ensure that the correct measures will be calculated and that they will be used by managers to improve the business.

The balanced scorecard should not supplant all previous measurement systems that a company uses to track its performance. There may be dozens or even hundreds of measures already in place that are extremely useful for the conduct of daily operations and that should be continued. The balanced scorecard is more for the use of the management group, who can use it to see how well they are directing the company's performance in reaching its major goals. To this end, it should be treated as a high-level set of measurements, under which lie a great many other measures that must still be used to transact daily company business.

Summary

Ratios are an analytical tool used for reporting and control. They have external and internal applications. Externally, trade creditors, bond-holders, and banks are interested in the ratios and the trends depicted by a historical progression of those ratios. Internally, financial and operating ratios depict how well the firm is doing and serve as an instrument of feedback for control.

In trying to determine what a ratio means, analysts sometimes resort to "rules of thumb." Rules of thumb are nothing more than averages. As such, they may be inapplicable, thus generating faulty comparisons and conclusions. Financial ratios generated internally over time may be the most useful for the firm's purposes. Next, one might compare other similar firms' ratios generated by trade associations.

For financial ratios, one might generate liquidity ratios, debt ratios, long-term liquidity measures, coverage ratios, and profitability ratios.

After financial concerns, operating ratios may be generated as a measure of how well the firm is doing, where bottlenecks occur, and where objective measures of performance can be established. Creating operating ratios is an individual endeavor for each business. Although some of the ratios established—for example, acceptable parts to parts produced—may be common, what is acceptable will vary from business to business. Also, where one wants to emphasize control will vary according to individual costs.

A five-step analysis of a process or system helps point out areas where a company may have critical steps or potential bottlenecks. These may be areas where one should expend some effort in generating ratios for control and reporting.

The generation of *useful* ratios is the guiding star for this analysis. If one undertakes to generate the information necessary for implementation of a ratio control or feedback system, the ratio should be meaningful and the information useful.

Ratios are guides, and that implies movement over time. Taking a snapshot look at ratios may tell management something, but that something may be misleading. Trends in ratios indicate what is going on with the business, and they may even indicate what might go on in the future.

Properly applied, analyzed, and interpreted, ratios are a powerful tool for internal and external reporting, control, and evaluations.

Chapter 7

Taxes and Insurance

$\mathbf{M}$any of the tax consequences to a firm are covered in Chapter 8 (Reporting). This chapter will point out how to manage taxes on a continuous basis in order to take advantage of the benefits associated with various liability-limiting provisions in the tax code. Without consideration on an ongoing basis, taxes can become a significant drain on the business's cash flow.

If one considers that under the federal corporate tax rates, one of the largest percentage deductions from a company's profits may come as payment of taxes on an annual basis, one quickly realizes that significant gains can be made if taxes can be deferred or, better still, eliminated. There are many tax choices available to businesspeople that may eliminate or defer payment of taxes on the profits. Although very few situations permit the permanent deferral of taxes, the law permits deferral of tax payments in certain situations. The deferral of taxes has many benefits:

- Deferring taxes lowers a company's cash flow commitment to the government. This means more cash will be available for withdrawal and use for profit-making opportunities.
- If taxes can be deferred long enough, there is a chance that the federal government will change the tax code so as to make the payment of taxes more favorable or eliminate some tax liability entirely. In effect, the deferred taxes may be less when paid after the law changes instead of before. The rate, or the method of calculation of liability, could change. Of course, the reverse may also be true.

- A tax deferral is, in effect, an interest-free loan from the federal government. It can be recognized as a valid financing source because there can be no more favorable rate than a zero interest rate for a loan.
- Many tax options are under the company's control. When one option fails to be favorable, it can change to another.

Tax planning can have significant advantages. It can help conserve cash flow by deferring the payment of taxes. It can make available interest-free capital for the financing and purchase of new fixed assets or expansion. It can free up additional cash and make more disposable cash available for payout.

Controlling Tax Liabilities

When planning for treatment of tax expenses, consider the following accounting methods and choices of accounting periods for controlling the amount of tax liabilities that may be incurred. Of course, one should discuss these issues with a competent advisor familiar with the circumstances.

Deferred Installment Sales

A company may be able to defer income if it makes sales of personal property on an installment sales basis. This deferral is permitted even if the overall method of accounting used is an accrual method. The company realizes a cash flow improvement by not having to prepay the tax on profits until they have been realized in cash payments. If you sell on installment sales contracts do not fail to utilize this deferral method.

An installment sale is defined for tax purposes as requiring two or more payments. Therefore, a company that sells personal property on a credit basis requiring only one payment in a certain period would not qualify for use of this deferral method.

Another consideration is the company's credit policy. In establishing a credit policy, one thing that the firm may wish to consider is the tax advantages of certain installment sales. This deferral gets particularly beneficial if the company is experiencing an increase in accounts receivable. Typically, big-ticket-item retail stores, such as furniture and appliance dealers, can take significant advantage of installment sales deferment. By looking to the installment sales method of tax deferments, the company may not only have the benefit of deferring income taxes, but it may also provide an opportunity to charge slow-paying customers interest in consideration for extended payment terms. In this manner, the company may be able to take advantage of a tax code benefit to improve the percentage return on its accounts receivable.

Bad Debt Method

One company may choose to recognize its bad debts for tax purposes at the point where these debts actually become known to be worthless. Another company may set up a reserve and obtain a tax deduction based on an estimate of the debts that will be bad. The reserve method simply accelerates the tax deduction for bad debts. This is true because the deduction is allowed in the year the reserve is established, based on the probability of some accounts going bad, rather than when the specific debt is determined to be bad.

Accounting for Inventory

Sometimes, by changing accounting methods, a company can eliminate short-term profits associated with inflation and the cost of inventory. In other words, if the company has significant inventory levels that were produced at lower costs and it is currently producing inventory at much higher expenses, by selling off the most recently made or purchased inventory items, the company will then realize a profit only between the current selling price and the current higher costs. In doing so, the company retains, as a matter of bookkeeping only old inventory at lower costs. This is a change from a first-in, first-out (FIFO) accounting system to a last-in, first-out (LIFO) system.

State Tax Considerations

When locating offices and plants, a company with multistate operations should take into consideration the states in which legislation has been passed giving lower taxes for business. Lower state taxes can substantially reduce tax liability and will not inhibit the business from engaging in interstate commerce.

Another important consideration is whether the state has a tangible personal property tax. In some states, on particular days of the year, tangible personal property located within the state will be subject to taxation. Many large companies (particularly airlines and railroads) ensure that the majority of their movable assets are not in states that levy tangible personal property taxes on the day of levy (and can prove it).

Consideration of the Taxable Entity

In planning the creation of a business, the principals should consider discussing tax liabilities associated with the various forms of business entities available. Consideration of whether to incorporate, enter partnerships, subchapter S corporations, or domestic/international sales corporations should be reviewed. Each of these has particular tax liabilities. Some of them are associated with particular types of businesses and may not be applicable to the business in which you engage.

Partnerships and subchapter S corporations can be useful to avoid double taxation, which arises because the corporation is taxed on its profits and again when the profits are distributed in the form of dividends. Again, there is an income tax liability associated with a receipt of the dividends by the owners.

Partnerships and subchapter S entities, however, shift income from the entity to the shareholders' or partners' tax return. Tax losses, as well, flow directly through to the owners or partners.

One of the criteria that should be considered when setting up the business entity is the relative tax rate for the individuals as compared to the corporate rate. The corporate rate may be higher than the rate at which the principals are taxed.

The qualifications for subchapter S status change periodically. The Internal Revenue Service (IRS) can provide up-to-date information on revisions.

Financing Considerations for Fixed Assets

Rapid Depreciation Methods.   When a fixed asset is purchased, new accelerated cost recovery systems can be used, which at the same time increase cash flow. The law in this area changes frequently, and consultation with a good tax advisor will help you to understand how the depreciation deductions work and what is currently available.

Investment Tax Credits. The laws regarding investment tax credits (ITCs) also change frequently. Congress permits and withdraws such credits as a means of altering tax revenue and/or stimulating the economy. The following describes the normal situation when an ITC is available.

An ITC affords the taxpayer an opportunity to reduce income tax liability by buying or constructing equipment or other qualifying properties. Property that qualifies for ITC normally includes tangible depreciable property. This property typically must have a useful life of at least three years. Due regard must be given to the fact that usually no ITC is permitted for buildings or permanent structural components.

In the case of leased property, a lessor for a qualifying piece of property may be able to pass the credit on to the lessee. The ITC or any portion may be carried back for three years or carried forward for 15 years. Unused credit for the current year is generally carried back for the earliest carryback year, and any other remaining unused credit is applied to each succeeding year in chronological order.

Again, serious consideration should be given to consulting with a tax advisor in this area. The tax laws are changing on a fairly regular basis, and before you make any capital decision, an ITC should be considered.

Leasing

There are certain tax benefits to leasing, although the controversy surrounding these benefits still exists. Leasing may have the following advantages:

- The cash needed to purchase the property is available for other uses.
- The lessor may pass through the ITC, if any, to the lessee for his or her use. This benefit probably will not be passed on without a corresponding payment to the lessor.

- The lessor bears the risk of obsolescence or loss.
- Lease payments may exceed depreciation and interest. In this respect, it may give the lessee a higher deduction in the form of immediate expense dollars.

Cash Management through Tax Planning

Compensation Plans.   There are three types of compensation plans: basic, deferred, and pension- and profit-sharing funds. Funded and unfunded deferred compensation plans offer numerous advantages. For example, in the funded pension plan, the employer's contribution to the fund is currently deductible as an expense. Any earnings generated internally by the trust fund are tax exempt. Finally, the employees are not taxed on an individual basis until after retirement. After retirement, the employee's income should be less than he or she is receiving as an active employee. The employee gets the benefit of a lower tax rate at a later date. This is an income-deferred plan available to employees through the cooperation of their employer. There are firms and businesses that plan compensation packages. These groups can be very helpful in demonstrating different ways in which a company may save cash flow through the design of compensation plans.

Employees' Stock Ownership.   Like compensation plans, many firms offer their employees participatory ownership plans. These plans offer two advantages:

1. By giving the employees some participatory ownership in the firm, there is greater loyalty and greater concern for the firm's well-being. Each employee has a vested interest in the success of the firm. As the firm grows and succeeds, so does the personal worth of the individual.
2. The second benefit of an employee stock ownership plan is that it offers an employer a deduction without the payment of cash. Be careful that the contribution of stock does not significantly change ownership. When significant dilution of the ownership is caused by a stock purchase plan, the company may become subject to a suit called a derivative lawsuit by those owners who have had

their percentage ownership decreased by sale of additional stock. This is generally associated with the issuance of new stock and is discussed more fully in Chapter 5.

An employee stock ownership plan may use a profit-sharing or stock bonus format. In a profit-sharing format, there are two basic limitations:

1. The employees' contributions to the stock ownership plan trust may come only from current or accumulated profits.
2. The plan may not borrow funds on the basis of corporate majority stockholder guarantees to purchase employee stock. There is a major advantage to a profit-sharing format: It allows distribution of benefits to employees in the form of cash or securities as well as employer stock. This may be an important consideration if the employer's stock is not publicly traded or does not otherwise have a ready market.

Risk Management

A company may have the best business plan on Earth, execute it with precision, and end up with extraordinary profitability—only to lose it all because it failed to consider and guard against the risks to which every business is subject. This risk can range from the effects of weather, such as floods or earthquakes, to lawsuits, such as by competitors for patent infringement or employees for sexual harassment. In this section, we review the policies and procedures that a company should adopt and follow to ensure that it has identified and protected itself against a wide range of risks.

The first step in developing a risk management system is to have the board of directors formally review and approve a set of risk management policies, such as the one shown in Figure 7.1. These policies predominantly address the types and minimum amounts of required insurance coverage, though there should also be a policy regarding the completion and periodic review of a risk management plan.

This policy forces the management team to not only obtain insurance from qualified independent insurance providers, but also (and

FIGURE 7.1

Risk Management Policies

1. The company will obtain insurance only from companies with an A. M. Best rating of at least B++.
2. The company will create a comprehensive risk management plan, which will be reviewed by the board of directors at least once a year.
3. No insurance may be obtained from captive insurance companies.
4. The company must always have current insurance for the following categories, using the following minimum amounts:
   - $5 million for director's and officer's insurance
   - $10 million for general liability insurance
   - Commercial property insurance, matching the replacement cost of all structures and inventory
   - Business interruption insurance, sufficient to support four months of operations

Source: James Willson, Jan Roehl, and Steven M. Bragg, *Controllership* (New York: John Wiley & Sons, 1999), p. 1317. Reprinted with permission.

more importantly) to create a risk management plan. This plan is designed to identify the major risks to which a company is subject, as well as specify how those risks may be mitigated. A very important point is that, when determining forms of risk mitigation, insurance should be considered the last resort. This is because insurance is designed to pay a company compensation for damages that have already been incurred, whereas a true risk mitigation strategy will prevent losses from ever occurring, so that there would be no loss for an insurance company to cover. Accordingly, the steps outlined in this section to develop a risk management plan address only the need for insurance at the end of the process.

A management team should use the following 12 steps to create a risk management plan:

1. *Appoint a risk manager.* There should be one person in charge of a company's entire risk management program. The reason for this is that, if too many people are involved, it is possible that some high-risk areas will not be addressed, simply because everyone involved thinks that someone else is addressing the problem. Also, this position should be a full-time one in a larger company and

occupy a significant proportion of one person's time in a smaller company, which ensures that a sufficient amount of attention is paid to the subject area. The risk manager's job description should include the review of all corporate risks, estimating the probability of loss for each one, selecting and implementing the best methods for reducing the highest-probability risks, ensuring compliance with all governmental insurance requirements, supervising the work of the company's designated insurance broker, maintaining loss records, and periodically reviewing the company's performance under its loss prevention program.

2. *Determine risk areas.* This step involves a detailed review of all possible risk areas in a company. A considerable aid in completing this step is to use a checklist of insurable hazards, which is available from most insurers. Another approach is to review the past history of insurance claims that the company has filed, though this method will not cover any risks that have not yet been realized. If neither of these approaches are available, then at least review the company's risks based on four key areas: facilities and equipment, business interruption, liabilities, and other assets. The review of facilities and equipment should include a detailed assessment of the risks to which each facility is subject (e.g., flooding, fire), while the equipment review should take note of explosion and damage risks for each piece of major equipment. The business interruption review should focus on the amount of cash required to keep the business from going bankrupt during a business shutdown. A crucial review is that of liabilities to other parties that are caused by the company's products, employees, or operations. This review must include an examination of a company's sales and purchase orders, contracts, and leases to see if there are any additional liabilities that the company has undertaken. Finally, there must be a review of a company's cash, accounts receivable, and inventory to see if they are subject to an inordinate risk of loss for any reason. When the review is complete, all of this data should be summarized in preparation for the next step.

3. *Identify risk reduction methods.* Once the key risks have been outlined, they can be reduced. There are three ways to do so. The first is to use *duplication,* which means that a company can make copies of records to avoid the loss of original documents, or duplicate key

phone or computer systems to ensure that there is an operational backup, or even set up duplicate fire suppression systems to reduce the risk of fire damage. The second way is to institute *prevention* measures. These can include safety inspections and safety training for employees, as well as the use of mandatory safety equipment, such as hearing protection, to ensure that identifiable risks are eliminated to the greatest extent possible. Finally, a company can *segregate* its assets, spreading them through numerous facilities, to ensure that losses will be minimized if damage occurs to a single location. All of these risk reduction methods must be documented so that they can be used in the next step, which involves their implementation.

4. *Implement risk reduction methods.* Implementing the risk reduction methods just outlined is not that simple, because they usually involve either a capital expenditure (such as for a fire suppression system) that requires prior approval by senior management, or some kind of training or inspection that requires the participation of multiple departments. Because of the additional time needed to complete some of these items, it is best to divide them into two groups—those that can be implemented at once without any further approval by anyone, and those requiring approval. The risk manager should implement the first group right away. The second group should be laid out on a project timeline, including expected completion dates, so that the risk manager can methodically work through the various approvals and required meetings prior to implementing them. This approach will ensure that risk mitigation steps are completed in as efficient a manner as possible.

5. *Schedule periodic risk reviews.* Initially setting up a risk management plan is not enough. Though it may initially provide an adequate degree of risk mitigation, the types of risk will change over time, while the types of risk reduction activities being followed may fall into disuse. To keep these problems from occurring, it is important to schedule recurring risk reviews that delve into any changes in risks, as well as the degree to which current risk reduction systems are being used. The result of these reviews should be a report to management and the board of directors regarding any deficiencies in the risk reduction system, as well as recommendations for improvements.

6. *Require insurance from third parties.* We have just outlined a plan for reducing the level of risk in a company's activities without the use of insurance. To take the concept one step further but without going to the expense of purchasing insurance as a form of risk coverage, it may be possible to force customers to *pay* for insurance coverage. A good example of this is in the rental business, where the renting company can require a customer to provide a certificate of insurance from the customer's insurance agency, proving that the customer's insurer will provide coverage for the specific equipment being rented. This approach allows a company to avoid paying for the same coverage itself, though there is some administrative hassle involved in obtaining the certificate of insurance.

7. *Select a broker.* Most insurance companies operate through brokers who are either their sole representatives or independent, and therefore represent numerous insurance companies to their clients. It is generally best to use an independent agent, since this person will work on the company's behalf to search for the best insurance deals from amongst the most financially stable insurance companies. This person should be thoroughly conversant in the particular insurance needs of the company's industry and be willing to provide in-depth advice regarding the company's insurance needs. The brokers to avoid are those who overemphasize the need for additional insurance coverage when the apparent risks do not warrant the extra insurance expense. These people are more concerned with earning a few extra commission dollars than with giving a company only the insurance it needs and no more.

8. *Specify types of insurance to acquire.* Review the risk management plan to determine the types and extent of risk that require extra mitigation through the purchase of insurance. For reference, go to the list of standard insurance types that is listed in the next section. It is important to not only identify the types of insurance needed, but also the amounts. For example, coverage for business interruption insurance should cover all reasonable ongoing expenses during the time period one would reasonably expect a company to require before the business is once again fully operational. Most insurance brokers have standard forms that assist one in determining the correct amount of insurance coverage needed.

9. *Acquire insurance.* It is the job of the company's insurance broker to find insurance coverage. This will usually result in a flurry of forms from interested insurance companies that want more data about the organization and the level of risk to be covered. The risk manager must fill out and return these documents in a timely manner in order to facilitate the insurance acquisition process. In addition, there will likely be inspections by the potential insurers for some types of insurance, such as boiler and machinery insurance, since they must evaluate the condition of the equipment and facility. The risk manager should be on hand to facilitate these tours and provide any additional information needed by the insurance company representatives. The insurers will then submit their bids to the broker, who will evaluate them with the risk manager, resulting in the selection of a group of insurance policies, possibly from a number of insurance companies, that will comprise the company's insurance coverage for the upcoming year.

10. *Create a claims administration process.* Once insurance has been acquired, the risk manager must set up a standard process for claims filings. It is best to have a standard process already in place before the first claim incident occurs. This will speed up the filing process, thereby improving the company's chances of receiving rapid and full payment from the insurer. The first step in this procedure should be instructions regarding the mitigation of further damages beyond those that have already occurred, because an insurer can rightfully claim that it will provide compensation only for damages that occurred before company personnel were aware of the problem—after that time, the company is responsible for reducing further damages as much as is within its power to do so. The procedure should also include instructions for compiling a complete list of damaged items, including their book values and replacement costs. This procedure should also include the contact name and phone number of an appraiser, in case a quick outside appraisal of damages is needed. The procedure should also include the contact names and phone numbers for insurers, so that the correct insurer representatives can be contacted as quickly as possible. Further, the procedure should note the names of all internal personnel who are responsible for investigating damages and filing claims, as well as the employees who fill in for them during

their absences. In addition to this basic filing procedure, the risk manager should have a standard investigation form, which is used to inquire into the reasons why damage occurred; though this information may not be requested by an insurer, it is of great value to the risk manager, who can use it to determine the most common causes of damage and then work to reduce those causes.

11. *Create an insurance documentation filing process.* There must be a well-organized filing system in place that will assist the claims administration staff in storing and retrieving insurance documentation. For each insurance claim, there should be a separate file that is indexed by type of insurance. Within each claim file, there should be a complete description of each incident, as well as a sequential record of all events and outcomes, plus the reserves established against each one and its current status. There should also be a tickler file regarding the expiration dates of all insurance policies, so that the risk manager will be warned well in advance that renewals must be negotiated. If a policy requires a report to the insurer at regular intervals, this tickler file should include that information. Finally, there should be a fully updated insurance policy summary that contains the key information about each current policy, such as the name of the insurer and broker, contact names and phone numbers, the effective dates of each policy, insurance premiums and surcharge information, plus an abstract of the coverage, listing all inclusions and exclusions. These files are not difficult to create or maintain, but make a great difference to the risk manager in running a tightly organized function that has all relevant information immediately at hand.

12. *Schedule periodic insurance reviews.* In addition to the risk review noted earlier, there should also be an insurance review. This is a review, with the insurance broker present to provide additional clarification, of all risk coverage provided by insurance, as well as a discussion of all risks that are not covered and that may require insurance. This step should immediately follow every risk review, so that management can custom-tailor its insurance portfolio to more closely match its current risk situation. The normal outcome of this review should be slight adjustments to the types of insurance coverage, the amount of coverage for each type of insurance, and the size of deductibles.

The key document that a risk manager uses is the risk management report. This document summarizes a company's full range of potential risks, analyzes their probability of occurrence, and itemizes the exact ways to mitigate those risks, which may include the use of insurance. It is the result of the work done in the second and third steps of the risk mitigation process noted in this section. An example of a risk management report is shown in Figure 7.2, which includes a short extract from the report for a rock climbing school (an endeavor in which the control of risk is a major and continuing concern).

The risk management report can be expanded to include a set of policies and procedures that support the actions of the risk manager, as well as a calendar of report and insurance review dates. When complete, this

FIGURE 7.2

Example of a Risk Management Report

Section I: Review of Risks
- Risks related to climbing education:
  1. Risk of school equipment failing.
  2. Risk of accidents due to improper instruction.

Section II: Ways to Mitigate Risks
- *Risk of school equipment failing.* School equipment is reviewed and replaced by the school governing body on a regular basis. Instructors are also authorized to immediately remove equipment from use if they spot unusual damage that may result in equipment failure.
- *Risk of accidents due to improper instruction.* School instructors must first serve as assistant instructors under the supervision of a more experienced instructor, who evaluates their skills and recommends advancement to full instructor status. The typical instructor has previously completed all prerequisite courses and has considerable outdoor experience. All instructors must have taken a mountain-oriented first aid class within the last 12 months.

Section III: Supplemental Insurance Coverage
- *Risk of school equipment failing.* The general liability policy covers this risk for the first $500,000 of payments to a claimant. The umbrella policy covers this risk for an additional $5 million after the coverage provided by the general liability policy is exhausted.
- *Risk of accidents due to improper instruction.* This risk is covered by the same insurance coverage as for the risk of school equipment failing.

Source: James Willson, Jan Roehl, and Steven M Bragg, *Controllership* (New York: John Wiley & Sons, 1999), p. 1325. Reprinted with permission.

report should be the governing text that the risk manager uses to administer the primary aspects of the risk management function.

Insurance

The preceding section focused on the checklist of activities that a company should pursue to ensure that it has an adequate risk management system in place. Part of that process included the acquisition of a sufficient amount of insurance to cover a company's risks that cannot be mitigated in any other way. In this section, we describe the types of insurance that are most commonly available. These will provide adequate coverage for most situations. The most common types of insurance are as follows:

- *Boiler and machinery.* This is particularly valuable insurance, because the most reputable insurance providers not only provide coverage for damage to boilers and machinery, and payments for injuries caused by them, but also a complete on-site review of the condition of the equipment, which includes recommendations regarding maintenance and repairs. This extra advice is consistent with the reasoning behind having a risk management plan, which is to keep potential risks from becoming a reality.
- *Business interruption.* This coverage pays for a company's continuing business expenses, and sometimes even the profits it would otherwise have achieved, during a shutdown period. For example, a company would claim payments under this insurance coverage if its facility had burned down, thereby forcing the insurance provider to cover the cost of the company's operations while it rebuilds the facility.
- *Commercial property.* This insurance is sold in two varieties. One is the "basic form," which covers losses due to vandalism, explosions, windstorms, fires, and hail. The "broad form" is an expanded version of the same coverage, which also includes water and snow damage, falling object damage, and some causes for the collapse of buildings.
- *Comprehensive auto liability.* There is usually no choice with this insurance—state law requires it in most locations. States require

specific minimum amounts of coverage for losses due to property damage and bodily injury that is caused by company vehicles, or employees driving their own vehicles while on company business.

- *Comprehensive crime.* This policy covers losses due to burglary, robbery, and theft from employees or company premises.
- *Directors and officers.* This is a type of insurance that the board of directors will be adamant about obtaining, especially if a company is publicly held. This insurance protects officers and directors from personal liability for actions they take in association with a company. This is extremely important in today's increasingly litigious environment, where directors and officers can be sued for almost any actual or perceived transgression.
- *Fidelity bond.* A company purchases a fidelity bond to cover either a specific person or job position, or a group of employees. In either case, the insurer will pay the company for losses brought about by the dishonesty of the person(s) covered under the bond. This bond is most commonly used for people in the accounting and finance areas.
- *General liability.* Though not mandatory, a management team should strongly consider obtaining general liability insurance, since this provides coverage against incidents that can have such large payouts that they will ruin a company. The incidents covered are liability arising from accidents at any company facility, as well as ones caused by its products, services, or agents. The dollar amount of the coverage can be greatly increased with an umbrella policy, which provides extra coverage after the first round of coverage is used to settle claims. This umbrella coverage is relatively inexpensive in comparison to the initial general liability policy on which it is based, since it is so rarely used.
- *Group life, health, and disability.* These types of coverage are offered separately and are intended to be a benefit to employees, rather than a form of risk management. Group life insurance is typically offered to employees either for free or at a nominal charge, with the possible option of added coverage at each employee's expense. Health insurance coverage is usually offered to all employees after a short trial period, such as 90 days of employment; a company may offer this insurance at the full price charged by the insurer, or discount it to varying degrees as an added benefit. Finally, a company can offer its staff both long-term and short-term dis-

ability insurance, either at full price or at a discounted rate. For all these types of insurance, the primary benefit to the employee is that the coverage is simply being made available to them, because many would otherwise be unable to obtain coverage at any price due to preexisting medical conditions.

- *Inland marine.* A better name for this coverage is "transportation insurance," since it covers damage to company products that are being transported, such as marketing displays or finished goods.
- *Ocean marine and air cargo.* This covers damage to or loss of transportation equipment, such as a freight-hauling truck, plus its cargo and liability claims against the owner of the vehicle. This coverage is most commonly obtained by freight hauling companies and is of little concern to organizations that contract out their freight hauling to third parties.
- *Workers' compensation.* This coverage is required by government. It pays employees for medical and disability expenses for injuries sustained on the job. Its main advantage from the employer's perspective is that having the insurance legally keeps a company from being liable for additional payments to employees. However, the allowability of negligence lawsuits varies in accordance with the statutes of individual states. This can be very expensive insurance for those companies in high-risk fields, such as manufacturing. A company can greatly reduce the cost of this insurance by working with the insurance provider to reclassify some employees into insurance classifications that are perceived to be less risky, and therefore less expensive, such as office workers and sales staff.

For other types of specialty insurance that are not listed here, a company should work with a broker to obtain them through specialty insurance providers. Examples of this type of coverage include damage to an actor's voice, a dancer's legs, or a pianist's fingers. However, most companies can obtain adequate coverage with the more common types of insurance just noted in this section.

Split-Dollar Life Insurance

A split-dollar life insurance plan is a way in which a company can create significant cash reserves through the payment of employee life insurance while at the same time offering the employee a benefit in the form of a term life insurance policy. The insurance policy is not actually a term insurance policy except as it appears to the employee. The employee is sold life insurance protection at low cost, but the company owns the cash surrender value of the policy. Under such an agreement, the employee has the benefit of the insurance and the company has a significant portion of the cash surrender value. Under most policy provisions, the cash surrender value can be borrowed against. This offers a low-cost source of additional capital.

Summary

Detailed coverage of tax liabilities, exemptions, and deductions can be readily obtained at no cost from the IRS. Two good federal publications are publication 334, *Tax Guide for Small Businesses,* and circular E, *Employer's Tax Guide.*

A company should plan for the tax effect of its decisions on a daily basis. Certainly each financial decision and most operational decisions have direct, if not immediate, tax consequences. Knowing what the tax effects are may enable the company to defer the payment of taxes. Many large firms use tax deferral methods to postpone the payment of some taxes indefinitely.

The form of the business—whether a corporation, an S corporation, a partnership, or a sole proprietorship—changes the form of reporting and the nature of the tax liability. One should look at the tax rates applicable to the entities at various income levels.

Liabilities should be calculated using various scenarios dealing with both the level of income and the payment of that income under various business formats. As incomes grow and the business prospers, changing the business form may be an integral part of the business plan. Methods of financing capital assets have tax consequences that should be part of the acquisition plan.

Overall, the business should integrate tax planning as part of the operating budget and capital budgeting functions of the business. When taxes cannot be reduced, they sometimes can be deferred, which in some cases can be almost as good as nonpayment.

Finally, review the company's insurance coverage on a regular basis, including coverage on employees, from an investment or financing perspective. Often, opportunities to reduce costs are available and overlooked in acquiring insurance. Policies may be changed, consolidated, discontinued, or altered. Deal with insurance planners and not just claims takers. Insurance can be a liability or a valuable asset.

Chapter 8

Reporting

Every business organization has numerous reporting responsibilities. In this chapter, we will discuss some of the reporting requirements of the federal, state, and local governments; creditors; and equity owners. In view of the variety of responsibilities that governmental units place on various types of businesses, you are advised to use the services of a competent accountant and/or attorney to assure compliance with all reporting requirements. Because they change so frequently, specific rates, caps, and eligibility rules have been avoided.

Federal Government Requirements

Federal Employer Identification Number

Every new business must file for and obtain a proper federal employer identification (FEI) number from the federal government. This number identifies the business and is the key for filing and reporting taxes. All federal taxes paid or filed by a business use the FEI as a reference. It is obtained upon request by filling out Federal Form SS-4. Some states also use an employer identification number of their own. Information concerning this requirement may be obtained by contacting your state's department of revenue or taxation.

The FEI number is used to identify the business entity for more than tax purposes. Other federal agencies reference the number for compilation of other information relative to business activities such as employment statistics. It is comparable to an individual's Social Security number.

Employment Reports

When a business employs and pays wages to even one employee, it becomes subject to the provisions dealing with payroll taxes. As an employer, the company is responsible for the state and federal income taxes and Social Security taxes withheld from its employees' paychecks and for the taxes assessed directly against it, such as Social Security and unemployment. Payroll taxes must be deposited by specific dates, which vary according to the amounts payable. Contact the Internal Revenue Service for booklets that provide this information.

- *New employees.* Employers are required to have each new employee fill out a W-4 form. This form requires the employee to produce a Social Security number. On the W-4 form, the employee specifies the number of withholding allowances claimed. With that number, and the marital status and salary of the individual, withholding tax amounts can be computed.
- *Social Security taxes.* Social Security taxes are calculated at rates which vary almost annually. The important thing to remember is that this tax is paid by both the employer and the employee. The employer not only has to withhold appropriate amounts, but also contributes to this fund.
- *FUTA (Federal Unemployment Tax).* This tax is deposited, reported, and paid by the employer only. The employee does not pay this tax. The tax applies to wages paid to each employee during the calendar year up to a maximum. Once an employee reaches this cap, no additional tax is due.

The income tax and the Social Security tax must be withheld, deposited, reported, and paid by employers to the government. The Social Security tax withheld from the employee is matched by the employer when deposited.

What Wages Are Subject to Taxes? The Internal Revenue Service (IRS) makes available publications on what constitutes wages for the purpose of tax liabilities. It is difficult to do the subject justice; however, wages subject to taxes include all compensation given to an employee for services performed. The pay may be in cash, vacation allowances, bonuses, and commissions. Other special considerations to be checked in current IRS publications include:

- Partially exempt employment.
- Moving expenses.
- Fringe benefits.
- Taxable tips.

Depositing Taxes. Federal deposit coupon books (Form 8109) are used to deposit paid and withheld taxes. The preprinted coupons are basically a form with boxes for the amount of each tax paid, the FEI number, and the tax period against which the payment is being made. The coupon is mailed or delivered along with a single payment covering the taxes to a federal reserve bank (serving the employer's area) or, more likely, to an authorized financial institution. The frequency of payment depends on the amount due at the end of the month; one should determine the required deposit periods in consultation with an accountant or attorney.

Filing Returns and Reporting Taxes. FUTA taxes are reported quarterly, using Form 940. The deposit is due by the last day of the first month after the quarter. If the amount due for any quarter is less than $100, it may be carried over and paid in the next quarter's report.

For income taxes withheld and for Social Security (FICA) taxes, the employer files a quarterly report on federal Form 941. There are some exceptions to this rule related to agricultural employers, household employers, state and local governments, and some others.

Willful failure to file returns and pay taxes when due will result in criminal and civil penalties. The same is true for willful filing of false or fraudulent returns. In some cases in which income and Social Security taxes are not withheld and not paid to the IRS, individuals of the corporation or partnership may be held individually liable for the payment of these taxes along with a penalty of up to 100 percent of the taxes wrongfully uncollected.

Following are some hints on filing:

- Do not report more than one quarter of taxes on a return.
- If your business is seasonal and you temporarily stop paying wages, file returns even though you have no taxes to report.
- Use the IRS's preprinted forms and envelopes for filing returns and reports.

Wages and Tax Statement.   By January 31 of each year, an employer must provide each employee a statement of wages and taxes. This report, form W-2, includes all wages, tips, other compensations, and withheld income and Social Security taxes. Other payments may be included when applicable: bonuses, vacation allowances, severance pay, moving expenses, taxable fringe benefits, some kinds of travel expenses, and others.

Income Tax Return

Tax rules vary according to whether the operation of the business is as a sole proprietorship, a partnership, a regular C corporation, or an S corporation. These tax rules may affect how the firm carries out its business activities.

Sole Proprietorships.   In order to qualify as a sole proprietorship, one must be self-employed and the sole owner of an unincorporated business. Schedule C is filed with a federal Form 1040 (personal tax return) by April 15 of the year following the fiscal year reported.

   In a sole proprietorship, there is no tax effect for taking money out of the business for personal use or transferring personal money to the business. However, one should set up and keep separate accounts to keep track of identifiable business expenses and personal withdrawals. Failure to keep adequate business records has been the downfall of many sole proprietorships.

Partnerships.   A partnership is the relationship between two or more persons for the purpose of carrying out a trade or business for a profit. Each person contributes money, property, labor, or skill, expecting to share in the profits or losses of the enterprise.

If a husband and wife carry on a business together and expect to share in the profits and losses, they may come under the definition of a partnership for the purposes of taxes. This may occur even by operation of law, where the husband and wife have not executed a form of partnership agreement.

Income from a partnership is reported on Form 1065, U.S. Partnership Return of Income. Also included will be a separate schedule SE, Computation of Social Security Self-Employment Tax. These are "information only" returns. Taxes will be paid in quarterly estimates as a part of the partners' personal (1040) tax reporting.

But for a few exceptions, a partnership determines its income in much the same way that an individual determines his or her income. In determining their income tax liability for the year on their own income tax returns, partners must take into account, separately, each partner's *distributive share*. This consideration must be made whether or not the following items are distributed:

- Gains or losses associated with the sale of capital assets.
- Gains or losses from sale or exchange of certain property used by the business.
- Charitable contributions.
- Dividends or interest for which there is an exclusion or deduction.
- Other items of income, gains, or losses, as explained in Schedule K, Form 1065.

Corporations.   Many areas of corporate taxation are quite complex and cannot adequately be dealt with here. For a more complete discussion of corporate tax consequences, the IRS publication 542, Tax Information on Corporations, may be helpful to you.

Every corporation must file a tax return, even if it had no taxable income for the year and regardless of the amount of its gross income for the year. The income tax return for the regular corporation is Form 1120. As in the case of individual taxpayers, the federal government has a short-form application for taxes of small U.S. corporations; Form 1120-A, U.S. Short-Form Corporation Income Tax Return. In order to qualify to use the short form, the business must meet certain requirements, which have usually been:

- Gross receipts do not exceed $25,000.
- Total income does not exceed $25,000.
- Total assets do not exceed $250,000.
- No foreign owners, direct or indirect, of 50 percent or more of its stock.
- It is not a member of a controlled group or a personal holding company.
- It is not a consolidated corporation return filer.
- It is not undergoing liquidation or dissolution.
- It is not an S corporation, life or mutual insurance company, or other company filing a specialized form. For more information, use the instructions for Forms 1120 and 1120-A.

If the corporation files a return on a calendar-year basis, then the return is to be filed by March 15 following the calendar year. If the corporation uses a fiscal year other than a calendar year, then the report must be filed by the 15th day of the third month after the fiscal year. The return is filed with the Internal Revenue Office serving the area where the corporation maintains its principal office—that is, where it maintains its principal books and records.

A corporation will receive an automatic six-month extension for filing a return by submitting an application for an extension on Form 7004. The IRS can terminate this extension at any time prior to the expiration of the six-month period. Interest is charged on the difference between the tentative tax reported on Form 7004 and the actual tax the corporation must pay when it files its Form 1120.

Failure to file on the date required without good cause shown may result in the imposition of a delinquency penalty of 5 percent of the tax due. This penalty will apply to the first month due and may be increased by 5 percent per month for each subsequent month, up to a cap of 25 percent. To avoid penalties, you will have to give an explanation of good cause; that statement will be made under penalty of perjury.

If after filing Form 1120 or 1120-A you wish to correct an error on the return, you may do so by filing a Form 1120X, Amended U.S. Corporation Income Tax Return. You can use this method when you discover that you may have misstated income, or failed to claim a deduction or credit.

Estimated Income Tax. Many, if not most, corporations are required to file and pay an estimated tax. A corporation's estimated tax is the amount of its expected tax liability less its allowable tax credits. This estimated tax must be deposited with an authorized financial institution or a federal reserve bank. Each tax payment must be accompanied by a federal tax deposit coupon, according to the instructions in the coupon book.

S Corporations. Some business owners prefer not to be subject to federal corporate income tax liability. If the corporation qualifies, its income will be taxed to the shareholders individually, like a partnership, rather than the corporation. For a complete discussion of the tax liabilities and calculations, the Internal Revenue Service provides publication 589, *Tax Information on S Corporations.*

To qualify as an S corporation, the following requirements have normally been applicable:

- All shareholders must elect to be an S corporation.
- The corporation must have a permitted tax year.
- The corporation must file Form 2553, *Election by a Small Business Corporation*, indicating the choice to be treated as an S corporation.
- It must be a domestic corporation.
- It must have only one class of stock.
- It must not have more than 35 stockholders.
- It must have only individuals or their estates as stockholders.
- It must not have a nonresident alien as a shareholder.
- It must not be a member of an affiliated group of corporations.
- It must not be:
  - A domestic international sales corporation.
  - A company that serves as a financial institution, taking deposits and making loans.
  - An insurance company taxed under Subchapter L.

The permitted tax year is generally a calendar year ending December 31. Other years may be requested but require approval from the IRS.

Other Specialized Reporting Areas

Specialized Business.   Certain businesses have specialized reporting for reasons of the exercise of the federal police powers clause. Businesses such as those dealing in firearms sales and transportation, tobacco sales, liquors and spirits, ethanol production, travel agencies, and others have special reports. Most have some relation to the health, safety, morals, and welfare of citizens. These reporting requirements vary for different businesses. For example, dealers in firearms require federal licenses depending on whether the dealer sells rifles and shotguns or handguns, or transports weapons in interstate commerce. In addition, sales have to be reported on various forms prepared and submitted by the dealer.

Special Agencies.   Many federal agencies require periodic and regular reporting of various business functions. For example, the Environmental Protection Agency (EPA)—air and water quality, Occupational Safety and Health Administration (OSHA)—workplace safety and employee health, (FERC)—utility fuel costs, Interstate Commerce Commission (ICC)—motor and rail carrier rates and charges, (FCC)—depreciation rates, service charges, and terms and conditions of service. This is not meant to be an exhaustive list. Such a list would comprise a book in itself.

The discussion of federal reporting requirements has been, by necessity, brief and general. An accountant and/or attorney should be consulted to assure compliance with all reporting requirements. Also, it is a good idea to make use of the publications provided by the various agencies.

State Government Requirements

Unemployment Insurance

Unemployment insurance provides a temporary source of income to make up a part of the wages lost by workers who lose their jobs through no fault of their own and who are willing and able to work. Although the programs may vary from state to state, the following description is representative.

The employer generally pays for unemployment insurance as one of its businesses expenses. Typically, workers pay no part of the premium. The premiums go into a reserve fund to pay claims as they arise. Many states consider the stability of an employer's employment history when establishing a tax rate.

New employers are required to report initial employment in the month following the calendar quarter in which employment begins. The regulating agency then determines whether the employer is liable for taxes. Typical state eligibility requirements include:

- That in a calendar year a business has a $1,500 quarterly payroll or one or more employees.
- Liability for federal unemployment tax.
- Purchase of a liable business.

If the employer is liable for the payment of unemployment insurance, it will be required to make periodic reports and payments of taxes. It may be required to report:

- Total wages paid to covered workers, excess wages, taxable wages, and taxes due.
- Individual wage listings with each employee's Social Security number, name, weeks worked, and total wages paid.

This report is usually required to be filed along with the proper amount of taxes one month after the quarter in which the qualifying employment occurred. Timely filing is necessary in order to:

- Receive the maximum amount of credit against the federal unemployment tax for the state unemployment taxes paid.
- Get proper credit for calculating the experience rating.
- Avoid penalty and interest charges established by law for late payment and late reports.

Sales and Use Taxes

Sales and use taxes vary greatly from state to state. Their applicability, rates, and exemptions from taxation are dissimilar across state boundaries. In addition, many counties and cities have local option sales and special use taxes. Information relative to the employer's state and local government should be obtained from the offices of the state department of revenue or taxation *and* from the county or city government. The following discussion will serve as an example but may not be typical of your state.

Registration. Every person, partnership, corporation, or S corporation desiring to engage in business in the state will generally be required to secure a certificate of registration for each place of business within the state. A business may not have to comply with this requirement if it is engaging in an enterprise not subject to sales and use tax. There is usually a nominal fee ($5–$25) associated with the filing for a certificate. Sales tax of about 4 to 8 percent is levied on qualifying sales made within a state. A use tax is generally the same rate, but the tax is paid on qualifying items brought into the state to be used, consumed, distributed, rented, or stored for use or consumption.

Exemptions in some states include:

- Groceries and produce, except those prepared within a premise for consumption.
- Medical—prescription and household medicines.
- Telephone and utility service (other taxes, however, may apply to these transactions).
- Sale of livestock, poultry, and produce if the sales are made by the producers.
- Professional services.
- Subscriptions.
- Rentals.

Payments. Sales taxes are usually payable to the state by a certain date, for example, the 20th day of the month following the collection of the tax. Some states offer quarterly filing of the tax. Some offer quarterly filing for small businesses and even monthly estimated filings for businesses that collect large sums of tax in any one month. Some states allow the business or person collecting the tax to retain a portion of the collection as a fee for the collection process itself. Finally, items purchased for resale may be exempt from the tax. This is usually the case, to avoid double and sometimes triple taxation of an item.

State Corporate Income Taxes

Many states have a form of corporate income taxes. These taxes are imposed on all domestic and foreign corporations for the privilege of doing business or earning or receiving income within the state. Generally, individuals, partnerships, and estates or trusts are not liable for this tax.

Reporting.　A return is generally required by a state if (1) a federal income tax return is filed or (2) the taxpayer is liable for payment of taxes. The return is usually filed on the first day of the fourth month after the close of the taxable year or the 15th day after the due date for the filing of the related federal returns for the taxable year. Some states allow for automatic extensions. However, they usually require payment of estimated taxes. Any underpayment of estimated taxes will usually be assessed both penalty and interest. These can be as much as 12 to 15 percent on the amount of underpayment. Remittance of the tax is due at the same time the return is filed. Some states have provisions related to the federal penalty provisions for nonfiling without just cause. Interest is generally applicable at a fixed rate, and the state may even penalize a company for fraudulent returns. Some states assess a penalty for failure to file a return even when no taxes are due.

Tax Basis and Rates.　The tax is generally applicable to all forms of income, including capital gains at (usually) a uniform rate. States typically model their code provisions so as to be consistent with applicable federal code provisions.

Individual Income Tax

If the business operates as a sole proprietorship, a partnership, or an S corporation, the profits may be subject to individual state income taxes. One of the initial considerations that should be made in setting up the form of business is the tax considerations of the entity and the individuals involved. Therefore, the state's individual personal income tax (if it has one) may be a valid consideration in the operation of the business and the policy for the distribution of profits.

Other Possible Tax Returns

Intangible Tax.   Intangible taxes are levied on the ownership, control, or custody of taxable intangibles such as notes, bonds, and other obligations to pay money that are secured by a mortgage, deed of trust, or other lien on real property within the state. In addition, the state generally levies this tax on shares of stock in incorporated businesses, bonds, notes, accounts receivable, and other obligations for payment.

Ad Valorem Tax.   Ad valorem tax is a tax on the value of real estate as assessed by a duly authorized appraiser appointed or elected to serve in that capacity. The rate of taxation—the millage—is usually expressed in one-thousandths of a dollar. For example, 23 mils means $.0023. Various states and even counties within a state apply various rates (and even various values) for tax purposes. This tax applies to land, buildings, fixtures, and all other improvements to real estate physically located within a jurisdiction.

Some states may have special taxing districts that assess an ad valorem tax on the property for special services (water management, flood control, fire, school, and many others).

Documentary Stamp Taxes.   Documentary stamp taxes are taxes assessed against the execution of certain documents. Although varying in rates across states, this tax is generally applicable on promissory notes, mortgages, trust deeds, security agreements, and other written promises to pay money. Typically not a significant tax (usually being about $.15–$.20 per $100 face value), it is an obligation that must be met in the consummation of certain financial transactions.

Tangible Personal Property Tax.   Tangible personal property taxes, like ad valorem (real property) taxes are generally assessed by counties at a rate sometimes equal to the ad valorem tax. This tax is based on the assessed value or the value declared by the owner, for business supplies, fixtures, furnishings, and so on. Some states extend this tax to motor vehicles, rail cars, trucks, buses, aircraft, and even ships and boats. Often, states that exempt these items from this tax collect a like amount through licenses. Some states include inventories and work-in-process in this class of taxable property.

Others. States may have enacted various other miscellaneous taxes and fees that may impose both a reporting and filing requirement. For example:

- *Charter tax:* A fee or tax associated with the filing of articles of incorporation, amendment to the articles, merger, consolidation, or dissolution.
- *Excise tax:* Tax usually collected directly from the ultimate consumer on the sale of utility services.

Local Government Requirements

Local governments—cities and counties—have varying amounts of licensing and taxing authority. These powers arise as a result of constitutional provisions, state statutes, county ordinances, special acts of state legislatures, and charters and municipal code provisions. Some of these requirements may include:

- *Occupational licenses.* Counties and incorporated municipalities may be authorized to levy a tax for the privilege of engaging in or managing a business, profession, or occupation within the jurisdiction. The basis and rates for license payments vary considerably. Inquiries concerning these restrictions can usually be handled by individual county or city clerks.
- *Zoning restrictions.* Land use restrictions and limitations may be governed by a local zoning board. This may be under the authority of city or county governments. Zoning restrictions are usually established for an area or a parcel. Variances to restrictions may be petitioned for on an exceptional basis. Often, the nature, character,

and use of parcels will change over time, bringing about updating and change to land use plans. For example, with the growth of suburbs, land previously zoned agricultural may be changed to residential; some may change to commercial to accommodate malls, shopping areas, and business activities.

- *Sales taxes.* Sometimes counties or cities impose local option sales taxes. These may be ongoing taxes or may have limited durations designed to meet specific needs (e.g., construction of a jail or courthouse, road improvement, modernizing a hospital or school). These taxes may be collected by the state and remitted back to the city or county.

- *Gasoline and special fuels taxes.* Generally all gasoline and diesel fuel used for on-road vehicles is taxed by the state and federal governments. However, counties may have an additional local option tax. Sometimes, special fuels sold for residential, agricultural, or commercial marine purposes are exempt from this tax.

- *Local income taxes.* Some large cities (notably New York) have local income taxes. These are levied in addition to federal and state income taxes. There is often a credit or deduction applicable for state and local income taxes against federal income tax.

Creditors

Companies that have advanced credit to a business or who have invested money in the enterprise want to know how their investment is faring. They will generally insist on some form of status report on a timely basis—weekly, monthly, quarterly, or other regular period. The frequency of the necessary reporting will depend on various factors: risk, volatility of the market, past performances, solvency, and others.

Often, several documents must be prepared (balance sheet, income statement, cash flow statement) to inform creditors of the business status and financial conditions.

Together these reports afford a comprehensive model of the operations, liquidity, and the past and current operations of the business. Creditors may also request pro forma or forward-looking financial statements to create an educated future forecast of the business operations of the enterprise.

When loaning money to a business, creditors may require notes and mortgages to carry conditions or covenants. In Chapter 5, we explained how the investors of debt capital will probably condition the loans on a showing of certain ratios. We also discussed how you can and should, to the extent practicable, negotiate these covenants. Covenants are conditions or assurances. They may include:

- Maintenance of specified current ratios or quick ratios.
- Limitations on payments or salaries to officers or directors.
- Ratios of debt to equity.
- Restrictions on dividend payments.
- Restrictions on additional debt obligations.

Again, these conditions are negotiable, and the reporting of changes of status are subject to the assessment of risk.

Equity Holders

Equity holders are not dissimilar to creditors in their interest in the business results. Secured debt holders have a lien against the property superior in claim to equity holders in the case of default. Debt holders have a superior claim to the equity holder's claim. Equity holders have claims to dividends in after-tax dollars (if any). Therefore, the risk to equity holders is higher and, with luck, so is the expected return.

Management Reports

Chapter 2 discussed how a business generates a budget for operations including targets for materials, and labor and overhead by product and/or by operation. These operating budgets are monthly projections and targets against which actual performance can and should be measured. An overall report against the business plan should be prepared to ensure that the objectives set are being approached.

These reports can be generated based on standards showing variances from plan. Variance reporting permits one to address variances with reports of performance and exception reports, which identify reasons for the various and curative steps taken. Finally, these reports can be economically generated—by centers, by departments, or in any other way.

Thus far, we have concentrated on reporting requirements to entities outside of a company. There are also a wide range of reports that a management team will want to see that clearly outline its internal performance. We will review some of the more useful internal management reports in this section.

In any operation, there are a number of statistics that management wants to review every day. These will vary by type of company, because every business operates in a unique manner that requires a tight focus on different performance measurements. Some information will be common to all such reports, such as the daily cash balance or sales from the previous day. Others, such as the production scrap percentage, will be useful only to a manufacturing company, whereas the number of meals served will be of more consequence to a restaurant. The key underlying reason for adding any measurement to a daily management report is that excluding it could harm operations. This criterion should keep the number of measures on the daily report quite low, usually in the range of two to six measures. Because there are so few of them, they are generally disseminated to management in an informal manner—not in a paper-based report, but rather by voice mail or e-mail. Following is an example of the daily management report, if sent by voice mail:

> Hello, here is the daily management statistics report. Sales yesterday were $120,000, and month-to-date sales were $1,320,000. The cash balance is $275,000. Yesterday's average machine utilization was 72 percent, scrap was 4 percent, and employee overtime was 14 percent.

By keeping the amount of information in the report to just the few key items that management needs to run the business on a daily basis, the report avoids bogging down the recipient in excessive detail. The report should be issued as early in the day as possible, so that the management team has the bulk of the day in which to follow up on the information.

In addition to the daily report, there should be a more comprehensive weekly report that summarizes a business's main operating statistics, as well as a few key financial figures. It is best to cluster the statistics within the report by department, so that department managers can spot all of the measures that pertain to them without any searching. Also, the report format should include the average measures for each of the last three months, plus the previous weekly measures for the current month; this format presents the reader with a trend line of information from previous periods that reveals any significant changes in the statistics. Finally, every effort should be made to keep the report to one page. The intent is not to overwhelm management with too much data, but rather to focus its attention on only the most important statistics. Very few businesses require more than one page to convey this information. An example of such a weekly management statistics report is shown in Figure 8.1.

Note that Figure 8.1 contains the key statistics for five departments and working capital, which is recorded as though it were a separate department. This is because working capital is an extremely important use of cash that must be kept clearly in front of the management team.

There are a few variations that can be included in the weekly management statistics report. One is to add a column that lists the goal for each statistic. For example, the inventory accuracy goal may be set at 95 percent, the backlog goal at $3 million, and the machine utilization percentage at 75 percent. This is a useful tool if the management team appears complacent in accepting performance levels that are lower than the goals. One can also add comments to the report. The simplest kind is to list unusual statistics in bold, to make them more prominent. For example, an unusually low cash balance can be highlighted in bold. Also, if the report is maintained on an electronic spreadsheet, such as Excel, one can include comment fields for any cell in the worksheet. These comments are most useful for describing the calculation methods used for each statistic, which readers can access if they have the file (which can be distributed to them each week by e-mail). A spreadsheet that contains the goals column and field comments is shown in Figure 8.2. All of these changes improve the informational content and clarity of the weekly management statistics report.

This weekly report is the primary one that management will use to ascertain the condition of a business. However, the information

FIGURE 8.1

Weekly Management Statistics Report

	Current Month							
	Week 5	Week 4	Week 3	Week 2	Week 1	March	February	January
Engineering								
Bill of Material Accuracy	92%	90%	87%	85%	80%	72%	68%	64%
Finance								
Cash Balance (000s)	$172	$198	$154	$123	$191	$208	$175	$163
Loans Available	$1,071	$1,203	$1,541	$1,678	$1,400	$1,378	$1,205	$1,556
Logistics								
Inventory Accuracy	99%	91%	83%	80%	89%	85%	79%	76%
On-Time Shipping	81%	90%	85%	84%	79%	75%	74%	73%
Customer Returns (000s)	$27	$25	$21	$36	$29	$78	$102	$139
Production								
Machine Utilization	65%	64%	60%	78%	81%	75%	70%	71%
Overtime	8%	10%	12%	7%	11%	10%	9%	12%
Production Schedule Completed	94%	92%	99%	100%	79%	81%	85%	83%
Scrap	4%	3%	4%	2%	1%	5%	4%	3%
Sales								
Backlog (000s)	$2,806	$2,809	$2,819	$2,876	$2,901	$2,904	$2,611	$2,605
Lost Customers	0	−2	−3	−1	0	−2	−7	−11
New Customers	2	3	1	4	0	0	5	8
Period Sales (000s)	$317	$289	$309	$321	$350	$1,251	$1,279	$1,321
Working Capital								
+ Accounts Receivable (000s)	$1,218	$1,327	$1,287	$1,285	$1,270	$1,300	$1,325	$1,330
+ Inventory (000s)	$1,707	$1,754	$1,732	$1,702	$1,659	$1,654	$1,632	$1,607
− Accounts Payable (000s)	$1,100	$1,103	$1,145	$1,307	$1,245	$1,301	$1,247	$1,225
Total Working Capital (000s)	$1,825	$1,978	$1,874	$1,680	$1,684	$1,653	$1,710	$1,712

FIGURE 8.2

Weekly Management Statistics Report with Enhancements

	Goal	Week 5	Week 4	Week 3	Week 2	Week 1	March	February	January
Weekly Management Statistics Report									
				Current Month					
Logistics									
Inventory Accuracy	95%				80%	89%	85%	79%	76%
On-Time Shipping	99%				84%	79%	75%	74%	73%
Customer Returns (000s)	$0				$36	$29	$78	$102	$139
Production									
Machine Utilization	75%				78%	81%	75%	70%	71%
Overtime	5%				7%	11%	10%	9%	12%
Production Schedule Completed	98%				100%	79%	81%	85%	83%
Scrap	2%				2%	1%	5%	4%	3%
Sales									
Backlog (000s)	$3,000	$2,806	$2,809	$2,819	$2,876	$2,901	$2,904	$2,611	$2,605
Lost Customers	N/A				-1	0	-2	-7	-11
New Customers	N/A				4	0	0	5	8
Period Sales (000s)	N/A				$321	$350	$1,251	$1,279	$1,321
Working Capital									
+ Accounts Receivable (000s)	$1,100	$1,218	$1,327	$1,287	$1,285	$1,270	$1,300	$1,325	$1,330
+ Inventory (000s)	$1,500	$1,707	$1,754	$1,732	$1,702	$1,659	$1,654	$1,632	$1,607
- Accounts Payable (000s)	$1,300	$1,100	$1,103	$1,145	$1,307	$1,245	$1,301	$1,247	$1,225
Total Working Capital (000s)	$1,300	$1,825	$1,978	$1,874	$1,680	$1,684	$1,653	$1,710	$1,712

Callout (Logistics): Total number from a random sample of 100 counts that have accurate locations, quantities, and descriptions.

Callout (Production): Total hours used on actual production during the period. Does not include scheduled down time for preventive maintenance.

Callout (Sales): Number of new customers who have applied for credit and who have placed firm orders exceeding $10,000.

presented in it does not give management a sufficient level of detail to determine the exact causes of problems that are affecting the statistics. To resolve this issue, additional reports are needed. For example, if a company is plagued with high overtime costs, then managers need to know which departments, as well as which people within those departments, are incurring the overtime. Armed with this information, managers can determine the exact causes of the overtime and correct them. An example of such a report is shown in Figure 8.3. The example is sorted by department and lists every hourly employee within each one. The report lists the percentage of overtime for every pay period (the example assumes two periods per month), so that one can quickly scan the report and see if there are consistently high overtime figures for particular departments or individuals.

FIGURE 8.3

Employee and Departmental Overtime Report

	1/15	1/30	2/15	2/28	3/15	3/31	4/15	4/30
Accounting								
Banuelos, Abel	15%	12%	13%	14%	0%	5%	10%	8%
Errett, Cynthia	18%	15%	16%	17%	3%	8%	13%	8%
Hick, Maggie	10%	7%	8%	9%	0%	0%	2%	4%
Knopf, Tom	14%	12%	12%	14%	2%	4%	9%	6%
Departmental Total	14%	12%	12%	14%	1%	4%	9%	7%
Engineering								
Belval, Tom	0%	1%	2%	6%	5%	4%	3%	8%
Fine, David	8%	8%	8%	8%	8%	8%	8%	8%
Holland, Drew	4%	3%	8%	5%	6%	7%	9%	2%
Kramer, Ted	10%	14%	12%	16%	20%	18%	14%	11%
Department Total	6%	7%	8%	9%	10%	9%	9%	7%
Logistics								
Bowker, Abby	14%	14%	16%	16%	16%	18%	14%	15%
Galleher, Patti	12%	13%	11%	10%	9%	8%	12%	15%
Jimenez, Brenda	3%	5%	4%	2%	1%	6%	16%	0%
Laramie, Connie	4%	7%	9%	2%	4%	6%	8%	2%
Department Toal	8%	10%	10%	8%	8%	10%	13%	8%
Production								
Castaneda, Jerry	16%	15%	14%	25%	2%	5%	8%	1%
Goick, Gina	11%	15%	12%	20%	8%	8%	8%	8%
Josephson, Mike	4%	0%	3%	21%	6%	6%	4%	3%
Lomheim, Louis	9%	2%	4%	24%	4%	20%	6%	14%
Department Total	10%	8%	8%	23%	5%	10%	7%	7%
Sales								
Drexler, Tom	2%	0%	5%	12%	20%	25%	12%	6%
Gordon, Frank	8%	3%	8%	10%	15%	20%	10%	5%
Kennedy, Dennis	6%	0%	0%	8%	16%	21%	8%	4%
Mansfield, George	4%	2%	4%	6%	19%	24%	6%	3%
Department Total	5%	1%	4%	9%	18%	23%	9%	5%
Company Total	9%	7%	8%	12%	8%	11%	9%	7%

Another measure on the weekly report that will result in a request for more detailed analysis is the on-time shipping statistic. If the percentage is low, managers have no way of knowing what shipments were delayed or why, so that they can correct similar problems in the future. To remedy this issue, one can distribute a listing of all customer orders that were not shipped on time, which should include the reason for the problem. There are generally a standard number of reasons, so the problem section of the report can be a simple matrix that lists the standard error at the top and a check mark in the underlying grid for each delayed shipment. This is a sufficiently detailed amount of information for managers to use in conducting their own investigations. An example of the report is shown in Figure 8.4.

Similarly, an additional report is needed if management wants to know more detail about the reasons for changes in the level of machine utilization. An example of such a report is shown in Figure 8.5. This report groups machines by type, so that one can determine the overall usage of each group. If the usage level for an entire group is low, and there is a consistent trend line of results at that level, then management can eliminate some of the machines in that group in order to raise the average utilization level. The reverse decision, that of buying more machinery, may also result if a group utilization number is consistently tracking at a very high level. Also, if utilization suddenly drops to zero for a specific machine, there may be a maintenance problem that is bringing it down. This level of detail is generally sufficient for management to obtain a clear understanding of the reasons for changes in machine utilization.

In the machine utilization example, we are tracking the usage of machines that are employed in the production of candy. Three utilization issues arise in the report. The first is in the candy extruder machine group, in which the total machine usage approximates 50 percent in most months. Assuming that this trend will continue, management could consider selling one of these machines, which would bring the utilization of the remaining machines to approximately 75 percent. The second issue is in the candy wrapper machine group, in which a new machine (CW-01) was added in the beginning of the year, and gradually ramped up to full production by April; however, utilization in this area is extremely high, so the purchase of yet

Figure 8.4

Delayed Shipment Report

Customer Name	Customer Order No.	Part Description	Part Number	Due Date	Problem Matrix						
					Freight Carrier Was Late	Insufficient Production Capacity	Machine Breakdown	Missing Materials	Missing Packaging	Scrapped Parts	Tools Broken/Missing
Avery Arials Inc.	00348	Ski Carrier	SK-412	05/02/2001	X			X		X	
Bufford Bump Co.	01982	Snowboard Rack	SN-023	05/03/2001			X		X		
Chameleon Co.	7701	Ski Edging Tool	SK-401	05/01/2001			X	X	X	X	
Duffy Mogul Co.	3278	Boot Heater	BT-213	05/04/2001			X				X
Entry Designs	1195A	Boot Rack	BT-214	05/03/2001	X	X		X		X	
Force Powertrain	5004C	Hand Warmer	HA-003	05/02/2001		X					
Gander Aviation	65481	Ski Locks	SK-410	05/03/2001		X			X		
High Fliers	AB-021	Ski Wax	SK-409	05/01/2001			X				X
Itchty Skier	5562	Ski Tuning Kit	SK-413	05/04/2001	X				X		
Jump Ski Co.	905	Ski Decals	SK-423	05/05/2001			X				X

FIGURE 8.5

Machine Utilization Report

Machine Description	January	February	March	April	May	June	July	August	September	October	November	December
Candy Mixer												
CM-01	70%	68%	63%	75%	80%	77%	71%	70%	69%	80%	75%	76%
CM-02	67%	65%	69%	75%	73%	70%	65%	64%	66%	68%	69%	71%
CM-03	69%	67%	65%	76%	75%	73%	68%	67%	68%	72%	72%	73%
Group Subtotal	69%	67%	66%	75%	76%	73%	68%	67%	68%	73%	72%	73%
Candy Extruder												
CE-01	52%	59%	60%	59%	58%	54%	59%	52%	54%	55%	54%	50%
CE-02	51%	52%	54%	55%	51%	52%	57%	58%	52%	53%	55%	60%
CE-03	43%	44%	51%	40%	43%	45%	41%	40%	39%	38%	37%	35%
Group Subtotal	49%	52%	55%	51%	51%	50%	52%	50%	48%	49%	49%	48%
Candy Wrapper												
CW-01	15%	20%	50%	100%	90%	95%	88%	93%	90%	91%	95%	99%
CW-02	100%	98%	99%	97%	98%	100%	99%	93%	98%	95%	98%	99%
CW-03	100%	100%	100%	90%	100%	100%	100%	90%	100%	100%	100%	90%
Group Subtotal	72%	73%	83%	96%	96%	98%	96%	92%	96%	95%	98%	96%
Candy Packager												
CP-01	80%	85%	90%	92%	89%	87%	83%	81%	85%	86%	87%	85%
CP-02	78%	76%	75%	74%	70%	78%	72%	76%	75%	73%	71%	75%
CP-03	79%	79%	81%	82%	81%	79%	75%	79%	79%	75%	83%	78%
Group Subtotal	79%	80%	82%	83%	80%	81%	77%	79%	80%	78%	80%	79%
Candy Cane Twister												
CCT-01	0%	0%	0%	0%	0%	100%	100%	100%	100%	0%	0%	0%
CCT-02	0%	0%	0%	0%	0%	100%	100%	100%	100%	0%	0%	0%
CCT-03	0%	0%	0%	0%	0%	100%	100%	100%	100%	0%	0%	0%
Group Subtotal	0%	0%	0%	0%	0%	100%	100%	100%	100%	0%	0%	0%
Total for All Groups	**54%**	**54%**	**57%**	**61%**	**61%**	**81%**	**79%**	**78%**	**78%**	**59%**	**60%**	**59%**

another machine for this group appears to be justified, especially if the breakdown of any machine in this group would result in a bottleneck that could cut into total facility sales levels. Finally, the candy cane twister machine group, located at the bottom of the report, produces a seasonal item. Because of its seasonality, there is no cause for alarm when seeing utilization jump from 0 percent to 100 percent and then back to 0 percent—this is just the nature of the manufacturing process for a seasonal product. These are some of the issues that will be revealed by a machine utilization report.

The "Lost Customers" statistic on the weekly management statistics report yields only the number of lost customers, not who they are or why they left. This information can be included in another report, such as the one shown in Figure 8.6. This is a more free-form document, since there may be lengthy explanations for losing a customer that cannot be readily included in a problem matrix format, such as the one shown in Figure 8.4. The standard information to include in this report is the name of the customer, the date on which the company first learned of the lost business, the names of the salesperson and customer service person who were responsible for the customer, and the reason given by the customer for leaving. The names of the two contact people are important to track, in case one or more of them have a history of losing customers. The information in this report should be stored for at least a year, so that managers can review the historical data to see if there are repeated problems that are consistently causing the company to lose customers. This report can also be modified slightly to track lost quotes. The only difference is that the identifying quote number should be listed on the report. All other fields remain the same.

The lost customers report in Figure 8.6 reveals a consistent problem with a single customer service person, about whom three customers complained at the time they dropped the company as a supplier. By using this report format to discover continuing problems such as the one with the customer service person, a company can identify and correct ongoing problems that irritate its customers.

The preceding sample reports were all connected to the statistics shown in the weekly management statistics report. The next report is not, because it focuses on a variety of errors that are not easily summarized. It is intended to put the spotlight on repeated transactional

Figure 8.6

Lost Customers Report

Customer Name	Notification Date	Name of Salesperson	Name of Customer Service Person	Reason for Losing Customer
Parrot Graphics, Inc.	2/15/2001	O. Harmsen	M. Pierce	Consistently late deliveries.
Little Designs	2/19/2001	H. Davidson	R. Kontmann	Damage to shipping carton for the last three deliveries.
Central Label	3/14/2001	H. Davidson	M. Pierce	Incorrect shipment quantities for four of the last seven deliveries.
Country Art	3/21/2001	O. Harmsen	R. Kontmann	Incorrect bar code labels on shipments, despite repeated requests to change them.
Cloud Designs	4/1/2001	F. Anderson	M. Pierce	Part quantities in boxes were lower than the amounts listed on the box labels. Had to repeatedly request credits for short quantities.
Graphic Industries	4/5/2001	O. Harmsen	B. Zeltmann	Customer service person did not call back in a timely manner, and did not call back at all on three occasions.
Graphical Overlay Company	4/19/2001	D. Schwandt	R. Kontmann	Shipments sent to wrong company location for approximately one-half of all orders.
Water Based Paints, Inc.	4/30/2001	F. Anderson	R. Kontmann	Products sent were correct, but the color was wrong.
Honey Color Graphics Co.	5/11/2001	O. Harmsen	B. Zeltmann	Had repeated problems with overpricing on invoices, because customer service person set prices based on incorrectly low purchase quantities.
Interior Design Associates	5/17/2001	H. Davidson	M. Pierce	Shipments were an average of two days late in arriving, which stopped the production line in which those parts were used.
Candy Stripe Artists Co.	5/19/2001	D. Schwandt	B. Zeltmann	Low-quality parts. Rejected an average of 12% of parts in each order delivered.
Paint by Color Company	5/25/2001	F. Anderson	B. Zeltmann	Had great difficulty in obtaining credits from the customer service person, who did not return phone calls.
Coordinated Label Company	5/29/2001	O. Harmsen	R. Kontmann	Too many extra shipping charges tacked on to invoices. Customer considers these charges to be two times higher than normal.

errors, so that the management team can focus on correcting corporate systems before they cause errors. To create this report, which is shown in Figure 8.7, one must extract all error correction transactions from the computer system. These are, for example, credits given to customers to adjust originally invoiced amounts, or cycle counting adjustments to correct inaccurate inventories, or scrap transactions for discarded materials. This information can be gleaned from the computer system by extracting the detail on these transactions—credits, adjustments, or scrap entries—and summarizing them into a report that notes the type of error, the date on which it occurred, the amount of the error in dollars, and the reason for the error. When the information in this report is summarized for a number of months, the summary-level report reveals where the bulk of a company's problems are occurring, so that management can focus its attention on these areas.

The main problem with a system errors report, such as the one noted in Figure 8.7, is that it can be used for a "witch hunt" by management, since it is possible to target the people who are repeatedly involved with errors, rather than the systemic problems that cause errors to arise. When employees realize that management is targeting employees instead of the system as a result of this report, a common response is to not make any adjusting entries in the computer system, so that the number of reported errors drops to zero, even though the errors are still occurring. This is a very detrimental result, for the accuracy of the data in the company database will rapidly decline when the staff stops correcting the information contained in it. Consequently, it is very important for the management team to use this report for systemic improvements, or else it will rapidly lose the trust of employees as well as database accuracy.

The reports in this section give management a comprehensive view of company operations. There are daily reports for the small number of crucial daily activities, as well as a more all-encompassing weekly report for which there are a number of supporting detailed reports that give management a thorough view of why there are problems with specific measurements. This type of interlocked internal reporting system is a good way to ensure that the management team is thoroughly apprised of company performance and the reasons for changes in it.

FIGURE 8.7

System Errors Report

Error Type	Error Date	Error Amount	Reason for Error
Customer Credit	7/01/2002	$278	Incorrect pricing that was based on a smaller order quantity than the order the customer actually placed.
Inventory Adjustment	7/12/2002	$1,204	Adjusted item was consumer product that may have been stolen by an employee.
Scrap	7/17/2002	$4,009	Caused by an incorrect setup with improper horizontal dimensions on large jig.
Scrap	7/22/2002	$57	Caused by damage to packaging, allowing welding materials to fall and be damaged.
Inventory Adjustment	7/29/2002	$12,471	Ran job with incorrect specifications for two days before noticed the problem. Had to scrap all completed parts.
Customer Credit	8/03/2002	$710	Shipped wrong product to customer by transposing part number in the order.
Customer Credit	8/14/2002	$654	Shipped too late to meet customer deadline, so product was returned for credit.
Scrap	8/15/2002	$98	Parts were painted the wrong color, due to color being labeled incorrectly.
Inventory Adjustment	8/23/2002	$170	Item was incorrectly counted during the year-end physical count. This entry adjusts back to actual quantity.
Scrap	8/23/2002	$249	Caused by excess sheet metal on sheet after required parts were punched out of it.
Customer Credit	9/05/2002	$1,298	We billed the customer for a larger quantity than was actually in the box.
Inventory Adjustment	9/06/2002	$2,500	Cannot find finished product, part number ABK-5402. Still investigating possible issues.
Inventory Adjustment	9/16/2002	$6,500	Incorrect unit of measure used for tape. Engineers changed it to rolls, which greatly increased the on-hand value, since the quantity had been recorded in inches.
Scrap	9/20/2002	$3,207	Extra wood scrap due to operator error. The machine operator was not well trained in how to use the equipment, and cut 142 planks too short.
Scrap	10/03/2002	$578	Product is missing, may have been stolen during the weekend.
Customer Credit	10/19/2002	$540	Incorrect pricing on product. Used standard pricing on the invoice, but this was a special deal with the sales staff that was not forwarded to the accounting department.
Customer Credit	10/24/2002	$821	Invoice could not be collected because customer went into bankruptcy. Wrote off as bad debt expense.

Profit Center Reporting

The previous section was primarily concerned with reporting on operational issues, such as machine utilization and scrap rates. However, these are of no import if a company cannot consistently create a profit or spin off enough cash flow to keep those operations running. In this section, we review the concept of profit centers, and how one should report their results.

Every company creates and issues an income statement that reveals the financial performance of the entire company. For smaller organizations that deal with just a single line of business, such as a plumbing service company, this is sufficient. However, if there are several lines of business, such as a plumbing service group, a plumbing hardware store, and an air conditioning repair staff, then the revenues and costs of each one should be recorded separately, so that management can see if some areas are less profitable than others. An example of this report is shown in Figure 8.8. In this report, we list a separate income statement for each profit center, which summarizes into the summary-level income statement for the entire company, as shown at the far right side of the report. Also in the report is a separate column for corporate overhead. These are costs that cannot be specifically allocated to a profit center. The basic rule for making the allocation determination is whether or not an overhead cost will disappear if a profit center is eliminated; if not, then do not allocate the overhead cost to the profit center. Also, there is an interest expense charged to each profit center, based on the amount of fixed assets and working capital that each one uses. Finally, after the profit figures at the bottom of the report, we add back the depreciation expense for each profit center (since this is a noncash expense), which yields the actual cash inflow or outflow to or from each profit center. The report reveals that the plumbing hardware store is making very little money, partially because of the interest expense charged to it that covers the cost of funds for the store facility and inventory. Both service groups, having no significant assets, have a much lower interest expense, and so earn a larger profit. Based on this analysis, it is evident that the hardware store is a drag on the overall corporate earnings percentage.

FIGURE **8.8**

Profit Center Income Statement (000s)

Description	Plumbing Service	Plumbing Hardware	Air Conditioning Repair	Corporate Overhead	Summary Income Statement
Revenue	$1,400	$1,750	$972	$0	$4,122
Direct Expenses:					
Material	625	1,115	410	0	2,150
Direct Labor	450	250	350	0	1,050
Total Direct Cost	1,075	1,365	760	0	3,200
Total Direct Margin	325	385	212	0	922
Direct Margin Percentage	23%	22%	22%	0%	22%
Overhead Allocation	14	57	14	375	460
Gross Margin	311	328	198	−375	462
Gross Margin Percentage	22%	19%	20%	—	11%
General & Administrative	25	85	25	175	310
Interest Expense	42	193	29	0	264
Net Profit (Loss)	244	50	144	−550	−112
Net Profit Percentage	17%	3%	15%	—	−3%
+ Depreciation Expense	21	81	21	37	159
Cash Inflow (Outflow)	264	131	165	−513	47
Capital Usage:					
Working Capital	325	1,578	175	0	2,078
Fixed Assets	145	565	145	258	1,113
Total Capital Usage	470	2,143	320	258	3,191

To create a profit center analysis, the accounting staff must track billings and expenses by specific profit center, rather than recording them all in a single set of account numbers, which is a slightly more complicated accounting transaction. Also, all assets should be recorded in accounts that are specifically assigned to profit centers, so that interest expenses can be charged based on these amounts. The

most difficult item to track is working capital for each profit center, because this requires the identification of all accounts receivable, inventory, and accounts payable by profit center. To accurately record working capital, it may be necessary to either maintain a separate set of accounting records for each profit center or manually compile this information whenever the accounting staff creates a profit center financial statement. Given the amount of detailed information that results from this report, the added work is well worth the effort.

Customer Margin Reporting

If a company creates an income statement report by profit center and the management group still feels that it does not have enough information, the next logical step is to create a customer margin matrix, because it reveals an additional level of detail by showing profits by customer for each profit center. This method results in a matrix, as shown in Figure 8.9, that segregates all company customers into one of four quadrants on a profitability and volume chart. The quadrant in the lower left corner contains those customers that are marginally profitable and also have minimal sales volume. The quadrant in the lower right corner is the worst one, for it contains those customers with low profit margins and high volume (e.g., the company is expending much effort for little result). The company's objective for the customers located in these first two quadrants is to either eliminate them or raise their prices to improve profits. The quadrant in the upper left corner contains customers with high margins but low sales volume. The objective here is to improve their purchasing volume. The final quadrant, which is in the upper right corner, is for high-volume, high-profit customers, and contains all the prized customers that a company absolutely does not want to lose. This report format is extremely revealing in terms of which customers should be dropped and which given special treatment, and, with some deft customer management, can result in a much more profitable mix of customers. The cutoff figures for margin and volume, as noted in the example, will change depending on the business. The dividing line for high and low margins may not be 25 percent, as shown in the example, nor may the volume demarcation be $100,000. A company can set its own boundaries with different figures. Also, the margins on which

FIGURE 8.9

Customer Margin Matrix

No. of Customers = 8 Total Sales = $450K Average Margin = 41%		**No. of Customers = 5** Total Sales = $800K Average Margin = 38%	
	Margin		Margin
All Day Fitness	52%	Central City Gym	41%
Better Body Fitness	38%	Fitter Bodies Co.	47%
Body Builder Warehouse	41%	Nationwide Gyms	33%
Custom Bodies Co.	43%	Powerbuilder Plus	35%
Fitness Designs	45%	Runner's Palace	34%
Jump Higher Aerobics	39%		
Weights by Design	62%		
Weights Warehouse	29%		
No. of Customers = 7 Total Sales = $325K Average Margin = 1%		**No. of Customers = 4** Total Sales = $1,417K Average Margin = 11%	
	Margin		Margin
All Round Fitness	−3%	Barbells Plus	13%
Dumbells Only	0%	Fitness Distribution Co.	7%
Fit by Night Inc.	3%	Kids Gyms and Day Care	11%
Ladies Workout Co.	7%	Southern Fitness	10%
Midwest Fitness	5%		
Powerhouse Bodies	0%		
Pumped Workouts Co.	−14%		

Margin axis (left): 25%, $100K, Revenue Volume

this information is based can be calculated in several ways. One is to use direct costing (i.e., price minus direct labor and material costs), because of its simplicity. Alternatively, the margin calculation can include fully burdened costs, though this approach may result in overhead costs being assigned that have little real basis in fact. Accordingly, if margins are to include overhead costs, use activity-based costing to ensure that there is a justifiable reason for assigning costs to a customer.

With the operations reports, profit center analysis, and customer margin matrix, a management team will have a plethora of information on which to base its decisions to improve company profitability.

Summary

Businesses have varying reporting responsibilities to federal, state, and local jurisdictions. They have other external reporting requirements to creditors and investors. Finally, they have internal reporting functions used for planning and control.

The federal reporting requirements include employment reports on wage-earning employees, tax reports, and Social Security taxes. Employers pay unemployment taxes for their employees. The federal government has arranged for banks and federal depositories to receive taxes collected from employees and those paid by the employer. The employer withholds federal income tax and Social Security taxes and pays those into the federal depository pursuant to IRS guidelines. Annually, the IRS requires employers to report to their employees the wages and taxes paid and withheld.

Depending on the form of the business organization, there are various reporting requirements for federal tax liabilities. Sole proprietorships, S corporations, and partnerships pay income taxes for the business entity. However, S corporations and partnerships file information returns. Corporations are taxed as a separate legal entity.

Other reporting requirements arise out of the nature of the business. For example, dealers in firearms are strictly licensed and regulated by the United States Treasury Department. Other businesses are regulated as to rates, charges, and services offered. Utilities, transportation companies, banks, and other such industries are closely regulated. Some, because of the dangers associated with working conditions, are closely scrutinized. Coal mining, toxic chemical companies, and airlines are just a few such activities.

State governments also regulate and tax many businesses and activities. States generally tax the real property of businesses and the structures attached to the property through their ad valorem taxing authority. A business's equipment, fixtures, appliances, and even inventories might be taxed using tangible personal property taxes. Intangible items of ownership, such as stocks, bonds, and notes, are taxed through intangible personal property taxes. In some cases, sales and even purchases made in other states are taxed. Some products, such as groceries, medicines, and telephone services, are exempt in some states.

Local governments may impose taxes, licensing requirements, and zoning restrictions on the operations of some businesses. Some county or city governments may have franchise requirements for the provision of services; these may be exclusive rights to provide services, such as cable television.

Creditors have or seek certain information to ensure the likelihood of payment. Balance sheets, income statements, and statements of cash flow may be prepared and distributed. Investors, likewise, are concerned with these reports.

Finally, businesses have internal reporting requirements for planning and control. These needs vary with the size and type of business and with the style of management used.

Index

Index

Police powers clause, 236
Preferred stock, 158–159, 175
Prepayment penalty, 173
Present value:
  defined, 66
  index of, 67
  table of, 81–83, 95
Pricing, C-V-P analysis and, 10–11, 16–26
Product discontinuance, 88–90, 91
Product matrix analysis, 71
Product specifications/design:
  C-V-P analysis and, 7–8
  capital budgeting and, 69
Production schedule, 128–130
Profit center, 43
  reporting on, 256–258
Profitability, 161–162
  ratios for, 190–192
Property:
  insurance on, 223
  taxes on personal, 212, 240–241
Proposals, capital:
  evaluation of, 72
  follow-up to, 73–74
  implementation of, 73
  solicitation/generation of, 69–71

Quantity discounts, 16

Rapid depreciation methods, 212–213
Ratios, 179–180, 206–207
  balancing use of, 204–206
  financial, 180–196
  operating, 196–203
Receivables, *see* Accounts receivable; Inflows
Refinancing, 173
Regression analysis, 24–25
  in Excel, 30–34
  in Lotus 1-2-3™, 96–99
Reports, 229, 260–261
  to equity holders, 243
  to federal government, 229–236
  to local government, 241–242

to management
  customer margin, 258–259
  operational, 243–256
  profit center, 256–258
to state government, 236–241
Required rate of return, 79–80
Research and development, 71, 170
Responsibility accounting, 41–53
  costs for, 43–51
  responsibility centers for, 42–43
  revenues for, 51–53
Revenue center, 43
Revenues:
  projected for operating budget, 51–53
  updating for budgeting process, 39
Risk management:
  plan for, 216–222
  policies for, 215–216
  report on, 222–223
Risk manager, 216–217
Risk, of investments, 106
Risk/return relationship, 74–75
Rules of thumb, for financial ratios, 181–182

S corporations, 212
  reporting requirements for, 235
Sales forecasts, 51–53, 57–58, 128, 129
Sales taxes, 237–239, 242
Sensitivity analysis, C-V-P and, 28–29
Short-term debt, 115
Small Business Administration (SBA) loans, 169–170
Social Security taxes, 230, 231
Sole proprietorship, 232
Split-dollar life insurance, 225–226
Standby costs, 23
State taxes, 211–212, 237–241
Step cost, 27–28
Stock, *see* Dividends; Equity financing
Strategic planning, 26–27
Sunk costs, 12

Tangible personal property tax, 212, 240–241